Popular Historiographies in the 19th and 20th Centuries

New German Historical Perspectives

Series Editors: Jane Caplan (Executive Editor), Timothy Garton Ash, Jürgen Kocka, Gerhard A. Ritter and Margit Szöllösi-Janze

Originally established in 1987 as an English-language forum for the presentation of research by leading German historians and social scientists to readers in English-speaking countries, this series has since become one of the premier vehicles for the dissemination of German research expertise on contemporary academic debate and of broad topical interest to Germans and non-Germans alike. Its coverage is not limited to Germany alone but extends to the history of other countries, as well as general problems of political, economic, social and intellectual history and international relations.

Popular Historiographies in the 19th and 20th Centuries

Cultural Meanings, Social Practices

Edited by

Sylvia Paletschek

Berghahn Books

OXFORD • NEW YORK

First published in 2011 by
Berghahn Books
www.berghahnbooks.com

Library of Congress Cataloging-in-Publication Data
Popular historiographies in the 19th and 20th centuries : cultural
meanings, social practices / edited by Sylvia Paletschek.
    p. cm. – (New German historical perspectives ; v. 4)
Includes bibliographical references and index.
ISBN 978-1-84545-740-2 (hardback : alk. paper) 1. Germany–
Historiography. 2. Historiography–Germany—History. I.
Paletschek, Sylvia,
DD86.P57 2010 2011
907.2'043–dc22

                                                      2010018546

British Library Cataloguing in Publication Data
A catalogue record for this book is available from the British Library

Printed in the United States on acid-free paper.

ISBN: 978-1-84545-740-2 (hardback)

Contents

Part III: Memory Culture and Popular Historiographies: Case Studies

List of Figures

1

Introduction: Why Analyse Popular Historiographies?

Sylvia Paletschek

At this point in time, popular presentations of history are booming – not only in the Western world, but worldwide. Recent allusions to history as the 'new gardening' by a BBC representative[1] or its characterization as the 'new cooking' by historian Justin Champion (2008a) suggest that in Britain history-related television programmes are on their way to outdoing the highly successful gardening or cooking formats in terms of popularity. While this may be a slight exaggeration, the fact is that there has been a rising interest in history since the 1980s. From the second half of the 1990s this interest has reached an unprecedented peak (Winter 2001: 5–16; 2006: 19–39).

In Germany, this trend was first observed in relation to increasing numbers of visitors to historical exhibitions and museums (Korff 1990). Similarly, considerable public attention was paid to controversies among historical experts. For example, in the second half of the 1980s, the *Historikerstreit* – the debate about scientifically adequate perspectives on German National Socialism among German history experts – was, in part, carried out in the public media where it reached a broad audience (Augstein et al. 1987; Evans 1991; Peter 1995; Schneider 1995). In the late 1990s, the *Wehrmachtsausstellung* – the German Army exhibition focusing on the war crimes of the *Wehrmacht* committed on the eastern front during the Second World War – caused a major public debate about the role of the German army in the Second World War (Klotz 2001; Hamburger Institut für Sozialforschung 2002; Hartmann and Hürter 2005). And in 2001, a fierce discussion between ancient historians and archaeologists about Troy caused a sensation in the public (Ulf 2003; Weber 2006).

Somewhat less spectacular, yet of equal importance, has been the evolution of new historical movements 'from below' which emerged from the 1970s on. Examples include the *Geschichtswerkstätten* (history workshops) and women's history groups, both of which indicate (among other things) an increasing interest both in regional history and in the history of everyday life. Initiated in

Scandinavia (*Grabe-wo-du-stehst*, Sven Lindquist) and in Great Britain (Raphael Samuel), the history workshop movement reached Germany in the early 1980s (Heer and Ullrich 1985; Böge 2004).

With the unprecedented success of the American television series *Holocaust* on German television in 1979, which was watched by 10 to 15 million people (Brandt 2003; Bösch 2007), German broadcasting and especially ZDF (a national public television broadcaster), discovered history as a *Quotenbringer* (a reliable deliverer of high ratings). Against this background, German television saw the emergence of new forms and formats for the presentation of history. From the 1980s on, and especially since the 1990s, television increasingly drew on historical subject matter for various documentary, semi-documentary and fictional formats. The period between 1995 and 2003 brought a doubling of the percentage of historical programmes presented on television; today about 5 per cent of broadcasting content is related to history (Lersch and Viehhoff 2007). On average, a history format can rely on an audience share of between 7 and 13 per cent, that is 2 to 5 million viewers (Wirtz 2008: 11). Thus, television has emerged as the *Leitmedium* – the medium in dominance with regard to historical culture. According to a representative survey in 1991, 90 per cent of Germans stated that they engage with historical issues on a regular basis and that they primarily rely on television (67 per cent) and on fictional material (38 per cent) for this purpose. In this regard, academic and other educational institutions (such as schools) involved in mediating history are of lesser importance (13 per cent) (Crivellari et al. 2004: 12).

In addition to this, the last decade saw a major boom in popular historical productions in the print media, in historical non-fiction books, in periodicals devoted to history as well as in popular magazines. For example, during the last few years most of the well-known German magazines – such as *Der Spiegel, Die Zeit* and *Geo* – released a specialized history format in the context of their diversified output (*Geo Epoche* since 1999; *Die Zeit Geschichte* since 2005; *Spiegel Special Geschichte* since 2007). Also, the decade saw an increase in the number of (historical) biographies and autobiographies published along with the rise of fictionalized forms, such as historical novels and historical crime fiction, in the book market. In addition, numerous historical websites on the internet, history articles on Wikipedia, CD-ROM productions as well as historical computer games attest to the phenomenon's expansion into the new digital media and to the creation of new forms of mediation.[2]

Moreover, re-enactments and living history, which have both been known since the late nineteenth century, have mushroomed in recent years. In their recent versions, both forms involve an experimental, 'live' re-enactment of historical events or living conditions and, thus, intensify the rise of new or updated forms of mediating history (Carlson 2000; Cook 2004; Hochbruck 2006). Such forms are used for historical performances by private associations as well as by museums and theme parks. What they suggest is the possibility of experiencing the past in much more sensual ways. Similarly, TV documentaries, such as the docudrama, offer the same kind of promise, and this has contributed to the immense popularity of historical docu-soaps such as *The 1900 House* in Great Britain and *Schwarzwaldhaus* and *Gutshaus* in Germany (Hunt 2006; Ebbrecht 2007; Müller and Schwarz 2008). Through these old and new media and formats, popular representations of history now reach a mass audience and are received by broad fractions of the population. Thus, it is legitimate to suggest that they have a much stronger impact on people's perceptions of history than academic studies.

The History Boom: Some Background Information

This history boom can be conceived of as an integral part of, and a response to, contemporary societies' accelerating changes and to what has been called 'second modernity'.[3] Traditional orientations, life styles and work patterns have gone through radical changes, if not disruptions, since the last three decades of the twentieth century. National boundaries as well as the construction of nations, states and ethnicities have gone through rapid changes. The same holds true for the significance and implementation of gender, religion, class and age. An unspoken belief in progress has become obsolete and many people experience the present as a period of crisis and uncertainty. In such a situation, the turn to history can serve the function of constructing continuity, orientation and identity – be it national or regional, sub-cultural or individual. An increased level of education, greater prosperity and more leisure time has also supported this new interest in history which can be seen as a result of the emergence of modern knowledge society since the end of the nineteenth century (Szöllösi-Janze 2004: 277–312). Yet, the engagement with history, particularly through popular display formats, also satisfies the need for emotional and aesthetic experience and for adventure, for a risk-free encounter with what is strange, different or 'other' and, finally, for relaxation and diversion. Moreover, public and state organizations, social elites and political groups draw on popular forms to strategically use history for legitimizing either the status quo or political changes.

Since the emergence of modern historiography in the early nineteenth century, its increasing incomprehensibility by non-specialists has been deplored particularly in Germany. Characterized by its ever-intensified specialization, modern historiography is based on empirical sources and decidedly sets itself apart from popular representations. Thus, scientific historiography has moved away from the philosophy of history as well as from various forms of literary historiography (Hardtwig 1982, 1990f). By doing so, academic historiography has lost its 'entertainment value' and also, to some extent, its ability to deal with vital issues. Meanwhile, questions about the meaning of history have come to take a back seat in scientific accounts. The development of modern historical science in the nineteenth century saw the emergence of a paradox: the rise of academic science, its instiionalization and specialization – which meant its moving away from 'universal history' (*Universalgeschichte*) to source-saturated national history – was inextricably related to the rise of the nation and of new, bourgeois elites. Thus, modern academic history owed its early and successful expansion in German universities to its legitimizing function. On the other hand, increasing 'scientification' and specialization, partly facilitated by the German tradition of freedom of research and teaching (*Lehr- und Forschungs-freiheit*) and the single states' competition in the cultural sector, led to a form of academic historiography which notably forfeited much of its appeal to broader bourgeois audiences, though never completely losing it. Academic historiography additionally reinforced existing power structures and the world-view of male, bourgeois, protestant, nationally conservative elites, with the result that it did not fulfil its legitimizing function for newly emerging political forces such as the Catholic or Socialist milieu or the emerging women's movement.

Definitions and Interrelations

By using the term 'popular historiography', I refer to representations of history in written, visual, artefactual and personal forms of presentation addressing a broad, non-expert audience. Within the field of popular historiography one could further differentiate between 'public history' – that is, the political use of history by nations, states, institutions and political elites – and 'popular history' – the use of history by civil society, families, groups, commercial or private associations and individuals (Black 2005). However, this differentiation should be only conceived of as a heuristic one because both forms are often interrelated. In simple terms the relationship between popular and scientific, or non-academic and academic, representations of history can be sketched as follows:

Popular historiographies are typically characterized by mediating strategies such as reduction, narration and dramatization; they personalize, emotionalize and often scandalize their subject matter. Their subject matter and representational forms are shaped by their respective medium's conditions of production and distribution and/or their respective institutional context – in terms of audience, quantitative reception, time budget, commercial aspects, potential for re-usability and for international distribution, and so on.

Yet, conventions and characteristics such as reduction, narration, and political exploitability also apply to academic historiography. Reduction and simplification are basic practices which scientists must necessarily rely on in order to communicate their results within the scientific community (Shinn and Whitley 1985: viiff). According to research on scientific knowledge, there is no fundamental or basic difference between popular and academic knowledge. Rather, the difference is one of degree. In research on the popularization of science, the interactionist model also suggests interdependence and mutual interference of academic knowledge producers, popularizers and recipients.[4]

Frequently, academic history tends to raise more questions than it provides answers and – at least ideally speaking – conceives of its results as a kind of knowledge that is methodologically reflected and sound, yet always open to scrutiny, always provisional and never definite. By contrast, popular representations of history are not interested in ambivalence and instead favour not-too-complex answers, providing meaning and political legitimation.

In spite of the provisional character of the interpretations produced by academic historiography, the latter tends to serve a controlling function in the public use of history. Thus, academic historiography points to incorrect facts, ahistorical assessment criteria and problematic comparisons and actualizations, even though academic history itself can never be completely free of such problems. Conversely, popular historiography can provide stimulation to its academic sibling; for example, where it picks up marginal or innovative issues or makes use of new methods, sources and representational forms.[5]

Research Fields: Public History, the History of Historiography and Memory Culture

In 1994, the British socialist historian and founder of the history workshop movement, Raphael Samuel, pleaded for opening up academic historiography to popular historical narratives characterized by their great impact-related potential:

> In any archaeology of the unofficial sources of historical knowledge, the animators of the Flintstones ... surely deserve, at least, a *proxime accedit*. Stand-up comedians, such as *Rowan Atkinson* whose Blackadder series re-animated the legendary moments of British history for a generation of television addicts, might get as much attention as the holder of a Regius chair. The impresarios of the open air museum, and their ever-increasing staff, would be seen to have made a far more substantial contribution to popular appetite for an engagement with the past than the most ambitious head of a department. (Samuel 1994: 17)

In Germany, there were similar calls by historians such as Rudolf Vierhaus, who as early as 1977 claimed that researching the history of historiography must exceed 'what has been common practice so far' by moving beyond traditional academic historiography to look at historical representations in education, museums, popular historical literature and monuments, and who also called for an investigation into 'historical awareness, its political and social function' (Vierhaus 1977: 111). Yet, pleas such as this did not lead to a systematic scientific engagement with popular presentations of history. What is beginning to show, meanwhile – particularly in the context of public history and the now booming interdisciplinary research on memory culture, as well as, in part, in the history of historiography – are clear steps toward an intensified and more systematic engagement with popular presentations of history.

Emerging in the U.S. in the late 1970s as a new segment of academic history, public history – also conceived of in the beginning as 'practising history', 'applied history' or 'consulting history' – has been institutionalized in study programmes, scientific associations and scientific journals.[6] Public history refers to the employment of historians and the historical method outside academia (Kelley 1978: 16). It trains historians to transform their work so that it reaches audiences outside the academy. Public history is 'history that is seen, heard, read, and interpreted by a popular audience'; it asks questions about the practical value of history and is also seen as 'history that belongs to the public'.[7] Meanwhile, there are more than 100 universities, mostly in the U.S. and Australia, which offer study programmes (at the BA or MA level) in public history.[8] In American historical science, the field of public history in particular has produced investigations into popular presentations of history.[9] This can partly be accounted for by public history's advanced institutionalization in the U.S. through study programmes, journals and expert associations.

Meanwhile in Australia, public history is now an up and coming field of history. Yet there are also some signs of its institutionalization in Great Britain through the establishment of study programmes and of new initiatives by historians such as the website Doing Public History, launched in 2008, which aims at promoting 'public debate about the nature and role of history in Britain'.[10] This site calls for a sustained discussion about the relationship between academic historians and the public. Indeed, it seems paradoxical that despite a broad interest in history within British society and the media, and 'despite a sophisticated and passionate debate about the nature of the heritage industry and National Trust', there is little 'engagement with the public value of historical discourse' among British academics (Champion 2008b).[11]

Turning to Germany, there have been a number of lively public debates about history, particularly about an adequate commemoration of the Holocaust and the Second World War, to which academic historical science and university historians have also made major contributions.[12] A lively public interest was also caused by the fact that coming to terms with the past – particularly in relation to responsibility for the consequences of the Second World War and the Holocaust – has led to various 'waves' of intensified engagement with National Socialism since the end of the 1950s. In the beginning, there was much hesitancy and stagnation in efforts at taking on this task. Yet, particularly since the 1980s, these attempts have played a central role in national identity formation in the Federal Republic of Germany. In comparison to other European states which have only recently taken on the task of addressing aspects of their past such as crimes against humanity or dictatorship, Germany has sometimes been alluded to as a 'master of coming to terms with the past'. Partly because the crimes committed by the national socialists have made historical responsibility disproportionately more burdensome, this 'coming to terms with the past' has succeeded because the country has practised an active politics of history, additionally flanked by academic research (Danyel 1995; Frei 1996; Wolfrum 1999; Reichel 2001; Welzer 2002). Meanwhile, there are numerous accounts which have engaged with this politics of history, and the coming to terms with history, in Germany. These accounts, however, have tended to focus on National Socialism, state action or the political elite. Thus, in Germany, history, and primarily the history of National Socialism, has been much more present in the political public than in other states since the 1980s. Yet this has not led to an investigation of popular forms of appropriation and presentation of history or to a more thorough reflection on public history. This may also be due to the widespread separation of and lack of contact between academic historical science and the didactics of history in Germany, and also to the rare occasions of cooperation between academic historians and 'practitioners' of history such as teachers, historians working in museums, archivists and historians or historically trained creative personnel in the media.

Lately, however, there have been tentative steps toward an institutionalization of public history, firstly in the form of study programmes[13] and, quite recently, by means of the formation of research groups (*Forschergruppen*) as well as through conferences and anthologies dedicated to the broad phenomenon of a popular historical culture that reaches beyond the engagement with National Socialism and a state-related politics of history.[14] At present, there are signs indicating the rise of the question *Wozu Geschichte?* ('History – what is it for?'), an intensified engagement with perceptions of history, or with history as a commodity.[15] In 2006, the annual convention of the Deutsche Historikertag (Society of German Historians) was dedicated to the issue of *Geschichtsbilder* (perceptions of history). Here, two panels dealt with the ongoing popularization of history on television. Existing research on history in film and on television reveals the above mentioned observation that National Socialism is the best researched topic (Bösch 1999; Classen 1999; Kansteiner 2006; Keilbach 2008). Yet there are also recent and quite promising shifts into other historical periods, new formats and efforts towards developing a more systematic approach (e.g., Crivellari et al. 2004; Lersch and Viehoff 2007; Fischer and Wirtz 2008; Steinle 2008).

The analysis of popular presentations of history might also be seen as part of the research on collective memory which has particularly flourished in Germany recently.[16] So far, this quite vivid, interdisciplinary research on memory and remembrance has focused on questions of 'how': how the memory of societies and of individuals works, how remembrance is constructed and how it shapes the identity of nations, groups and individuals, and how, in general, the past interacts with the present.

Research on memory culture started in the 1920s with Maurice Halbwachs (1985) who coined the term 'collective memory' and emphasized the constructed and socially determined character of individual remembrance. Halbwachs's theory was further developed by Jan Assmann, who introduced the concept of cultural memory and focused on the interrelation of public memory, collective identity and political legitimization. Jan Assmann also introduced the distinction between communicative and cultural memory. Taking up the notion developed by Halbwachs (and also by Pierre Nora) that generational memory is limited to eighty to one hundred years, Assmann describes communicative memory as immediate commemoration passed on informally though communication. Cultural memory, in contrast, is organized and institutionalized, bound to objects and rituals. It includes any given society's and era's stock of 'reusable texts, images and rites ... whose "cultivation" serves to stabilize and convey that society's self-image. Upon such collective knowledge, for the most part (but not exclusively) of the past, each group bases its awareness of unity and particularity' (Assmann 1995a: 132). Aleida Assmann (1999) suggested a further differentiation between functional and storage memory. Functional memory conveys the segments of the past which are regarded as functional and serve the creation of political and social identity in a society, group or nation. Functional memory can be described as acquired memory that constructs meaning. Storage memory, in contrast, also includes currently useless historical knowledge which was meaningful once but is not longer made use of, though it can be reintroduced into functional memory when necessary. Recent work on historical remembrance also emphasizes the contested and continuous reinterpretation of remembrance which leads to a coexistence of numerous, hegemonic and marginal, cultures of memory (Winter 2006: 1–13). Popular presentations of history belong to memory culture, even though research on this topic has not paid much attention to these popular forms of appropriation, such as living history, historical docu-soaps and so on.

Apart from these concepts of memory culture, there is the concept of historical culture (*Geschichtskultur*) formulated by Jörn Rüsen and others (such as Wolfgang Hardtwig or Bernd Schönemann), which also looks at the social/ societal significance of historical commemoration. *Geschichtskultur* points to presentations of history existing in a broad variety of cultural institutions and media which integrate

> the functions of instruction, entertainment, legitimation, criticism, diversion and education. By historical culture, we mean the historical interpretations of diverse cultural institutions, e.g. by the university, school, the museum, administration or mass media, which turn into an ensemble of locations for collective remembrance and integrate the functions of instruction, entertainment, criticism, diversion, education and other modes of recollection into the comprehensive unity of historical commemoration. (Rüsen 1994: 4)

However, existing works on *Geschichtskultur* are primarily of a theoretical nature and are oriented at traditional institutions and authorities for the mediation of history. Empirical studies have primarily addressed the nineteenth century – its middle classes as well as the more 'high culture' products of that time such as memorials and monuments.

Popular presentations of history might also be understood as an analytic object in the history of historiography. Up to this point, the history of historiography has mainly concentrated on academic historiography, focusing on the (hi)story of great historians, on canonized works, on work-immanent interpretations and on the ex post tracing of methodological developments that became successful later on. However, a 'modern' history of historiography should also address the structural conditions of the production of historical knowledge, its political, institutional, material and social determinants as well as the relation of historiography to society, the state and the public. Also, and very importantly so, it should also include non-academic historical works and their interaction with the expert world – something done, for example, by Bonnie Smith in her book 'The Gender of History' (Smith 1998) which not only analyses institutional conditions but also academic and non-academic historiography (by women). It is particularly gender (along with other aspects of social difference) and an interest in bringing to light a female historiography which account for the importance of expanding the history of historiography to popular forms of presentation (Paletschek 2007). Of course, this opens up the question whether women as both producers and recipients of historiography, as well as issues of women's history and the history of gender relations, become more visible (or not) by including non-academic historical presentations in the history of historiography.

Presently, we are seeing more and more work which argues for the inclusion of non-academic forms of historiography in the history of historiography (Jordanova 2000) or specifically inquires into the scope of and the relationship between academic historiography, the state and the public (e.g., Tyrell 2005). First steps towards such an 'expanded history of historiography' and a new reflection on historiography and the public can also be seen in Germany.[17] To name just a few examples, this includes work on commemoration, historiography and gender (Regnath and Riepl-Schmidt 2007; Paletschek and Schraut 2008; Epple and Schaser 2009), Valentin Groebner's lucid work on views of the Middle Ages in the nineteenth century and in contemporary popular culture (Groebner 2008), the discovery of the thriller as a historical source for the twentieth century (Schwarz 2006), as well as the work done by Dieter Langewiesche (2008a) and Wolfgang Hardtwig, whose edited anthology of popular historiography in twentieth-century Germany contains 'history for readers'; for example, popular biographies of Emil Ludwig from the 1920s and C.W. Ceram's bestseller *Gods, Graves and Scholars* (1949). Last, but certainly not least, Martin Nissen's dissertation provides a first, condensed account of popular historiography in the second part of the nineteenth century, and particularly of the interaction between historians, publishers and the German public (Nissen 2009).

Contributions to this Volume

To date little research on popular presentations of history has been done in Germany. Thus, the articles in this volume[18] attempt to provide a pathway into this new field of research and introduce some of the work which has emerged in Germany over the past few years. While mainly (though not exclusively) focusing on Germany, the articles analyse different forms of popular historiography and popular presentations of history since 1800. By doing so, they try to provide some answers to a set of basic questions: What kinds of history and which perceptions of history are presented? What kinds of interrelations are to be found between popular and academic history? What kinds of challenges and opportunities were created by popular historiographies?

The contributions presented in Part I focus on popular histories in the nineteenth century, predominantly presented in written form. While differing in their respective object of interest, the articles share a concern with the relationship between popular and academic historiography. Thus, Angelika Epple investigates popular historiography produced by women writers from the mid eighteenth to the mid nineteenth century. As she points out, it was particularly the history of historiography which blocked out these successful popular historians. Female historians of popular historiography such as Catherine Macauly, Therese Huber, Louise von Blumenthal and Johanna Schopenhauer employed innovative methods (such as closeness to sources, oral history) early on; in fact, they partly took up this practice prior to their academic colleagues. As a strategy for proving the authenticity of their accounts, these women authors pointed to their 'correct' moral and political attitude and their respective history's significance for the present. Thus, they set themselves apart from an increasingly more academic historiography, which considered scientific objectivity to be founded in the depiction of causality (Hume) or in the methodological criticism of sources (Ranke). Through their radical subjectivity, popular female historians not only challenged the canon's strategies of striving for 'truth' but also dealt with thematic fields excluded by professional academic historiography such as ethical values, friendship and family issues, death, birth, childhood, love and hatred. Angelika Epple concludes that the division of labour between popular and professional historiography was legitimized two hundred years ago: 'It was an attempt to create a professional identity by excluding important themes and "unimportant" people'.

My own contribution provides an overview of the emerging institutions and forms of the popular mediation of history in the nineteenth century. Concentrating on the press as the most successful mass medium of its time, the article analyses presentations of history in the pictorial family magazine *Die Gartenlaube* for the years between 1863 and 1900. As the analysis shows, the perceptions of history circulated in these popular presentations were much more pluralistic than those provided by academic historiography in the second half of the nineteenth century. Simultaneously, however, *Die Gartenlaube's* popular presentations of history were of a decidedly affirmative nature and strongly related to the present. As the analysis shows, the *Die Gartenlaube*'s historical presentations were most notably dominated by contemporary history. Secondly, many of these accounts addressed topics of cultural history and the history of everyday life which were hardly touched on by contemporary academic historiography. Similar to present-day strategies, the magazine strongly drew on anniversaries as anchors of commemoration. Moreover, the analysis reveals traits of dealing with respective historical events by drawing on a broad spectrum of existing forms and formats of popular mediation. This suggests that in Modern Times, the period captured by communicative memory occupies the centre of a given society's functional memory. For one thing, this means that the time span covered by all living contemporaries along with topics and issues attached to their immediate everyday lives and to individual experience form the centre of a given period's primary interest.

Hartmut Bergenthum investigates the 'world histories' around 1900 which so far have been neglected by historiography. These works were bestsellers in Germany, with several hundred thousand copies in circulation around the turn to the twentieth century. Bergenthum looks at the kinds of issues and geographical spaces represented in these popular histories. He also considers the assumptions about history's driving forces on which these works were based and asks whether this sets them apart from academic historiography. For the most part marked by a strong Eurocentric signature, these popular 'world histories' were dominated by the idea that history begins with the formation of states and that the state, (male) elites and religion are history's driving forces. Yet, these 'world histories' also contained innovative approaches in that history could be organized according to a fundamentally new spatial concept, that of *Völkerkreise* ('circles of peoples'), which meant that African history was for the first time included in this type of historical account. Some of these 'world histories' drew on an interdisciplinary approach by using sociological, anthropological, ethnic, linguistic and also racial patterns of interpretation. Bergenthum concludes that the 'world histories' responded to their contemporaries' need for orientation by trying to 'stabilize a conventional world-view while adapting to globalization. New methods were adopted to justify old identities'.

The articles collected in Part II deal with popular historiographies in the twentieth century and cover both 'old' and what in their respective time were 'new' media. Wolfgang Hardtwig looks at successful books that focus on history in the twentieth century and particularly at the works of Sebastian Haffner and Golo Mann. Hardtwig raises basic questions with regard to the object of research and conceives of popular historiography as a challenge for the future. In his perspective, popular historiography is an answer to the audience's ethical and aesthetic needs, which are no longer adequately served by modern academic historiography. According to Hardtwig, 'research should focus on the contribution of popular historiography to the formation and change of historical and political awareness in Germany, as well as on the problem of whether popular historiography can be seen as a source which is useful to the analysis of these historical processes'. However, the fundamental tension between academic historiography and memory culture, this binary way of approaching the past must itself be historicized.

Taking the example of contemporary history's presentation on radio in the German Democratic Republic (GDR) as his case in point, Christoph Classen takes a look at the way history functions to stabilize the political system and at the popular media's general potential within the context of dictatorship. He stresses the frequent reference to history, and particularly to contemporary history, in the GDR, which was so 'omnipresent that one might be tempted to talk about an obsession with history'. Yet, in comparison to the current history boom, Classen states that the GDR radio presentations provided 'a quite different form of popular history'. The history programmes on GDR radio were characterized by a personalized presentation, an emotional language and frequent recourse to witnesses of history, all of which served as strategic means of establishing authenticity. The prevailing style was that of a marked 'historical presentism'; that is, an instrumentalization of the past for confirming the respective present's political status quo, and of a predominant recourse to historical analogies, particularly in terms of delineating the GDR from the West. Constraints inherent to the political system foreclosed the possibilities of exploiting the new medium's potentials. This is particularly evident in the case of the historical radio play, which was extremely popular with audiences. Frequently, there was no way of synthesizing the writer's creative potential and a successful narrative structure with political constraints.

Frank Bösch investigates films (on cinema and television) released over the past thirty years and thematically devoted to the period of National Socialism, with a particular focus on German productions. He argues that 'audiovisual history about the Third Reich is seen as a key element of self-assurance with regard to historical and national identity'. His analysis points to the interactions and correspondence of issues and approaches in academic and popular accounts of history. Since the groundbreaking success of the mini-series *Holocaust* in 1978/9, numerous films about National Socialism have been made internationally, thus constituting a transnational phenomenon, which nevertheless is endowed with its respective national peculiarities. Taking German films as his case in point, Bösch traces three phases in German film production over the past thirty years. Each phase has been characterized by distinctive topics and modes of representation, which reflected its period's particular zeitgeist. Thus, Bösch emphasizes that historical research and film are closer connected to each other than seems to be the case at first sight. Since historical research does not necessarily function as an emitter for popular history, Bösch argues for a reconsideration of the term 'popularization' since films do not merely simplify scientific results. He also identifies a severe lack of research concerning audience studies of these historical movies.

The contributions collected in Part III are devoted to popular historiography as part of memory culture. They either address the relationship between memory culture and popular and academic historiography in general (Langewiesche, Lenz) or provide case studies (Schraut, Ceranski, Brüggemeier). These chapters investigate persons or events which have been present in popular memory culture throughout the second part of the twentieth century but which have not so far figured in general historical overviews or in the kind of special research authorized by academic historiography, with the consequence that they have escaped the latter's grid of significance. This applies both to the Austrian Empress Elizabeth, better known as Sissi, and the German soccer team's victory in the 1954 football World Cup. Some of the contributions point to the vital significance of gender by showing that both in popular and scientific historiography contemporary gender relations function as the frame of reference and, thus, influence what can be said, thought and (re)presented.

Dieter Langewiesche's chapter investigates the relationship between memory culture and academic historiography. Langewiesche takes as his point of departure the topical finding of today's international responsibility for history, which he substantiates by various examples. He interprets this new, and historically unprecedented, international responsibility as an outflow of globalization and, more particularly, as signifying the democratization of the use of history in pluralistic societies, something which goes along with a deprofessionalization of historiography. The new type of 'lay history' can develop imaginative forms and follow unforeseen paths, quite independently and untouched by academic history writing. Departing from these findings, Langewiesche goes on to discuss the relationship between memory culture, popular historical narratives and historical science by drawing on historical propositions made by Johann Martin Chladenius, John Herald Plumb, Reinhart Koselleck and Paul Ricœur. A critical historiography can be practised in a given society only if historical science is linked to that society's memory culture. 'The possibility of historical writing having an effect on society depends on its ability to make the connection between "faithfulness to memory" and "historical truth"… This is only possible however, if historical writing puts forward a view of the past which is accessible to the experience of contemporaries'.

Wartime memories provide a good example for illustrating how modified social conditions and power relations form the preconditions whereby certain historical facts or actors become acknowledged. Claudia Lenz takes a look at the depiction of the Second World War and the period of German Occupation in Norway's popular memory culture. She looks at how stories considered worth remembering emerge in both the private and the public context. What authorizes those considered to be valuable narrators so that they can narrate their past? Lenz assumes that negotiations about the meaning of the past fulfil the crucial function of legitimizing a subject's former and present actions and, furthermore, of constituting the subject as an agent. In this regard, gender is a central category in the process of historical narration and of attributing authority. Lenz shows this in the analysis of popular recollections of the Second World War in Norway and by drawing on examples taken from films, photographs as well as the orchestration of exhibitions and public honours. It was the rise of feminism and the societal changes which occurred from the 1980s onwards which gave way to a new historical culture of representation offering 'new images of courageous and active women who had participated in the struggle for national independence – both by means which traditionally had been regarded as "female" (smuggling food, hiding and helping refugees to flee) and by weapons in their hands'. Nevertheless, the demystification of male-biased narratives about 'boys in the woods' brought about by adding female heroines remained linked to the myth about the 'resisting nation' so that further deconstruction was – and is – yet to come.

Sylvia Schraut looks at popular presentations of the Austrian Empress Elizabeth (1837–1898), known as 'Sissi' in the German-speaking world in differing media, genres and formats throughout the twentieth century. Surprisingly, despite worldwide 'Sissimania' and a successful global marketing of her story, there has as yet been no scientific investigation of the Sissi 'myth' nor of Empress Elizabeth's political work and her impact. Popular historiography has primarily focused on her private life and her 'tragic fate' and is characterized by a mixture of fact and fiction. Interestingly, the Empress herself and her contemporaries respectively laid the foundation for her later mystification. The example of Sissi shows that presentation and, thereby, presence, across a variety of mediating forms –monuments, books, journal articles, pictures, exhibitions, plays, films, musicals, figures, artefacts or spatial representations at tourist sites – and recurring interpretations of the myth, topically refreshed and streamlined into the respective period's particular character, are prerequisites for entering, and lasting in, popular memory culture. Rounding up her contribution, Sylvia Schraut argues that the core of the fascination with Sissi as subject matter – in addition to the general attractiveness of power and royal splendor – lies in the fact that an ambiguous character resisting any unproblematic understanding can be utilized as screen on which can be projected almost any content for which there is demand in the popular engagement with historical matters.

Beate Ceranski turns our interest to the presentation of Marie Curie and Albert Einstein in popular biographies published between the beginning of the twentieth century and today. Her analysis reveals perplexing parallels as well as significant differences between their respective presentations. Both Einstein and Curie laid the foundations for their future image in their own lifetimes. After their respective death, it was close collaborators, friends or relatives who exclusively administered their estates and wrote the first, and extremely successful, biographies. It was only the new zeitgeist of the 1970s and 1980s, coupled with a new access to sources, which brought about a change in the earlier hagiographic and stereotyped images. Influenced by the pressures exerted by the second-wave women's movement and by altered moral conceptions, both the popular and academic history of science turned to an engagement with the relationship between gender and science. It was this engagement, which allowed for the development of a modified perspective on both protagonists, which nonetheless remained characterized by significant differences related to gender. When analysing the semantic fields associated with these exceptional scientists, the presentation of Einstein still stresses his genius while that of Curie emphasizes her obsession (a trait connoting the realm of emotion and even that of the non-rational) – and this applies to both the popular and academic history of science, both of which must therefore be seen as reproducing gender clichés. When looking at the history of historiography, this case study reveals an interaction between the popular and academic history of science. As Beate Ceranski notes, the popular history of science's late success led to a rehabilitation of biography as a genre of the academic history of historiography.

Finally, Franz Brüggemeier takes a look at the so-called *Wunder von Bern* ('miracle of Bern'), the German football team's winning of the World Cup in 1954 and this event's role and function in popular memory culture. As an issue of national recollection, the 'miracle of Bern' slowly evolved from the 1980s onward. The major excitement that surrounded the fiftieth anniversary of the Bern victory in 2004, and the broad soccer enthusiasm of the summer of 2006, when Germany once again hosted the World Cup, firmly rooted the event in popular memory culture. In the mass media, the 'miracle of Bern' was retrospectively celebrated as the Federal Republic of Germany's proper founding act and as the decisive event in the formation of national identity after 1945 and the division of Germany into two separate states: East Germany (the German Democratic Republic) and West Germany (the Federal Republic of Germany). In strong contrast to this, the event is not even mentioned in relevant scientific overviews of the Federal Republic's history. Taking this finding as his point of departure, Franz Brüggemeier traces the meaning given to the event by its contemporaries. As his findings suggest, the World Cup victory of 1954 caused an intense, but rather short-lived mass enthusiasm and was not granted any meaning with regard to national identity formation at that point in time. It was only in the context of a decidedly altered societal situation, one which emerged in the 1980s, that the 'miracle of Bern' could be endowed with a new kind of meaning. Among the preconditions for this act of (re)writing popular history was an increased softening of the high culture/popular culture divide, the assumption of new economic, political and cultural functions by competitive sports, and a Federal Republic conceived by major parts of the population as a postnational society which has been gradually developing a more relaxed relationship to national identity since the turn of the millennium. The example of the 'miracle of Bern' reveals that new facets of popular memory culture and altered historical attributions fulfil a burning glass function and imply the potential for uncovering social and societal changes.

In Conclusion

The articles collected in this volume show that popular presentations of history present a discrete and original form of knowledge production rather than one which has branched off from historical science. Many of the contributions point to the multifaceted interdependences and interactions between popular and academic historiography. This means that popularizing history must not be conceived of in terms of a unidimensional and hierarchical process in which the body of knowledge created by historical science trickles down into other representational forms. What must be discussed is whether, when it comes to public awareness and the popular presentation of knowledge, not only history but the humanities in general ask for different models than those applied to the natural sciences.

The contributions clearly show popular history's adjustment to a given period's respective zeitgeist. Like a burning glass, an analysis of the popular images of history reveals an epoch's respective societal, political and social changes and provides insights into changing mindsets and social relations. Thus, this analysis is not just one of 'official' state-related historical politics or the big public controversies of academic historians but one which pays special attention to so far marginalized appropriations of history in popular culture and holds out the promise of gaining insights into vital political and societal developments.

The presently evolving academic interest in popular presentations of history might also be interpreted as an expression of a process of diversification and pluralization in the context of a generational change in academic history and a changing relationship between high and popular culture in the postmodern era. An engagement with popular history forces academic historical science to intensify its self-reflection and to always define its position at a given moment in time. It is exactly this reflexivity which ultimately should provide the decisive criterion of differentiation between popular and academic historiography. An analysis of popular historical accounts also provides an occasion for questioning the terms of academic historiography's societal and political functions, its conditions of production, its politics of lending significance to certain issues and of excluding others, its dominant discourses and its inscribed, past and present power relations. We should not abstain from the innovative impulses provided by an engagement with the 'other' (and sometimes not all that different) history of popular culture.

Acknowledgements

I want to thank Gabriele Kreutzner for discussing and translating this article. For assistance with editing the volume I want to thank Kerstin Lohr, Olaf Schütze and Christa Klein: their help was essential to successfully finish the project. The same holds true for the reliable editing of Tom Williams. I also want to thank Jane Caplan, who supported not only the publishing of this book but furthermore created a very inspiring and cordial atmosphere during my stay at the European Studies Centre, St Antony's College, Oxford, during the academic year 2006/7.

Notes

1. *Süddeutsche Zeitung*, 21 July 2006.
2. For history on the internet, see Epple and Haber (2005); on Wikipedia, see Lorenz (2006) and Rosenzweig (2006); on history in computer games, see Poblocki (2002), Fritz (2003) and Uriccio (2005).
3. See Beck and Giddens (1996), Beck and Bonß (2001) and Beck and Lau (2004). For a survey of the potentials and limits of different theories of modernity, see Degele and Dries (2005).
4. Research on the 'popularizaton of science' differentiates two approaches (Schwarz 1999: 38–48, 89–107; Kretschmann 2003: 7–22): Older work advances from a diffusion model (i.e., from a linear and hierarchically structured distribution of knowledge from experts to lay people): knowledge production and mediation seem to be distinctly separate processes. In contrast to this, the interaction model argues in favour of interdependency and the mutual impact of knowledge producers, popularization and recipients (Shinn and Whitley 1985; Shapin 1990; Cooter and Pumfrey 1994). The interactionist model is substantiated by recent work on laboratory research (Latour and Woolgar 1979; Knorr-Cetina 1984) and on the construction of scientific facts (Fleck 2002[1935]; Daston 2001: 20). These studies show that scientific facts or theories are not purely empirical and rational constructs but are created through interaction and communication in a collective process of negotiation and depend on the existing balance of power relations and on institutional structures. They also challenged the division between a sphere of 'pure science' and a social and societal sphere.
5. In this respect, a particularly good example is provided by experimental archaeology: see Keefer (2006).
6. See, e.g., *Public Historian* (since 1978) and *Public History Review* (since 1992).
7. Source: New York University's website for its graduate program in public history. Retrieved 7 August 2008 from: http://www.nyu.edu/gsas/dept/history/publichistory/main.htm. See also Evans (2000) and the definition given in the following synopsis from the Australian journal *Public History Review*: 'Otherwise known as the History of the Present, Public History concerns the historical in the everyday, and the sense in which we are all historians – historians of our families, our homes and our lifetimes'; it also 'explores history as the terrain we traverse – battlegrounds, graveyards and television' (*Public History Review* 9: (2001)). For a 'classical' text, see Becker (1932: 221–36).
8. See 'Where to Study Public History' at the website of the Public History Resource Center. Retrieved 7 August 2008 from: http://www.publichistory.org/education/where_study.asp.
9. See, e.g., Rosenzweig and Thelen (1998) and Glassberg (2001).
10. Retrieved 9 August 2008 from: http://www.doingpublichistory.org/. The mission statement continues:

> Indeed, for example, the current discussion of a national memorial day, as well as TV series like *Monarchy*, *Great Britons*, and others, indicates there is popular context and demand for such discussion. Beyond engaging with the local commemoration of important anniversaries, centenaries and bicentennaries (think of recent events associated with 1807, or more traditional moments like the Gunpowder Plot, Trafalgar Day, Magna Carta Day, Holocaust Memorial Day, Black History Month and a number of WW2 events) there is little cogent

reflection on the relationship between the academic historian and the public. On the contrary in the USA, Australia, and France during the late 1980s and after (for example the 500th anniversary of Columbus, the bicentenary of white settlement/First Fleet in 1988 for Australia, the 200th anniversary of the 1776 and 1789 Revolutions) the public events were driven by, reflected in and prompted considerable scholarly and public debate.

11. In 2006 a series of British public history conferences was launched (History and the Public, 13–14 February 2006). The first conference was organized by the Institute for Historical Research, which brought together a broad range of people from universities, archives, museums, publishers and the media to discuss the public study and consumption of history. Follow-up conferences were organized in Wales (Swansea University, 12–14 April 2007) and Liverpool (April 2008).

12. See, for example, the *Historikerstreit* debate (1986 onwards), the debate about the *Wehrmachtsausstellung*, the *Denkmal für die ermordeten Juden Europas* (Holocaust memorial) in Berlin (Heimrod 1999; Kirsch 2003; Leggewie and Meyer 2005) or the highly controversial discussion about the planned foundation of a centre against expulsions in Berlin.

13. E.g., at the Free University in Berlin.

14. See, e.g., the Freiburg DFG Research Group 'Historische Lebenswelten in populären Wissenskulturen der Gegenwart' which organized a conference on *Geschichte in populären Medien und Genres* in April 2008. For more recent publications, see, e.g., Korte and Paletschek (2008).

15. See, e.g., the jubilee issue of the *Zeitschrift für Österreichische Geschichtswissenschaft* 15 (2005), devoted to the question 'What is history for?' (*Wozu Geschichte?*). In Greifswald, a conference held in January 2006 discussed *Wahre Geschichte – Geschichte als Ware* ('True history – history as a commodity') and the question of the historian's responsibility vis-à-vis science and society. For the role of images of history and foundation myths as forms of intentional history: see, e.g., Gehrke (2001).

16. See, for example, the numerous works provided by the DFG Sonderforschungsbereich (Collaborative Research Centres) on memory culture in Gießen. For an overview on approaches to memory culture, see Erll (2005: 13–39).

17. As for publications that have been released after this book was issued, see Kork and Paletschek (2009), Hardtwig and schug (2009), Horn and Sauer (2009), Oswalt and Pandel (2009) and Pirker et al. (2010).

18. Most of the articles collected in this volume are based on contributions to a lecture series at the European Studies Centre, St Antony's College, Oxford University, in Hilary term 2007.

PART I

Popular and Academic Historiographies in the Nineteenth Century

2

Questioning the Canon: Popular Historiography by Women in Britain and Germany (1750–1850)

Angelika Epple

Edward Gibbon, David Hume, Jules Michelet and Leopold von Ranke are all well-known and important historians from the eighteenth and nineteenth centuries who earned fame for their role in the making of modern historiography. They were all men, however. Did women of that period write history? Of course they did, but they solely wrote popular historiography. Women across Europe lacked access to scholarly training until the beginning of the twentieth century. Consequently one cannot find any academic history written by a woman that would belong to the traditional canon of European historiography of that time. This picture alters, however, if we consider historical texts written for non-academic readers. From the second half of the eighteenth century and into the nineteenth century popular historiography sold very well (Brock 2006: 48) and several authors made a living from their writings – even women (Davis 1980).[1] Thinking of Britain, Catharine Macaulay, Lady Wortley Montague and other women historians instantly cross our minds. Other European countries have their history women too, as can be seen in an excellent issue of the international journal *History of Historiography* (O'Dowd and Porciani 2004). Regarding Germany, however, no names come to mind. Successful female authors, and there were many of them in eighteenth- and nineteenth-century Germany, only wrote fiction. Why?

An adequate answer to this question has to deal with gender questions, with the history of historiography and the professionalization of history as an academic discipline (Epple 2003). A comparison of the British and the German situation will help us to disentangle this confusing complex. I will start by looking at the case of the famous British historian Catharine Macaulay and her female British colleagues. How did they deal with the problem of female authorship? As we will see, this issue leads to some even more difficult and troublesome questions, which were answered by Catharine Macaulay in her masterpiece *The

History of England (Macaulay 1763–83). What is, according to Macaulay, a good historian? How should a good historian tell their story? What is the duty of a good historian? And how does a good historian establish historical truth?

Secondly, and this is the main point of this chapter, I will contrast the British with the German situation. Why do we not find a German Catharine Macaulay? Who actually wrote history in eighteenth- and nineteenth-century Germany? Giving some consideration to the historiography of Leopold von Ranke I try to show why there were no professional women historians. However, if we look beyond the canon we do find a huge number of historical writings by female authors. Women historians of that time were non-professional insofar that writing history was not their academic profession. These women historians did not receive a university education; they did not use a specific historical methodology; and, therefore, they did not meet the requirements of the emerging academic discipline of academic history.

Nevertheless, women wrote history: they wrote about the past and interpreted historical events. Though they were often unskilled historians, they were professional authors and wrote stories to earn a living. These observations will lead me to challenge the male-dominated canon of German historiography from the eighteenth and nineteenth centuries. To learn more about German women historians I will ask the same questions I have already raised about Catharine Macaulay: How do German women historians deal with their female authorship? What do they expect from a good historian? And last but not least: How do they prove the historical truth of their histories? All the German women historians, and the historical narratives which I present here, have been excluded from historical tradition by what I will call the 'patriarchal' canon of historiography. This leads me to my last point where I analyse how this exclusion worked and what strategies lay behind it.

Catharine Macaulay and her Female Colleagues in Britain

The first volume of Catharine Macaulay's *History of England from the Accession of James I to that of the Brunswick Line* was published in 1763. During the next 18 years seven more volumes followed (Macaulay 1763–83). Macaulay began her masterpiece not at all timidly but with the following assertive statement: 'Though the rectitude of my intention has hitherto been, and, I trust in God! ever will be, my support in the laborious task of delineating the political history of this country' (ibid.: vii).

Even though Macaulay mentions here and there her inaccuracies of style due to her gender, she leaves us in no doubt about her competence: 'From my early youth I have read with delight those histories which exhibit Liberty in its most exalted state, the annals of the Roman and the Greek republics. Studies like these excite that natural love of Freedom which lies latent in the breast of every rational being' (ibid.).

It is therefore hardly surprising that these annals represent the ideals that Macaulay herself wanted to achieve.[2] If it was already remarkable that she announced quite directly her intention to write a political history of her country, it is even more extraordinary that she compares her own history with the annals of the Roman and the Greek republics. With this comparison she implicitly includes herself and other women as citizens in such a republic. After a long introduction, she concludes with an excuse: 'If I have digressed from the subject I set out with, which was to inform the public of my intention in writing this history, they will, I hope, excuse a warmth which national evils have excited in a breast zealous in the cause of Liberty, and attached with a servant devotion to the civil rights of my country' (ibid.: xvii).

For Macaulay it is beyond all questions that she was devoted to civil rights and the concept of liberty as strongly as her male colleagues were. For her, writing true history was not a matter of gender but a matter of the correct conviction. The ancient republics remained the famous model English history had to compete with (Wiseman 2001: 186). When Macaulay attacks Hume and his *History of England* (Hume 1754–62) in the sixth volume of her own work, it is mostly because of his – in her opinion – biased Tory point of view, one which she refutes ardently. She takes it for granted that, while being a woman, she is able to serve her country by helping the public to 'digest' the 'faithful representation of the important transactions of past ages' (Macaulay 1763–83). According to Macaulay, a good historian is a person who has the true political conviction – which means a Whig conception of the world. For her, a wrong political attitude is synonymous with historical bias and contrary to historical objectivity. Her understanding of prejudice is not embedded in a theory of the possibility of cognition. Macaulay still believed in the existence of an objective truth beyond the subjectivity of the historian. Hume thought that historiography should not intervene in political issues. He was convinced of the existence of an objective historical truth, which would be independent of a historical subject. He found the historical objectivity in the principle of causality.

Neither conviction excluded women theoretically from the production of historiography. From the outset their writing was not classified as dilettante. As to methodology, Macaulay, in a present-day sense, was even more professional than David Hume.[3] Hume did not use primary sources; however, Macaulay's *History of England* was based on her own research in the then new British Museum in London, which opened in 1753. This method, as Devoney Looser highlights, did not become a historical imperative for many decades (Looser 2000: 13).

Catharine Macaulay is probably the best known female historian of eighteenth-century Britain, but she is definitely not the only one – think, for example, of Hester Lynch Piozzi, who wrote about world history (Piozzi 1801). There existed a kind of professional network of female historians in the Anglo-Saxon world and Billie Melman has identified sixty-six English speaking women historians during the nineteenth century who wrote 782 books (Melman 1993). Women not only made history, they have also been writing history. For a British audience this is hardly a revolutionary idea. Maybe one could question whether British female historians were seen to be as important or as influential as their male colleagues, but nobody could deny their existence. The German case by comparison is more difficult. Most academics are still convinced that there was no equivalent to Catharine Macaulay and her ilk in the German speaking countries until the end of the nineteenth century.

Who Wrote History in Eighteenth and Nineteenth Century Germany?

At first sight the history of academic history in Germany is a success story of the late eighteenth century. The historians of the Enlightenment, above all the historians of the so-called Göttingen School gathered around Gatterer and Schlözer, established a new professional role: the academic historian.[4] Thanks to these historians, historiography from then on set out to explain past events rather than simply remembering or reconstructing them. Nobody expressed this concern more precisely than David Hume, who had a deep influence on the German Enlightenment (Reill 1975). One could say that the European Enlightenment introduced causal explanation into historiography (Gawlick and Kreimendahl 1987).[5] From the Enlightenment on it was the duty of a good historian to find the causes of past events and to show that a later event was an effect of a former one. Logically consistent, Hume was convinced that the proof of historical truth lay in the chain of argumentation. The chain of argumentation, however, from his point of view was nothing other than the verbal expression of a natural necessity. Even though teleology was less important for Hume than it was for Macaulay, history then appeared to be an objective process. The past seemed to be interesting not in itself but for its effect on the present.

The predominance of causality as a law of nature and history was questioned only a generation later. After the experience of the French Revolution and the Napoleonic wars it seemed obvious that history did not follow given rules. Contemporaries gave up the belief in historical causality; they could no longer see anything rational about history or predictable about future events. If a past epoch was worth dealing with – as the famous German historian Leopold von Ranke argued – it was not due to its effects on following epochs but due to its individual value or its inherent worth (Ranke 1970[1854]: 7). For Ranke, the principle of causality seemed to be far less important than the unique individuality of a historical epoch. Ranke and his contemporaries tried to free history from its reduction to a present political function. Today we know that they did not succeed and that Ranke's students notably contributed to a nationalistic German historiography. At the time, however, the new concept of historiography was based on the idea of political neutrality. Remember Catharine Macaulay's point of view: she was convinced that historical truth was a question of the correct political conviction. Ranke on the contrary argued that historical truth does not depend on political conviction. He also refuted Hume's suggestion that historical truth lies in the causality of past events.

Ranke's answer to the issue of historical truth sounds quite simple but is in fact revolutionary: historical truth lies, according to Ranke, in the evidence the historian presents, not in the form of a causal chain of arguments but in the form of an adequate historical methodology.[6] This new concept of historical truth had a big influence on ideas of what made a good historian and on the development of academic historiography. With the first historicists of the nineteenth century – among them Herder, Schiller and Ranke – a methodological framework was developed, which was meant to guarantee the quality and the truth of scientific historical studies (Fulda 1996). On the one hand this framework helped to create a professional identity for academic historians, while on the other it also helped to differentiate between professional historians inside and less qualified historians outside universities. This framework was thus both a definition of standards and a criterion of exclusion. At the same time, the canon of historiography was built up. The canon was fixed by historians at universities – like Ranke, Droysen and their succesors – who developed a specific methodology for the academic discipline. This creation of a canon was not a conscious act or a conspiracy by some male historians to gain power over female historians. A first step in the process was that, in their lectures or writings, these historians only mentioned and recommended certain academic works to their (male) students and to their readers of both sexes.[7]

When Leopold von Ranke delivered his lectures on the history of England in the 1860s he claimed that David Hume was the first and only historian to have succeeded in writing a concise history of the country.[8] Even though Catharine Macaulay was as successful as David Hume, she was never mentioned by Ranke (see Ranke 1937), and this tradition continued up to the late twentieth century. In an otherwise brilliant essay on British historiography, Jürgen Osterhammel (1992: 282) points out both the similarities and the differences between Ranke, Hume and Thomas Babington Macaulay, but ignores the work of Catharine Macaulay.

The construction of a fixed canon has some important implications for gender issues. If we look at the canon of German historiography it is true that there were no female historians. The early professionalization of the discipline defined the aforementioned methodological framework and the standards for doing history (Smith 1995). These standards relied on specific ways of proving the truth of historical events. They defined how a good historian should demonstrate the objectivity of their narrative (Epple 2007). In contrast to Catharine Macaulay's definition of a good historian, a professional historian now had to be objective in terms of political neutrality, this being one of Ranke's main concerns. This concern might also remind you of David Hume's effort at banning a Whig conception of history. Ranke's objectivity, however, no longer relied exclusively on the causality of past events and on the chain of argument. For Ranke, historical truth was seen to be affected by the subjectivity of the historian. This caused new problems. If historical truth depended on the subjectivity of the historian, how could historiography then claim objectivity? To defend history against arbitrary interpretations, the historicists created a historical methodology. Historical truth consequently had to be verified in terms of objective evidence, which mostly meant written documents. Women could not fulfil these standards, however, because they had no access to an academic education. Studying at a university was a precondition for true historiography. With the emergence of historical seminars (*Historische Seminare*), which had been institutionalized in most German universities by the 1870s and 1880s, students learned, for example, how to analyse manuscripts of the early modern period or how to interpret antique papers or coins critically. Only with these skills was the historian able to verify their narrative in terms of evidence.

As a result women and unskilled men were excluded from professional academic history writing. This fact alone would be enough to explain why we cannot find women historians in Germany in the nineteenth century. But it was even worse. The so-called modern way of doing history was not only a question of methodological standards. It was also a question of the very concept of history as such. It was a question of how historians thought about the past and thus how they narrated history (Epple 2003). During the Enlightenment, history seemed to be a teleological process: In Catharine Macaulay's history, for example, we read about the development towards liberty. Hume was less definite in this respect and made the first move toward a new concept of history. Instead of pure teleology with a given aim, he emphasized causality as the main historical principle. After the experience of the French Revolution and of the Napoleonic Wars this concept of history could not survive in Germany – at least not among the male intellectual elite. History could not be told any more as a story of a continuous development for the better. This is a well-known fact and many books have been written on this subject (Iggers 1968; Muhlack 1991; Rüsen and Jäger 1992). What makes it so relevant in the present context is that the historicist's concept of history not only gave birth to methodological standards, not only abandoned the belief in historical progress but, as a result, also changed the way history was told. It changed the patterns of narration in German historiography (Fulda 1996). If we compare Catharine Macaulay's *History of England* with Ranke's outline of the same subject we will notice that difference very clearly. Macaulay gives us a story of a continuous development for the better that leads up to a republican form of government. This story may include some set backs but, in the main, it is an illustration of historical progress. If we read Leopold von Ranke's history of England (Ranke 1859–69) in contrast we do not read such a story of progress. Neither do we read a story driven by the principle of causality. What we read is a self-contained story of an individual part of history. From Ranke's history, you cannot deduce directly any advice for people being in political charge.

Ranke's narrative finds unity in itself. His concern was with the investigation of the particular, even of the single point or moment (Megill 1995: 157–58). The narrated past was thus not tied to a specific function in the present of the historian. Ranke's pattern of narration answers to the historicist's concept of history: present and past are not connected teleologically, there is no visible progress. Instead of a connection there is a qualitative difference between the past and the present.

Historical narratives which imply a continuity between the recorded past and the present of the author, according to Ranke and his followers, can no longer live up to the expectations of academic historiography and the often-hidden claims of a good historian. This indeed marks an epochal turn. Following Michel Foucault (1974: 413–18), I would like to call it an epistemological break. It definitely changed the reception of the bygone patterns of historical narratives. According to the perspective of this new epistemology, all stories of continuity show up as old-fashioned, naive and unsophisticated; in a word: dilettantish. The new era of academic historiography in the twentieth century called itself modern. Non-professional historiography often followed patterns of narration which – according to the new epistemology – were by definition pre-modern.

Women as Historical Writers

Sixty per cent of all articles registered in the index of German periodicals between 1750 and 1815 were published anonymously.[9] Given this fact, it is notable that women often did not dare write under their own names. Therese Huber (1764–1829), the daughter of a philologist and librarian in Göttingen, was lucky to have access to a large amount of published writings of her time. Like Catharine Macaulay, she had never had a systematic training but relished the opportunity to learn on her own. History was one of her favourite subjects.[10] Even though she wrote many accounts of her journeys, a huge number of letters, narratives and essays during her two marriages, and even though both her husbands supported her writing, she did not publish anything under her own name until 1811 – after her father died (Leuschner 1999: 8). It took her twenty more years to write her first history book. In 1830 she published a history of the wars in the Cevennes, which dealt with the religious upheavals in early modern France (Huber 1834). Therese Huber was no exception in hiding her name from the public. More probably, one could say she was an exception in giving up anonymity. And there were other strategies for making women's achievements invisible. For example, women supported their famous husbands or relatives in collecting historical data, translating or even writing.

These female practices fitted better with the normative discourse of gendered role models. Yet despite this, even in late eighteenth and early nineteenth century Germany women had the agency to act. For example, women played an important role in the so called 'reading revolution', that is the rapid growth of a middle-class readership and the expansion of the literary market.[11] The growing number of published books and journals enabled more and more women to make a living from their writing. Though the public was more receptive to historical writing in Britain than in Germany, many German readers were also interested in historical settings, whether they be fictional or non-fictional. The enormous popularity of history provoked the conviction that it was desirable for women to have a certain knowledge of the past (Weckel 1998: 533). In contemporary periodicals for families, especially for ladies, one can find small historical portraits of, or comments about, famous persons. Nevertheless, there are no historical articles or essays in the corresponding periodicals explicitly written by a female author.[12] It remains only a suspicion that among these anonymous authors were many women.

If we want to know who wrote history in eighteenth- and nineteenth-century Germany, including women, we have to find a new approach to the definition of historiography. In this regard the successful writer Johanna von Wallenrodt is a good example. Johanna von Wallenrodt (1740–1819) wrote countless courtly novels and romances which were set in the Levant and the Far East. She used the Middle Ages, foreign societies or imagined countries to experiment with gender roles or social hierarchies. History was thus a kind of utopian playground and fiction a good way to conceal the provocative content of her work. Johanna von Wallenrodt is a good example of a female author who played with, but never crossed, the border of fictional and non-fictional narratives. She never wrote history in a narrow sense, though she published an autobiography in two volumes (Wallenrodt 1797), and using the history of her own existence she provided an insight into the everyday life of the lower nobility in the second half of eighteenth-century Germany (Epple 2003: 167–284).

Women did not have the skills to investigate primary sources in state archives and neither did they have access to official political documents. They did, however, obtain information from relatives and friends and they themselves were eyewitnesses of historical events. So if we do not only look at professional historiography but also at popular historical writings – including historical novels, autobiographies and biographies – we discover new texts beyond the canon, many of them authored by women.

Another example of a woman historian from the late eighteenth century is Louise Johanna Leopoldine von Blumenthal (1742–1808). In 1797 she published a biography of her uncle which was translated only five years later into English under the title *The Life of General de Zieten* (Blumenthal 1803). For the biography Blumenthal not only investigated Zieten's correspondence – among it an exchange of letters with King Friedrich II – and other primary sources, she also employed what we would nowadays call 'oral history' as she interviewed contemporary witnesses. Thus she wrote a detailed biography of her uncle who had served more than forty years in the army of Friedrich II. She did not, however, focus exclusively on her protagonist but also reconstructed the three

Silesian wars with extraordinary diligence. She even discussed the traditional historiography of her times critically and thus established a relation between her own book and other contemporary interpretations of events. She drew new conclusions from her sources and did not hesitate to question the version Friedrich II himself had given in his history. She also contradicted the contemporaneous historian General von Tempelhof (1783–1801). The latter still counts as an expert in the military history of the Seven Years War (1756–1763), while Blumenthal's detailed analysis has fallen into oblivion (Lindner 1993). There are some basic similarities between Blumenthal's concept of history and that of Catharine Macaulay, even though Blumenthal was not in favour of a republic; for example, she was convinced that history was a teleological process for the better. Like Macaulay she was quite self-confident about her female authorship and at the end of the book she named herself a *Geschichtsschreiber*, or 'historian' (Blumenthal 1797). This is the only occasion of a German woman describing herself in this way from this period I have found (Epple 2003: 363–97).

Another good example of a popular female historian is Johanna Schopenhauer (1766–1838), whose son was the famous and influential philosopher Arthur Schopenhauer. Johanna Schopenhauer was well known in the era of the *Weimarer Klassik* at the beginning of the nineteenth century. She ran a salon, a central meeting point for the literary world of Weimar and was a friend of Johann Wolfgang Goethe and other leading artists and intellectuals of the time. In 1810 she published a biography of her teacher and friend Carl Ludwig Fernow (Schopenhauer 1810).[13] Shortly after Fernow's death, the most important publisher in early-nineteenth-century Germany, Friedrich Freiherr Cotta von Cottenburg, asked Johanna Schopenhauer to write Fernow's biography. One reason why Cotta asked a female author and not a male one was probably the relative mediocrity of the protagonist, mediocre in comparison to famous contemporaries like Reinhold, Schiller, Goethe or Hegel. However, his mediocrity was not the main reason; rather, it was the friendship of author and protagonist. Cotta asked Johanna Schopenhauer because she and Fernow had been close friends (Weber 2000: 20), and Schopenhauer used Fernow's friendship to excuse her female authorship. It was important for her to underline that it had not been her idea to write a book; rather, she felt obliged 'to edit the following pages' (Schopenhauer 1810: i) because she knew some important details of Fernow's life exclusively. In comparison to her contemporary Catharine Macaulay, Johanna Schopenhauer is much more anxious about her female authorship. This is a striking and significant difference because it contrasts with similarities in their methodology: both women historians studied primary sources – Macaulay went to the British Museum and Schopenhauer read a large number of letters and analysed Fernow's diaries and travelogues.

Macaulay used the documents extensively to sustain her argument. In the first five volumes of her book she named sources in footnotes, but changed method in volume six: 'The author, having heard that long notes were tedious and disagreeable to the reader, has altered the method which she pursued in the five first volumes of this history, and at a much larger expense of labour has woven into the text every part of the composition which could be done without breaking into the thread of the history' (Macaulay 1763–83: 15).

The quote expresses her point of view that there is a 'thread of history' which can only be revealed by the historian. For Macaulay, historical truth is not a question of interpretation but of correct conviction and of using skills to find all the hidden documents. History is, according to this epistemology, like a puzzle: the more parts you find, the clearer the picture becomes.[14] Here Macaulay is in agreement with Leopoldine von Blumenthal. Blumenthal also believed that her male colleagues had made mistakes because they had missed relevant documents – and not because history could be a subject of discussion. This conviction fits into the concept of history as a teleological process.

Johanna Schopenhauer also quoted her sources at length, but here similarities with Macaulay or Blumenthal come to an end: Schopenhauer never wove the sources into the text. The biography of Fernow is not a narration but a compilation of what the protagonist himself would have said if he were still alive.

Schopenhauer used sources to re-present history; they were not testimonies of historical truth but history itself. The author disappears behind the sources of the past. Consequently Schopenhauer qualified herself as an editor. To prove the truth, Schopenhauer used alternative strategies: on the one hand she pointed out that she herself was an honest person with an upright and ethical personality. Schopenhauer's tactic of emphasizing Cotta's request thus appears in a new light. It is an excuse for her female authorship while also an excellent chance to demonstrate her modesty. But this is not the only truth strategy she employed. As important as her character is her familiarity and close friendship with the protagonist. Often she was an eyewitness of events in his life while friends sometimes entrusted her with details about Fernow's experiences. She made it very clear through which chain of persons information had come to her. This way she became an 'ear witness' of past events (Epple 2003: 329–46).

One could ask whether this difference in truth strategies was determined by the difference in genre. Schopenhauer wrote a simple biography of a not especially well-known contemporary, while Macaulay wrote a serious history of a country. This definitely makes a difference. But Schopenhauer did not just write a biography of a friend addressed to a small number of Weimarian intellectuals. Ultimately the biography was an economic project and Cotta had asked her for the book to make a profit. Apart from its biographical aspects Schopenhauer's book also analysed the intellectual milieu in Weimar in the first decade of the nineteenth century. And this made the book interesting for many readers all over Germany.

How did the Exclusion Work?

The difference between Johanna Schopenhauer's biography and Catharine Macaulay's history leads us back to questions of gender and the difference between the two genres. Johanna Schopenhauer was not an equal of those of the literary circle for whom she arranged meetings in her salon. When she wrote Fernow's biography she did not live up to the contemporaneous standards of what made a good historian. She did not dare adopt the position of a confident author. Schopenhauer as an author disappeared completely behind her protagonist and the written documents of his life. She tried to hide her subjectivity behind the objective facts of Fernow's life. At the same time, however, when the subjectivity of the author disappeared behind an assumed objectivity of facts, subjectivity came back as a truth strategy: Schopenhauer argued that her character was of such a high morality that the truth of her story could not be questioned. Somewhat paradoxically, the reader only hears the voice of the author when Schopenhauer tries to underline the truth of her writing. The truth thus lies in the subject of the author. Meanwhile Schopenhauer's concept of history is attached to naive objectivity.

This truth strategy has a long history and can be traced back to ancient rhetoric (Koselleck 1979). Even Macaulay's emphasis on the correct political conviction has something to do with this strategy.[15] Whatever the tradition, this moral truth strategy loses its power in the era of so-called modern historiography. Ranke wrote history with the knowledge of the subjectivity of historical recognition. Having this in mind, the emerging academic discipline of the time claimed scientific objectivity all the same. The historical methodology thus had to guarantee the objective truth of historical writings beyond the subject of their authors. To labour the point, once historical recognition had turned out to be affected by subjectivity, truth strategies had to rely on objectivity.

As a consequence, the morality of a character, the deep feelings of an author for their subject and all mention of emotion became a sign of subjectivity and thus of dilettantism. Historical methodology should both avoid obvious political manipulation and exclude all emotional subjectivity from historiography. Leopold von Ranke and other founding fathers of German academic historiography presumably did not read Catharine Macaulay's *History of England*. If they had, it would have been difficult for them to condemn it at first sight. According to the new rules of the discipline, Macaulay used a valid truth strategy: she proved the truth with written documents. On second thoughts, however, they would probably have rejected her work because of her old-fashioned concept of history. My main argument here is that Macaulay's *History of England* could only be a success in the historical context of the Enlightenment. As with Johanna Schopenhauer's biography of Fernow, it is closely attached to a naive concept of historical objectivity. The so-called modern concept of history, however, combined historical objectivity with subjective recognition. In Germany, where historiography became an academic discipline very early on, the new concept of history rejected the historiography of the Enlightenment. As a result women were completely excluded from writing professional history.

Schopenhauer's biography is a good example of how the new concept of history contaminated its 'other', which was excluded. Schopenhauer's book helps us to understand how this exclusion worked. Nevertheless there were other women historians who found a more appealing way to solve the problem. In contrast to Johanna Schopenhauer, who tried to hide her authorship behind her protagonist, they carried subjectivity to an extreme. This strategy was almost never combined with political history but with historical writings such as biographies, travelogues, diaries, autobiographies and other works. With their radical subjectivity they not only challenged the truth strategies of the canon but also dealt with an excluded field of professional historiography. Like Leopoldine von Blumenthal, Johanna Schopenhauer or Isabella von Wallenrodt, they dealt with the characters of their protagonists, with ethical values, with friendship and family questions, with death, birth, childhood, love and hatred. Only in the late twentieth century did academic history learn about the importance of what was excluded. What had been once excluded returned partially to the fold as micro history or the history of everyday life. The division of labour between popular and professional historiography was legitimized two hundred years ago. It was an attempt to create a professional identity for academic historians by excluding important themes and those who were seen as unimportant people. We, as professional historians, should leave nothing undone to regain that lost terrain.

Notes

1. According to Claire Brock it was the best selling genre of the period because it was acceptable reading for both sexes and a necessary part of the education (and enlightenment) of eighteenth-century children in Britain (Brock 2006: 48).
2. John Pocock has characterized Macaulay's commitment to the ancient ideal of active citizenship as being in contrast to her feminist attitude. Like 'an eighteenth century Hannah Arendt' she was 'wholly undeterred by its hyper-intense masculinity' (Pocock 1998: 251). Kate Davies (2005) argues, however, that the eighteenth-century version of the republican debate was basically different from classical republicanism. The latter relegated the feminine to a private sphere.
3. Claire Brock points out that Macaulay used her own work to reassert her claims to greater authority through continual enhancement of her more scholarly methodologies in comparison to her male rivals (Brock 2006: 49).
4. Horst Walter Blanke and Dirk Fleischer list sixty-nine universities in German speaking countries (including Austria and Switzerland) with a chair of history in the eighteenth century – church history not included (Blanke and Fleischer 1990: 103–23).
5. The German *Aufklärer*, according to Reill, admired Hume's *History of England* greatly (Reill 1975: 56).

6. This methodology relies on 'documentary, intensive, broad study' and also includes the search for a 'causal nexus' (Ranke 1975a: 78–79).

7. Concerning English history, Ranke mentions Carte, Hume, Lingard, Brodie, Mackintosh and Macaulay (Ranke 1975b: 367–71).

8. Ranke mentioned Hume consistently (Ranke 1937, 1975b: 365).

9. See the *Index Deutschsprachiger Zeitschriften 1750–1815*. Retrieved 18 August 2008 from: http://www.clio-online.de/site/lang__de/ItemID__17439/mid__10325/87/default.aspx.

10. According to Brigitte Leuschner (1999: 6), who analysed Huber's letters, Huber read, for example, Arnold's *Unparteiische Kirchen- und Ketzerhistorie. Vom Anfang des Neuen Testaments bis auf das Jahr Christi 1688* (Arnold 1967[1729]).

11. Thomas Nipperdey traces the reading revolution in Germany back to the first two-thirds of the nineteenth century (Nipperdey 1983: 587–95). This is certainly true regarding journals and newspapers. Concerning popular literature, the reading revolution began in the second half of the eighteenth century.

12. Except, that is, for small historical portraits in the style of lexicon entries.

13. See also the *Allgemeine Deutsche Biographie* (1877: 716–17), where the author of the entry refers explicitly to Schopenhauer's biography. Born the son of a farmer, Carl Ludwig Fernow escaped the Prussian army as a juvenile and, in Lübeck, met the painter Carstens, who became a close friend and teacher. He studied philosophy in Jena, and then worked in Rome for nearly a decade (1794–1803) where he became an art historian and aesthetician. Back in Germany he earned his living as a librarian at the famous Herzogin Anna Amalia library in Weimar. After Fernow's death in 1809 Goethe acquired 1600 Italian books which Fernow had brought back from Rome. See also the website of the Herzogin Anna Amalia library: http://www.klassik-stiftung.de/einrichtungen/herzogin-anna-amalia-bibliothek/ueber-die-bibliothek/geschichte/bestandsgeschichte.html. Retrieved 29 March 2007.

14. Claire Brock underlines the point that Catharine Macaulay wanted the public to gain a profound awareness of the 'living presence behind the composition' of her work (Brock 2006: 52). Macaulay's emphasis on her authorship is not necessarily in contrast to her objective concept of history. Her critique of Hume does not allude to the problem of the subjectivity of historical recognition but only to the problem of whether Hume's delineation was right or wrong.

15. Finally the truth strategy is based upon a certain understanding of civic virtue, attainable by both sexes. For details, see Brock (2006: 56).

3

Popular Presentations of History in the Nineteenth Century: The Example of *Die Gartenlaube*

Sylvia Paletschek

The Nineteenth Century as the Century of History

The nineteenth century has many names: the century of the bourgeoisie, the century of nations, the century of industrialization, and the century of natural science and technology.[1] However, it might just as well be called the century of history. From the late eighteenth century on, the engagement with the past, and particularly with 'patriotic' history (*vaterländischer Geschichte*), was an important means of shaping individual and collective identity. After the collapse of the *Alte Reich* (the Holy Roman Empire of the German Nation) in 1803–1806, and following the Congress of Vienna in 1815, the German states in their new patchwork arrangement placed an emphasis on history and on the construction of the single state's historical tradition. This served the purpose of securing the old and new population's attachment to the readjusted political system and of constructing a patriotic and national identity.[2] Yet, next to the German states of the first half of the nineteenth century and the newly unified Germany of the *Kaiserreich* (German Empire) of 1871 onwards, the national movement, newly emerging political movements such as liberalism and the women's movement, and an aspiring bourgeoisie also drew their legitimacy from history and made politics by means of history.

The end of the eighteenth century was marked by the experience of radical, unprecedented and unforeseeable changes. Thorough uncertainty brought about by the Enlightenment, the French Revolution, the collapse of the *Alte Reich* (the Holy Roman Empire of the German Nation) in 1803–1806, as well as the territorial reorganization of the world of German states, meshed with emerging economic, social and mental changes such as industrialization, transportation and communication revolutions and the implementation of a secularized world view. These cataclysmic transformations gave rise to a new perception of history. The so-far unquestioned perspective on history as something static, as an everlasting recurrence of some deathless kind of human behaviour, had become obsolete. The historical constellation promoted a divergence between the realm of experience and the horizon of expectations (Koselleck 1989: 349–75). History now became conceived of as a process and, thus, as something unique and changeable. In the course of the nineteenth century, historicism – the demonstration of the historical genesis of societal, political and mental phenomena – turned into a central paradigm of world interpretation and also determined the kind of thinking practised in the humanities and early social sciences. Thus, history took on new meaning in the decades around 1800: now its task was to explain each historical period's unique nature and the present's historicity as well as to help endure the future's open character. At the same time, however, its old functions of moral, religious, and political instruction remained.

Consequently, by the beginning of the nineteenth century historical developments had produced a demand for orientation through history which increasingly materialized in multiple civil and state initiatives for researching and mediating history. The establishment and expansion of academic historical science is just one component of this larger development. If history thus gained increasing importance in the nineteenth century, how exactly did it reach the members of society? What kinds of popular presentations of history existed at that time? Through what media did people learn about the historical past? What historical periods or issues were particularly attractive to them?

Very much like today, history was felt to be much too important to be left exclusively to academic historians. Following on from this insight, this chapter offers an investigation of nineteenth-century popular presentations of history. For my present purposes, the term 'popular presentations of history' refers to accounts in written, visual and audiovisual form which convey information about the historical past in a way that is attractive and accessible to a broad audience.[3] My aim is to provide a first outline of the topic since investigations into the popular culture of history and syntheses of a comprehensive culture of history in the nineteenth century are still to be accomplished. As early as 1977, Rudolf Vierhaus claimed that researching the history of historiography must exceed 'what has been common practice so far' and move beyond traditional academic historiography by looking at the presentation of history in schools, museums and popular historical literature as well as by investigating 'historical awareness, its political and social function' (Vierhaus 1977: 111). Yet existing work on historical culture is mostly of a more theoretical nature and geared to the traditional mediators of history and high culture. For the most part, the hitherto existing history of historiography has concentrated on academic historiography established in the universities without looking into possible interdependencies between this and popular forms of (re)presentation.[4]

In what follows, I start out with a cursory overview of the various institutions and media through which history was researched and conveyed in the nineteenth century. Secondly, I look at historical presentations in the context of the family journal *Die Gartenlaube*, a highly popular periodical which commenced publication in the mid nineteenth century.[5] I will conclude with a few arguments about the characteristics of popular presentations of history in the nineteenth century.

Forms of Appropriating History in the Nineteenth Century: An Overview

The Church, Schools and Universities

The attempt to gain knowledge about the past is closely related to the history of education and the media, but also to the history of religion and to intellectual history. In the early nineteenth century, the first, and in many cases only, encounter with history experienced by the lower social classes was their acquaintance with biblical history, provided by both the Church and elementary schools (*Volksschulen*). Here, history was not taught as a discrete subject but communicated via religious or reading lessons. As a discrete subject, history was established in elementary school in the second part of the nineteenth century (Pandel 1997: 526–27). At that point in time, lessons about the historical past were thought to support a nationally oriented and patriotic education (Kuhlemann 1991: 206). In higher boys' schools (*höhere Knabenschulen*) and gymnasiums, history made its first appearance in the teaching of old languages (particularly Greek and Latin). However, discrete history lessons also entered the curriculum in the first part of the century. As the syllabuses reveal, history teaching was frequently combined with geographical instruction. In terms of quantity, history lessons held a rather modest share of the overall teaching load and comprised two to three (at the most) hours of instruction per week (Schneider 1997: 495–501). Partly pressed by Wilhelm II, the school reforms of the 1890s were designed to place an emphasis on German modern history and on conveying a national, monarchical and anti-socialist attitude. Yet, this focus on shaping the 'correct' political attitude through history was also met by resistance by the school administrations; also, the first annual convention of the *Deutsche Historikertag* (Society of German Historians) passed a note of protest against the reform in 1893 (Albizetti and Lundgreen 1991: 260–61).

In universities, history was also taught only to a moderate extent until the mid century. Up to that point, a given university was usually endowed with just one history chair. Lectures were predominantly held for students of law and theology in their *Grundstudium* (the phase of basic studies) when they were obliged to visit a lecture on world history for two semesters. With its focus on working with historical sources and the creation of new insights, modern historical science necessarily implied specialization. Accompanied by rather fierce conflicts (see Paletschek 2002: 41–44, 55–57),[6] its broader institutionalization took place after 1850. Accordingly, academic history won its proper student clientele only in the second half of the nineteenth century when an increasing demand for teachers turned Schools of Philosophy (*Philosophische Fakultäten*) into institutions for the education of teachers. Simultaneously, classical philology was removed from the curricula of higher schools in favour of the so-called 'realities' (*Realien*), which included history along with modern languages and sciences. However, by the end of the nineteenth century, historical science's increasing specialization and scientism also did away with its former status as part and parcel of a general academic education which also meant that it lost a great deal of its attractiveness to students of other disciplines.

Museums, Historical Associations, Edition Projects

The task of mediating and researching history was not restricted to schools and universities as public institutions of learning. In response to the unsettling upheavals of the years around 1800, representatives of both the bourgeoisie and nobility began to collect historical artefacts and sources and founded the first historical museums. A well-known example is Hans von Aufseß who collected sources on the history of the *Alte Reich* and on 'patriotic archaeology' (*Vaterländische Altertumskunde*) from 1820 (Hakelberg 2004). His initiative ultimately led to the foundation of the German National Museum in Nuremberg. Another aristocratic initiative, this time by Freiherr von Stein, led to the establishment of the *German Historical Society* (*Gesellschaft für ältere deutsche Geschichtskunde*) and the Monumenta Germaniae Historica (MGH), a major project for editing the most important sources on the German Middle Ages (Fuhrmann 1996a: 11–28). Pushed by German high nobility, the project was ultimately financed by the states of the German Confederation (*Deutscher Bund*).

From the second half of the eighteenth century, bourgeois reading clubs and patriotic societies dedicated to serving the public good grappled with historical issues. The 1820s and 1830s saw the emergence of numerous regional history and antiquity associations. By 1860, there were about sixty societies of this kind (Kunz 2000: 59), and by 1900 their number had risen to about 150. These organizations conducted research on the history of their particular regional environment. By offering access to history they functioned as mediators of history, first to broader parts of the upper classes – the nobility, clergy, senior officials and high-school professors (*Gymnasiallehrer*) – and, later on, to ordinary elementary-school teachers (*Volksschullehrer*), small merchants and individual bourgeois women. By the end of the nineteenth century, these civic initiatives partly interlocked with others run by the state (Speitkamp 1996). Evidence for this is provided by the establishment of the historical commissions (*Historische Kommissionen*) from the 1890s onwards. Simultaneously, these associations also established links to the *Heimatschutzbewegung* – i.e. the movement for the preservation of the 'homeland', its countryside and culture –

and initiated the establishment of the *Denkmalschutzbewegung* – the movement for the preservation of historical monuments.

Visual and Animated History

There were also different visual and even 'living', animated types of historical appropriation – for example, in the form of monuments, history paintings, panoramas or dioramas, and the re-enactment of historical scenes via historical festivities (Hartmann 1976), pageants, living images (*lebende Bilder*) and through theatre plays and operas. Thus, for example, guilds and heralds in historical costumes made their appearance at the national feast (*Nationalfest*) in Nuremberg which was celebrated from 1825 onward. The idea behind this event was to provide a point of contact with the town's past as a free, imperial city. As one contemporary observer noted in 1833, 'figures from a previous world moved through the city in measured, ceremonial succession' so that people 'couldn't help but feel their minds returned to that romantic time' (Bauer 2006: 63). Through visual display, such pageants were able to reach broad strata of the population beyond the educated classes.

Sustained by the liberal and the national movement, and also partly supported by the single states' rulers, historical celebrations and commemorations emerged as distinctive types of historical recollection from the 1830s onward. Frequently in combination with the inauguration of a memorial, merited bourgeois heroes of the 'cultural nation' (*Kulturnation*) were honoured on these occasions. Thus, Nuremberg celebrated a Dürer festival in 1828, followed by a Gutenberg festival in Mainz in 1837 and a Schiller festival in Stuttgart in 1839. Apart from this, there was also the practice of commemorating important war events of the more recent past, such as the Battle of Leipzig (1813). Monuments were now erected not only to rulers, pictured on horseback, but also for bourgeois men who had rendered outstanding services to the *Kulturnation* (Nipperdey 1968). Thus, such memorials popularized the recollection of the bourgeoisie's historical achievements. Frequently, the implementation of major national memorials dragged on for quite some time. For example, the construction of the Hermann monument (*Hermannsdenkmal*) in the Teutoburg Forest began in 1838, but its inauguration was celebrated only in 1875 after interminable financial problems were finally overcome (Tacke 1995; Ritzmann 2006: 193–229). However, the (mediated) discussions about these memorials, the foundation of associations dedicated to their construction, drawn-out fundraising campaigns and splendidly staged inaugurations reached a broader public and popularized the historical events or personalities commemorated.

Information about history was also conveyed through commercial events, such as the presentation of historical sheets of pictures (*Bilderbögen*) at fairs. Looking back on his adolescence, Theodor Fontane (1819–1898) noted that his knowledge of the Greek war of independence in the 1820s or of the affiliated Russo–Turkish war of 1828/9 was gleaned from the images provided by a show which he visited at a fair. The images of these *Bilderbögen* were so strongly imprinted on his memory that 'in spite of all their crudeness and triviality or, perhaps, due to this, they did their part' so that he felt better informed about 'persons, battles, and heroic deeds of that period than the majority' of his contemporaries (Kraul 1982: 44). Apart from these images, Fontane's perception of history was also shaped by historical anecdotes picked up from journals and magazines which his father conveyed to him. According to Fontane, these two instructors taught him more about history than 'all teachers in secondary school and the gymnasium taken together' (ibid.).

The panoramas which became both extremely popular and economically successful between 1880 and 1900 were a modern continuation of the *Bilderbögen* shown at fairs and, in part, also of the historical and ethnological presentations found at world exhibitions (Weidauer 1996). Set up in purpose-built pavilions of about forty metres in diameter and fourteen metres in height, these elaborate painted panoramas particularly featured recent national battles and European contemporary history. Their sudden disappearance at the end of the nineteenth century is probably due to the rise of the cinema and other innovative forms of entertainment.

History in the Book Market

The communication and reading revolution of the first half of the nineteenth century (Nipperdey 1983: 587–94) – exemplified by the rise of literacy, the increased production of less expensive books and journals brought about by the invention of the rapid printing press, and the implementation of new distribution channels such as commercial lending libraries, bourgeois reading halls and the book hawking trade – increased the production and circulation of historical reading material. Inspired by the model of Sir Walter Scott, historical novels in particular became bestsellers throughout Europe from the end of the eighteenth century onward (Reitemeier 2001; Potthast 2007). This particular type of historical fiction endowed with historical information inspired a more thorough historical interest in many readers. This is evidenced by the example of Leopold von Ranke who is said to have found his way to studying history by reading Scott's novels.

If we look at non-fiction books, history (as a market segment) accounted for about 5 per cent of the overall book market in the second half of the nineteenth century (Nissen 2009). This matches the market share presently held by historical books in the market for specialized books. Between 1849 and 1914, historical works made up between about 3 and 5 per cent of lending libraries' total stock. In comparison to German academic historiography, which was decidedly protestant and national-liberal or national-conservative, popular presentations of history provided a much broader and more pluralistic view of history, both politically and in terms of subject-matter (Langewiesche 2008d: 88). According to the social, political and religious fragmentation of German society during the *Kaiserreich*, different social groups read quite different history books. Historical works with a decidedly socialist, Catholic or Jewish perspective were frequently found among the bestsellers.[7] Also, general or world histories authored by the enlightened historians of the late eighteenth and early nineteenth century consistently held top positions – in spite of the establishment of an approved national historiography in the universities from the 1850s onwards.[8] Even more surprisingly, in an age of accelerated nationalism, not only works on German history but also on French and British history became historical bestsellers.[9] What is also remarkable is that the field of cultural history, neglected by academic history, enjoyed great popularity.[10]

'Popular' history books were primarily written by clergymen, teachers and members of the military – and, incidentally, also by an impressive number of revolutionaries from 1848 (Nissen 2009). However, there were relatively few women among these authors, figures like Fanny Arndt or Lina Morgenstern being exceptions. Women, it seems, preferred to write historical novels rather than specialized history books. Before 1880, university professors featured more frequently as authors of popular histories, among them von Rotteck, von Raumer, Schlosser and von Ranke. After 1880, however, there seems to have been a break in this regard. This suggests that the then ongoing professionalization of academic historiography meant that academic historians' works were no longer accessible to the broader educated public. The historians recalled by the history of historiography as particularly influential were often considerably less successful regarding the broader educated readership. Leopold von Ranke is a rare exception here, though to some extent this also holds true for Johann Georg Droysen and Theodor Mommsen.[11]

However, popular historiography's success in the book market should not blind us to the fact that the readership of books constituted only a small segment of the overall population. As we will see below, a much wider audience was reached by illustrated journals such as *Die Gartenlaube*. As I will argue, many of the above mentioned characteristics of popular historiography in the book market in the second half of the nineteenth century also apply to the presentation of history in contemporary family journals.

As these briefly touched on examples of the appropriation of history demonstrate, the nineteenth century saw the gradual emergence of an enormously diverse and both politically and commercially successful historical culture which not only reached the higher levels of the nobility and bourgeoisie but also the petite bourgeoisie and, if only to a marginal extent, the strata below the middle classes as well as people of all genders and confessions.

Popular Presentations of History in *Die Gartenlaube*

Founded in 1853 by the former revolutionary Ernst Keil in Leipzig, *Die Gartenlaube* was both the most successful and most popular German family magazine of the second half of the nineteenth century; it is referred to as the first periodic mass press publication (Belgum 1998: 187). One of the trademark characteristics of this weekly were its numerous elaborate illustrations. By the 1870s, it had reached a print run of about 385,000 copies. This means that *Die Gartenlaube* presumably reached an audience of up to two million male and female recipients. By comparison, most of the major newspapers of the time had a print run of just 4,000 copies (ibid.: 11–27). Based on a liberal programme and endowed with the impetus of enlightened ideas and education, the journal strove for the implementation of the civil rights of both the individual and the nation-state. *Die Gartenlaube* popularized the nation and, thus, contributed to so-called 'internal nation building' (*innere Nationsbildung*) as well as to the emergence of a national communicative space (Koch 2003; Zamseil 2007).

Die Gartenlaube can be conceived of as a vehicle for the popular (re)presentation of history. Its primary goal was 'to entertain and to teach in an entertaining way' which also included the realm of history. Thus, the first issue stated that 'through genuine, well-written narratives, we want to introduce you to the history of the human heart and of peoples, to the struggles of human passions and of past times'.[12] About half of the articles in *Die Gartenlaube* were fiction, with the other half covering what we now call factual issues: the natural sciences, medicine, economic issues, travel descriptions, mixed news and historical contributions. As a review of the volumes of 1861 and 1898 reveals, historical contributions made up about 18 to 20 per cent of the journal's topical content.[13] Thus, history comprised the largest category among factual issues and was much more in evidence in family magazines than in the book market, where history comprised only 5 per cent of overall production. In *Die Gartenlaube*, history was preferably negotiated through biographies of historical figures (about 11 per cent), while more general political and cultural contributions and articles on cultural history made up about 8 per cent.

Designed to draw in subscribers, *Die Gartenlaube*'s advertisements primarily focused on the serialized novels that were published by the magazine. However, they also drew on the historical issues covered by the journal. For example, the advertisement for the 1899 volume contained a preview of Adalbert Stifter's *Nachsommer* as well as upcoming articles on ship collisions, the issue of apparent death, and castles in the Harz region. Also, it contained teasing headlines from its historical contributions; for example, 'Schill and His Officers' (concerning the 1809 *franctireurs*), 'Truth and Tell Tale about the Paris Bastille' and 'German Expatriates of 1848 in the United States'.[14] This suggests that the historical contributions not only pursued the political goal of a national *Volksbildung* – education of the general public – but also it seems that the subject matter was selected for both its entertainment and sales value.

The periodical's historical contributions were sometimes authored by permanent members of the editorial staff, journalists such as F. Hoffmann, who wrote suitable contributions on contemporary political history when occasion was provided by an anniversary. Alternatively, historical writers successfully established in the popular book market also published articles in *Die Gartenlaube*. Examples include the cultural historians Johannes Scherr, Karl Biedermann and Rudolf von Gottschall. Thus, the popular presentations of history in the family magazine clearly overlapped with those found in the book market and in lending libraries. In contrast to this, there seem to have been no crossover between the journal's historical accounts and coeval academic historiography. According to my provisional investigations, academics who held a chair in history were not among the journal's contributors. Moreover, there are hardly any references to books, vitae or public appearances of well-known academic historians; in the rare case of such a reference it is conveyed in the form of a short note. The only academic historians to whom the journal dedicated a more detailed and substantial article were Leopold von Ranke and Theodor Mommsen. Yet, even this exception adhered to the rationale of popular presentations in that both articles were published on the occasion of the fiftieth anniversary of their doctorates.[15]

Recent historical work on *Die Gartenlaube* stresses the journal's important contribution to nation building, its liberal potential undervalued by former research and its significance in the process of negotiating a modern identity by coping with the insecurity and conflicts experienced in the process of modernization (Belgum 1998: 188). In this respect, it was particularly *Die Gartenlaube*'s historical contributions that served the purpose of shaping a national and modern identity. For the time being, we can conclude that in *Die Gartenlaube* history stood for the popularization of the nation, for suspenseful and touching entertainment, and for instructive enlightenment. Moreover, it served as a means of modern identity formation. What, then, were the historical issues and periods covered by the journal and how were they depicted? The following represents the results of an initial analysis of the journal's historically oriented contributions.[16]

Contemporary History

Most strikingly, the majority of contributions is devoted to the history of the preceding one hundred years; that is, to recent and contemporary history.[17] Accordingly, one column in the annual index of contents is headed 'Descriptive and Historical Articles/Matters of Contemporary History (*Beschreibende und geschichtliche Aufsätze/Zeitgeschichtliches*).[18] It was predominantly historical facts and events pertaining to what Jan Assmann has called 'communicative memory' (Assmann 1995a: 125–33) that were at the centre of *Die Gartenlaube*'s historical coverage. Communicative memory covers the last three generations and a time span of about eighty to one hundred years. It is marked by more informal structures and oral communication, and overlaps in various ways with familial memory. As part of the culture of remembrance, communicative memory has a major significance for identity formation, both with regard to the individual person and to social groups. This also implies its significance in the formation of nations and political movements.

In *Die Gartenlaube*'s historical articles, the focus is on three contemporary historical events: the Napoleonic Wars, especially the so-called Wars of Liberation (1813/14); the Revolution of 1848/9; and, from the 1870s and 1880s onwards, the Franco–German War of 1870/71.[19] In the light of the journal's nationalist programme, it is not surprising that major space and attention was devoted to the Napoleonic Wars and, in the last decades before the turn of the century, the Franco–German War. However, what is striking is the consistent recollection of the 1848 Revolution. These historical events were an important part of German nation building, not least because all three were warlike occurrences in which family history, the history of the nation and world history converged. Moreover, the wars were excellently suited to personalizing, dramatizing and emotionalizing historical depictions and, thus, to a representational aesthetics which characterizes popular forms up to this day. Readers' individual access to these historical events was facilitated both through family members' involvement in them and via identification with well-known heroes and heroines – such as the stubborn officer Schill and his franctireurs and the young heroine Eleonore Prochaska.[20] These and others were model achievers in, as the magazine puts it, Germany's 'most arduous years' – that is, between 1809 and 1814.[21]

By recollecting these events, *Die Gartenlaube* also established a dialogue with its readership. Not least because the journal dealt with contemporary historical issues, this led to the active involvement of the journal's readership. Thus, on the occasion of the fiftieth anniversary of the Frankfurt parliament (*Paulskirchenparlament*), the journal published the following call for participation: 'However, we gladly take up a proposal which originated in the circle of our readers and hereby cordially request that all "veterans of the *Paulskirche*" who are still alive may soon delight us by sending us a short sign of life so that it will be possible for us to assess their total number'.[22] The names of those still alive were published along with their portraits later in the year.[23]

In additon to noting *Die Gartenlaube*'s clear focus on national contemporary history, we should not overlook the journal's policy of depicting national events in their concrete regional specificity. Moreover, the German states and regions also provided a self-evident issue which was dealt with by the journal. What recent research now refers to as the 'federal nation' (Langewiesche 2000: 55–79; Langewiesche and Schmidt 2000) also crops up in *Die Gartenlaube*'s historical contributions: the concept of the nation was made acceptable and comprehensible particularly by its regional wrapping, and by synthesizing both a broader and narrower sense of nation (*engeres und weiteres Vaterland*), as this was termed in contemporary parlance.

It should be noted that the journal also directed the attention of its readership to contemporary historical events outside the German territories – particularly in contributions addressing the French Revolution, the Crimean War (1853–1856) and the Russo–Turkish War (1877/8) – but also to the national histories of other European states.[24] While contemporary history was clearly tailored in a national way, it was by no means narrowly confined to national events. The journal practised a surprisingly broad, European and almost 'global' approach to history even though non-European history was preferably presented in terms of cultural history, and engagement with American, Chinese, Arabic or African history tended to be based on the oversees actions of German minorities. The depiction of non-German and non-European territories, especially in the context of cultural historical contributions, nurtured a contemporary longing for the exotic and the fabulous, even though they also revealed the transnational and global entanglements of the late *Kaiserreich*.

The Ancient World and the Middle Ages

It is striking that there is a scarcity of articles in *Die Gartenlaube* on the ancient world and the Middle Ages in comparison to those on the contemporary period. Yet, when the focus is on them, depictions tend to be endowed with lavish and decontextualized visualizations which serve the purpose of myth-making.

This scarcity is arguably due to the fact that ancient history was less suited to supporting the formation of national identity in the second part of the nineteenth century which may account for its minor presence in the journal. Another reason may have been that the journal's broader petit bourgeois clientele did not possess prior knowledge of ancient history – in contrast to the bourgeois class endowed with a higher education and acquainted with classical philological studies. An exception to this concerns events and personalities of antiquity which could be related to Germanic history (Belgum 1998: 172–76). This applies, for example, to contributions dedicated to Hermann resp. Arminius. Yet, the mythification and monumentalization of such figures was not accomplished through the written text, but exclusively through marginally comments and large and lavishly designed illustrations. The most striking characteristic of this 'mythic monumentalism' (ibid.: 174) was its decontextualized nature. The illustrations picked up national stereotypes and popularized a mythical national past. Thus, for example, the conflict between Kriemhild and Brunhilde in the Song of the Nibelungs, the return of the Germans from the battle in the Teutoburg Forest or the capture of Hermann's wife Thusnelda by Germanicus were presented in broadsheet, full-page pictures.

Topics of medieval history had a somewhat stronger presence in the journal, even though they were again scarcely contextualized and articles employed monumental illustrations of 'great individuals' that caught the eye. Furthermore, the journal also featured more unspecific scenes taken from cultural history which can be viewed as a tribute to a more simple, romantic era of national life.[25] Apart from attention devoted to singular heroic figures – such as Luther, Frederick the Great, the Fugger family, heroes from the Peasants' War (1524-1526) or the Thirty Years War (1618-1648) such as Konrad Wiederhold – the early modern period was covered more strongly through social and cultural topics which provided an occasion for their association with problems of contemporary society by means of critical retrospection.

The Functions of History

In line with an enlightened tradition, the usefulness of historical contributions was very much an issue in *Die Gartenlaube*. This 'usefulness' included the promotion of national identity, the shaping of a modern, bourgeois mentality, a critical assessment of politics and society and – last but not least – entertainment value.

   History was viewed as a means for criticizing the existing political and social status quo and for assessing one's position in the present. This was particularly apparent in contributions on cultural history. Unresolved contemporary problems – such as uncompensated orientation needs (Kocka 1990: 427–43) – often provided the peg for such a contribution. Thus, the first episode of the eight-part series 'Images of Cultural History' (*Culturgeschichtliche Bilder*) by Karl Biedermann, which started in 1854,[26] states that the observation of cultural history is unlikely to produce the kind of immediate usefulness provided by the observation of nature and the laws deduced from it. Yet, the author argues that the observation of cultural history is equally instructive in many respects even though it does not provide direct instructions for action. According to Biedermann, engagement with historical progress in commerce, science, art and technology reveals 'the potential of the human mind ... and, thus, incites us to such a suitable use, to the diligent development of our manifold mental dispositions and abilities'. At the same time, cultural history is said to teach 'modesty by pointing out how earlier generations also conceived of themselves as having arrived at a high level of perfection which, in part, was actually true, although they were outdistanced by far by their offspring'.[27] Thus, the author tells his readers that they must assume their collective fate to be a similar one in the future. Cultural history is characterized as something which can stave off despair when much in the present is not as one would like it, since it teaches the lesson that in former, sometimes not-too-distant, times such circumstances have been by far more unsatisfying and much has improved since. This legitimates the hope that circumstances will become even better and more satisfying in the future. However, cultural history is also seen to correct erroneous assessments by historical comparison. Briefly put: engagement with history indirectly stimulates new ideas, constitutes faith in progress while at the same time it teaches humility and qualifies current problems or puts them in a new perspective.

For the most part, the contributions on cultural history start from contemporary problems. For example, an 1854 article addresses the 'now dominant issue of price increase' (*Theure Zeiten*) and introduces the notion that in the past bread used to be cheaper and the middle classes used to be better off.[28] Generally speaking, the historical reflections of the author then deconstruct such a notion by criticizing the false idealization of the past and, instead, stressing the progress accomplished or producing a qualifying result. Thus, an 1898 article on servants in the sixteenth century offers a differentiated argument concerning complaints about bad servants and deconstructs the notion that things had been much better in the past.[29] The notion is refuted by recourse to historical sources: a councillor's book of economic accounts exhibited at the Germanic National Museum and to the so-called 'Devil's Theatre' (*Teufelstheater*) of 1587. The article suggests that complaints about servants survived the centuries as a quasi 'extrahistorical', anthropological attribute and supports this by making the observation that there is a general preference for complaints over compliments: good servants are less commented on than bad ones. Furthermore, it is argued that there are only a few sources which provide access to the servants' own perspectives which might present a rather different picture. This example illustrates the function of popular historical depictions of this kind, which provide orientation with regard to everyday problems and current social issues, looking at them from a different perspective.

It is the cultural and social historical contributions in particular which take up issues of everyday history frequently coded as female even in our time: the household, beauty, consumption, fashion, lifestyle and so on.[30] All in all, *Die Gartenlaube* covers both a colourful and broad spectrum of issues of everday life. Topics such as the history of beer or the history of male hair or beard styles and practices of shaving[31] indicate that the journal nurtured the cultural historical interest of a male readership and that the practice of gendering issues – for example, making political history 'male' and cultural history 'female' – was present while also being disrupted. This also applies to incidents when political and national history are depicted in terms of female protagonists – women rulers, freedom fighters and, of course, by the mother who sacrifices herself for the nation – which ensures the inclusion of a female readership.[32]

Commemoration and Remembrance

Anniversaries and jubilees functioned as major points of reference for *Die Gartenlaube*'s popular depictions of history. Similar to present-day practice, articles tended to be published some time in advance of the actual event. This kind of media coverage was thus designed to draw the national audience's attention to the actual event and to provide an informed interpretive framework for its reception. This kind of celebratory practice of particular anniversaries and jubilees ensured their periodic recurrence, their consolidation and their transmission through established social practice.

As we know from the work of Winfried Müller and Arndt Brendecke, the beginnings of the jubilee tradition go back to medieval religious and ecclesiastical traditions (Brendecke 2005: 61–83; Müller 2005: 29–44). This particularly relates to the introduction of the first Holy Year and the pontiff's granting of full indulgence and remission for all sins to the faithful who, having repented and confessed, visited the basilicas of the Apostles Peter and Paul in 1300. At that time, the intention was for this practice to be repeated every hundredth year in the future. Later on, this expanded to include indulgence decreed every fiftieth and, finally, every twenty-fifth year. Humanism linked this tradition with ancient traditions of secular celebrations so that the end of the sixteenth century saw the emergence of a secular Protestant jubilee culture, first practised at the universities and eventually adopted by Protestant rulers. From the nineteenth century on, the jubilee tradition was increasingly taken up by the bourgeoisie and expanded to political and cultural as well as to personal jubilees.

Recent research by Aleida Assmann and Heinz Schlaffer, for example, considers anniversaries or jubilees as 'memorials in time' (A. Assmann 2005: 313). As representatives of periodic time, anniversaries are situated between linear and ephemeral historical time and the kind of cyclical time attached to myth and nature which symbolizes the eternal return of the same. According to Aleida Assmann, the increasing acceleration of linear time is inextricably related to a growing significance of periodic time with its firmly recurring points of reference. For a certain point in time, anniversaries extract the non-recurring from linear order, allow for periodic remembrance, convey orientation and offer opportunities for a staging of collectivity. They are 'memory activists' (Carol Gluck), authorities for activating collective memory. Depending on temporal circumstances, such activations either facilitate new interpretations of actual historical events or make for their further consolidation as myth. Anniversaries stabilize recollection through repetition, offering a formation of meaning and a future-directed promise of action.

Returning to *Die Gartenlaube*, anniversaries, regardless of their particular rhythm or periodization, were consistently and almost excessively used for presenting historical issues. For example, the year 1863 initially offered an opportunity to look back at the *Befreiungskrieg*, the wars of liberation against Napoleon (1813/14), which took place fifty years earlier, but also featured several articles on the occasion of the fifteenth anniversary of the 1848 Revolution.[33] Anniversaries were covered by comprehensive or short articles or by full-page, elaborate illustrations. With regard to the latter, good examples include an illustration published in September 1898 in remembrance of the 1848 street fighting in Frankfurt.[34] In 1894, a full-page drawing of the arrival of Abbess Irmingard in Frauenchiemsee appeared on the occasion of the event's millennium, thus indirectly pointing to an alleged thousand-year-old German heritage.[35] Equally popular were historical articles composed as multipart mini-series which covered a jubilee topic. A good example is a series called 'From the Times of Arduous Adversity' (*Aus den Zeiten der schweren Noth*) which was published over several years and depicted the heroic deeds of well-known and not so well-known people during the Napoleonic Wars. The series featured the escalade of the *Crimmaische Thor* in Leipzig as well as the fates of a shepherd, a second lieutenant, a book-seller and a peasant of that time.[36]

The year 1898 brought about the fiftieth anniversary of the 1848 Revolution and saw the publication of an eight-part series authored by Johannes Proelß, lavishly illustrated with 105 drawings and entitled 'How the First German Parliament Came into Being' ('*Wie das erste deutsche Parlament entstand*').[37] It was proudly announced that the series was partly based on so-far unconsidered sources. Part one was published in the first January issue of 1898, a few months before the event's actual anniversary in March.

Also popular was the depiction of an anniversary that spoke to particular current events, using historical analogy to illustrate the concrete political function of history. Thus, an article published in 1864 criticized the contemporary political situation by comparing the lack of rights found in an assembly of delegates who convened in Frankfurt on 21 December of that year with the far-reaching authorization of the parliament which had met in the Frankfurt Paulskirche fifteen years earlier.[38] The recourse to contemporary history was thus used to critically hold up a mirror to the present political situation. However, such recourse could also celebrate past successes in an affirmative way and, by doing so, consolidate the status quo.

Die Gartenlaube also reported on public commemorations occasioned by anniversaries; for example, the construction of a memorial or the inauguration of a monument, on a wreath-laying ceremony or a commemorative speech.[39] The meaning of the event in terms of memory culture was thus once more consolidated via the interconnection of different media; for example, when a commemoration was taken up by the press or when popular historical bestsellers (such as the works of Wilhelm Zimmermann or Johannes Scherr) were reviewed in *Die Gartenlaube*.[40]

Results and Outlook

As the analysis of popular depictions of history in books and the family journal *Die Gartenlaube* demonstrate, the concepts and narratives of history which circulated in Germany in the second half of the nineteenth century were much more pluralistic – politically, confessionally and topically, but also in national terms via the integration of regional, national and world histories – than a focus on academic historiography of that period would suggest. From the point of view of popular historiography, German society looks much more pluralistic and open, even though social and cultural difference can also be traced in popular historiography.

Popular historical depictions definitely contain innovative approaches. Examples include cultural history and the world histories published around 1900 which, in part, pursued transdisciplinary approaches. However, popular historiography itself did not provide a methodological formulation or reflection on these approaches.[41] What also stands out is the strong reference for contemporary history and the affirmative character of discussions. These features result in a reductionism which foregrounds the topical facets of history prevailing in the respective period's functional memory. This already indicates academic historiography's important and indispensable function beyond the discipline's instructional tasks. These functions include the methodological reflection of the discipline's own actions and an engagement with issues less relevant to a given time's prevalent issues and preferred historical periods.

What seems to me to be significant about *Die Gartenlaube* is the journal's decided focus on contemporary history. This finding has its parallel in the dominance of contemporary history in popular presentations of history today – as can be seen, for example, in film and on television. We might conclude that in modern times the period enclosed in communicative memory and the time span covered by all living human beings in a given moment forms functional memory's 'natural' centre. Constituting such a centre also fulfils the function of providing intergenerational coherence. Apart from this, it is the mythical incipiencies (located either in antiquity or the Middle Ages) that inspire historical interest and determine the need for orientation while the 'in-between ages' recede against this. Exceptions to this trend are events or persons from such 'in-between ages' passed on through anniversaries, or fictional presentations in plays, novels and films, and thus enshrined in cultural memory on an intermediate to long-term basis.

There is currently a lack of empirical research on popular depictions of history and the diverse segments of nineteenth-century historical culture. Such research could provide stimuli for a renewed history of historiography. Also, such analytical work on historical culture could reveal much about the mindset of the nineteenth century. Finally, it could contribute to our discipline's self-reflection and to determining our present position as historians. The popular presentations of history, many of which drew on 'scientific' ways of proceeding and on methodological comprehensibility, partly took up new issues beyond academic historiography. There is considerable evidence substantiating the argument that in the humanities, these popular presentations constituted an innate, original form of knowledge production, rather than one deduced from academic historiography. This means that for the humanities in the nineteenth century, much more so than for the natural sciences, we may have to assume the existence of a discrete form of knowledge production outside academic institutions.

Notes

1. I want to thank Gabriele Kreutzner for translating this chapter as well as for her helpful and inspiring discussions.
2. This is demonstrated particularly well by the example of Ludwig I and Bavaria's historical politics. The Bavarian monarch supported research on Bavarian history and financed the construction of patriotic and national monuments. He encouraged the building of the 'Hall of Fame' ('*Ruhmeshalle*') 1853 in Munich, designed as a memorial to Bavarian figures of all times. Also, he inspired the construction of the Walhalla Hall of Fame and Honour (1842), designed as a collective memorial to the most dignified and famous German men and women of all times. Thus, he was able to skilfully link the shaping of a patriotic identity in new parts of Bavaria to a national identity politics which both aimed at strengthening Bavarian patriotism and consolidating the Wittelsbach dynasty.
3. The term popular 'presentations' is chosen in order to convey the notion that many of the depictions received by a mass audience were endowed with decidedly visual and performative traits; see, e.g., panoramas, pageants or the numerous historical illustrations found in family journals.
4. See also the remarks concerning the state of research on the subject of popular history in the introduction to this volume.
5. My study focuses on the period 1853–1900 (vols. 1–48) of this journal, published in Berlin by Scherl.
6. There were protests by representatives of the disciplines of theology and law when modern history professors refused to teach established lectures on universal history. This conventional form of history lecture, which offered a compilation of older historical works, not only failed to conform to the new professional and scientific standards of modern historiography, it also failed to meet the profession's national sense of mission. On the other hand, the new, more specialized lectures no longer met the educational ambitions of theologians and jurists whose interest was in a broader overview of history.
7. In the socialist milieu, history books which were critical of the Church as well as works dedicated to the history of revolutionary upheavals were very popular. See, e.g., the history of the Peasant War (*Geschichte des großen Bauernkrieges*) by the historian Wilhelm Zimmermann (1841–43) and the history of the 1848 Revolution by Wilhelm Blos (1893), a leading social democrat. With 47,000 copies sold, Blos's work was the most successful socialist history book until the First World War. While fiercely criticized by the Protestant expert league (and widely read by Catholics), Johannes Janssen's history of the German people since the end of the Middle Ages (*Geschichte des deutschen Volkes seit dem Ausgang des Mittelalters*, 1876–94) was one of the bestselling books on German history in the second half of the nineteenth century.
8. Thus, Karl von Rotteck's *Allgemeine Geschichte vom Anfang der historischen Kenntniss bis auf unsere Zeiten* (1812–27) saw twenty-five editions by the end of the nineteenth century and sold more than 100,000 copies. For the success of the new 'world histories' around 1900, see also Hartmut Bergenthum's contribution to this volume.
9. E.g., Thomas Babington Macaulay's *History of England* in four volumes was a historical bestseller, published in several German editions from 1849 onwards (Macauly 1763–83); the same applies to Henry Thomas Buckle's *History of Civilization in England*, first published in Germany in 1857. See Langewiesche (2008d: 87–88) and Nissen (2009).

10. This included books like Heinrich Riehl's natural history of the German people (*Naturgeschichte des deutschen Volkes*, 1851–55), Johannes Scherr's history of German culture and custom (*Geschichte der deutschen Kultur und Sitte*, 1852–53) and Gustav Freytag's 'pictures from the German past' (*Bilder aus der deutschen Vergangenheit*, 1859–67).

11. It was particularly the earlier works and the biographical studies that were successful: see, e.g., Droysen's *Geschichte Alexander des Großen* (1833) or overviews characterized by their strong references to the present like, for example, Mommsen's *Römische Geschichte* (1851). See also Lamprecht's *Deutsche Geschichte* (1891–1909) which, even though it was controversial within the circles of academic historians, sold comparatively well. The same applies to Treitschke's *Deutsche Geschichte im 19. Jahrhundert* (1879–94). However, in quantitative terms, it could not match the older enlightenment histories' success or the reception granted to the Catholic and Socialist historians.

12. 'An unsere Freunde und Leser', *Die Gartenlaube* (1853: x).

13. Further statistical analysis is still to be undertaken. My present data base is a first sample which counted the number of titles on various historical subjects published in *Die Gartenlaube* in the columns 'Biographien und Charakteristiken'; 'Beschreibende und geschichtliche Aufsätze, Zeitgeschichtliches, Vermischtes'; and 'Blätter und Blüten'. For an overview on the journal's content, see also Hofmann and Schmitt (1978[1903]) and Estermann (1995). Alexander Gall, who has analysed the visual content of articles on natural science and technology in *Die Gartenlaube*, took a 5 per cent control sample for selected years (1892, 1897, 1902) and evaluated the respective surface ratios of text, drawings, and photography according to content-related aspects. According to this sample, about 50 per cent of the available space in *Die Gartenlaube* fell on literature and about 9 to 13 per cent on history. For the most part, historical contributions form the biggest functional group, ranking above medicine (about 2 to 4 per cent) and geography (about 3 per cent). Only the categories *Verschiedenes* (miscellaneous) and *Gesellschaft* (society) which might also include historical contributions (particularly on contemporary history) hold about the same share or even exceed the history category.

14. *Die Gartenlaube* (1898: 893).

15. See *Eine goldene Hochzeit mit der Wissenschaft* (*Die Gartenlaube*, 1867: 100) on Ranke, and *Ein Gedenkblatt zu seinem 50jährigen Doktorjubliäum* (*Die Gartenlaube*, 1893: 747) on Mommsen.

16. The following points should be read as initial findings which need to be substantiated by further research. The coverage of history in *Die Gartenlaube* has not been systematically analysed so far and this still constitutes a desideratum. Belgum (1998) has focused on the presentation of Germanic history, and particularly on its visual representation.

17. This assessment is based on the evaluation of *Die Gartenlaube's Inhaltsanalytische Bibliographie* for the years 1853–1880 (based on Estermann 1995), content analysis of the years 1861 and 1898, and on Hofmann and Schmitt (1978[1903]). A more detailed statistical and qualitative evaluation of the historical articles in *Die Gartenlaube* is yet to be accomplished.

18. See the contents of *Die Gartenlaube* (1898).

19. For recollection of the Napoleonic Wars, see Planert (2007); on the Franco–German War, see Becker (2001); and on the 1848/49 Revolution, see Siemann (1998). None of these works on nineteenth-century memory culture drew on *Die Gartenlaube*.

20. See, e.g., the article 'Ein deutsches Heldenmädchen', *Die Gartenlaube* (1863: 596–600).

21. See also the series 'Aus den Zeiten der schweren Noth', *Die Gartenlaube* (1863: Nr. 3, Nr. 8. Nr. 9).

22. 'Wir folgen aber gern der Anregung aus dem Kreise unserer Leser und lassen hiermit an alle noch am Leben befindlichen "Veteranen der Paulskirche" die herzliche Bitte ergehen, uns durch ein kurzes Lebenszeichen baldigst erfreuen zu wollen, damit eine genaue Feststellung ihrer Zahl möglich werde' (*Die Gartenlaube* 1898: 35).

23. *Die Gartenlaube* (1898: 317).

24. Here priority was given to France, Austria, Britain and Russia, but also to historical articles about Belgium, Spain, Italy, Serbia and Greece.

25. See, e.g., the illustrations for 'Auf einer alten Handelsstraße in den Alpen' (*Die Gartenlaube* 1884: 77) and drawings such as 'Aus einer altdeutschen Stadt' or 'Sängers Werbung' (Belgum 1998: 172).

26. The series started with the first article on 'Theure Zeiten' (*Die Gartenlaube* 1854: 377–80). A footnote referred to Biedermann's (1969[1854]) then recently published book.

27. *Die Gartenlaube* (1854: 377).

28. *Die Gartenlaube* (1854: 378). A similar approach is taken in the next article in this series, devoted to the supposedly increasing phenomenon of begging and to greater altruism in the past. The article concludes: 'And yet in general nothing is more inaccurate than degrading the present and praising a former, supposedly better, time' (*Die Gartenlaube* 1854: 446).

29. 'Die Dienstboten vor dreihundert Jahren', *Die Gartenlaube* (1898: 749–50)

30. On cultural history in *Die Gartenlaube*, see the titles listed in Estermann (1995: 277–88). For example, the ten-part series by F. Helbig, 'Deutsches Frauenleben im Mittelalter. Eine culturhistorische Studie' (*Die Gartenlaube* 1878: 444–46, 509–11, 610–12, 710–12, 774–76; 1879: 30–34, 102–4, 217–19); 'Damentoilette sonst und jetzt' (*Die Gartenlaube* 1855: 590); 'Die geschichtliche Wandlung der deutschen Frauenmoden' (*Die Gartenlaube* 1880: 803, 819); 'Urbilder unserer Frauenmode' (*Die Gartenlaube* 1867: 726–27); 'Die Wäsche sonst und jetzt' (*Die Gartenlaube* 1878: 278–79); 'Aus der Geschichte des Traurings' (*Die Gartenlaube* 1876: 439–41); and 'Das Wasserglas. Eine geschichtliche, technisch-chemische und volkswirthschaftliche Skizze' (*Die Gartenlaube* 1857: 198–200, 278–80).

31. See, e.g., 'Rasieren. Alles hat seine Wissenschaft (Alte und neue Art das Rasiermesser abzuziehen)' (*Die Gartenlaube* 1864: 686–87); 'Die Geschichte des Bieres' (*Die Gartenlaube* 1855: 604–605); 'Ein Geheimniß im Bierreiche. Culturhistorische Skizze' (*Die Gartenlaube* 1872: 96–99); and 'Leute bei der Spritze. Alte und neue Feuerwehr' (*Die Gartenlaube* 1864: 732–34).

32. See, e.g., 'Die Damen auf dem Wiener Kongreß' (*Die Gartenlaube* 1880: 401, 431); 'Frauen als Entdeckungsreisende und Geographen' (*Die Gartenlaube* 1880: 163, 259); 'Frauen der französischen Revolution' (*Die Gartenlaube* 1875: 26).

33. See, e.g., the series 'Aus den Zeiten schwerer Not' (*Die Gartenlaube* 1863), the articles dedicated to recollections of the Battle of Leipzig (*Die Gartenlaube* 1863: 672, 688) and the articles on the heroic girl Eleonore Prochaska (*Die Gartenlaube* 1863: 596–600). In remembrance of 1848/49, articles on 'Kinkels Befreiung' (*Die Gartenlaube* 1863: 194), on Gustav Struve (*Die Gartenlaube* 1863: 208) and a relatively long article by Moritz Hartmann on the last days of the German parliament (*Die Gartenlaube* 1863: 40–44) were published in 1863.

34. *Die Gartenlaube* (1898: 613).

35. *Die Gartenlaube* (1894: 192–93).

36. On the escalade, see *Die Gartenlaube* (1862: 649–54); on the different fates, see *Die Gartenlaube* (1861: 500–504).

37. *Die Gartenlaube* (1898: 9–12, 44–47, 72–76, 104–10, 139–43, 168–74, 208–14, 254–57).

38. *Die Gartenlaube* (1864: 93–96).

39. See, e.g., the reference to the commemoration which took place from 16 to 20 October 1863 on the occasion of the fiftieth anniversary of the Battle of Leipzig (*Die Gartenlaube* 1863: 596). See also the report on the history of the monument in Altona in memory of the Schleswig–Holstein War (1848), the monument's inauguration and the reference to a public act of remembrance both in Altona and in Kiel in March 1898 on the occasion of the event's fiftieth anniversary (*Die Gartenlaube* 1898: 275–76).

40. See, e.g., several enthusiastic reviews and articles on Wilhelm Zimmermann's history of the Peasant War ('Ein Geschichtsschreiber der Wahrheit', *Die Gartenlaube* 1869: 292–94; also 1877: 799–800); on Johannes Scherr (*Die Gartenlaube* 1886: 877); and on Gustav Freytag (*Die Gartenlaube* 1886: 514).

41. See also Nissen (2009).

4

Understanding the World around 1900: Popular World Histories in Germany

Hartmut Bergenthum

Introduction

Around the year 1900 popular world histories blossomed in Germany.[1]

Why were so many people at that time interested in the history of the world? What factors caused this boom and what did this particular upsurge signify? What kind of stories do these universal histories tell and what do these reveal about Wilhelmine society? What are the functions of these popular historiographies? Why is it worthwhile analysing popular world history compendia in general? And what can be said about the relation between these popular historiographies and the academic mainstream?

Until today, popular world histories, apart from those of Leopold von Ranke and Oswald Spengler, have not been recognized as a source for historiographical studies. The history of historiography only deals with assumed scientific or more philosophical accounts of renowned scientists (Geiss 1993: 434; Middell 1993: 390–91). Like other popular forms of history writing, world history compendia do not feature in classical texts and comprehensive overviews.[2] Even current discussions of world history and new global history have not altered this situation (Stuchtey and Fuchs 2003; Kaelble 2004; Middell 2005a).[3] Therefore, new methods to analyse this partly voluminous material had to be evolved.

To begin with I will introduce world history compendia as a source and outline the methods used to analyse them.[4] In a second step the historical context around 1900 will be explored. The main part of the chapter shows the different ways in which these world histories attempted to understand the world and its changes. Finally some concluding remarks deal with the popular academic nexus.

World History Compendia

World histories try to describe and interpret the entire history of humankind in one volume or several from the earliest times to the present. Their titles or introductions claim to present a universal history of the world in a coherent compendium (Moore 1997: 948). Popular world histories are intended for a broad readership outside the academic context (Schenda 1988: 32–34; Daum 1998: 33–36; Hardtwig 2005d: 15, 20). The designated target audience can include both young and old people and even the working class. Some books were cheaply produced on low-quality paper, while others were lavishly illustrated and very expensive.[5] They had to be sold and had to be physically attractive to reach a popular audience. Beside the price, other strategies were adopted to make these compendia a success.[6] Firstly, some of these world histories or parts of them were also published in a different format, such as in the daily press. Secondly, the lively presentation and simple language employed allowed for quick and easy understanding. The stylistic devices of dense description and of fictitious speech were heavily used. Some authors also used a moralizing style. The dramatic, detailed and figurative style of presentation also had a memorizing function. For a quick overview, extensive tables of content and other indexes were employed, and important phrases were highlighted. Some world histories presented a headline or used short abstracts in the margin. They did not employ bibliographies nor exact quotations. However, occasionally secondary literature is mentioned and all world histories claim to have integrated the results of recent academic research. The illustrations were mainly portraits of people, and pictures of battles, buildings, coins and so on. Reviews always appreciated this visual content. In particular the authenticity of the images was stressed and the educational purpose was highlighted.[7]

The goal to educate turned out to be ambivalent. For example, the working class simply could not afford the expensive, beautiful six-volume world history edited by Julius von Pflugk-Harttung (1848–1919) and published by Ullstein.[8] These prestigious objects belonged instead to a bourgeois lifestyle and a copy could be found in every middle-class household (Herrmann 1991: 148; Wittmann 1991: 267–68). Reinhard Wittmann calls these book 'monuments' and 'typographic knickknack' (*typographische Nippesfiguren*) (Wittmann 1991: 249). Except for some autobiographical accounts (Schmitt 1950: 25), no one knows if, how and when they were read. In many respects they are similar to encyclopaedias (Moltmann 1975: 137; Kelly 1981: 6–7; Hughes-Warrington 2005a: 225, 234).

Why is it still worthwhile analysing popular world history compendia in general? Despite the simple fact that they exist in large numbers and editions, they also reveal insights into the historical culture of their time. As such, world histories are a specific cultural practice, an attempt to come to terms with the world. They are part of a particular 'historical culture' (*Geschichtskultur*) in the sense of Wolfgang Hardtwig (1990c) and Jörn Rüsen (1994b: 235–37; see also

Schulin 1998). They connect historical sciences and the public sphere. World histories popularized scientific results and offered their readers a standardized, common version of knowledge of the past. This collective knowledge had the potential to produce an identity-building effect and to determine action. World histories offered models with which to interpret life experiences in changing times. With the help of these histories, groups could better understand themselves. They were produced mainly by historians and teachers in order to cope with different challenges and to restore the basic assumptions of collective and cultural identity. In short, they offered coherent narratives of the past to provide a clear orientation in the present (Hughes-Warrington 2005b: 8).

How can and should they be analysed? How is it possible to cope with the sheer size, the universal regional and topical scope of these works, especially for individuals who are themselves an expert in only a few fields of study? The method I want to suggest consists of three sets of questions:

1. How did the world histories themselves define history and world history? What philosophy of history or models of progress do they adhere to? What criteria actually structure world history? What caesuras are used to divide world history and what epochs are defined with what characteristics (Graus 1987: 153; Dunk 1994: 22)?

2. What are the driving forces of history? Which categories are employed to characterize the main development of history? Drawing on Ernst Schulin (1974: 40) and Fernand Braudel (1969: 20–21), I employ the term 'universal factor' (*Universalfaktor*) to look at the protagonists, the driving forces and larger topics which have a bearing on history. Here it is necessary to avoid having a strict set of factors. Instead the categories used by the world histories themselves must be taken seriously. In this case six broad, universal factors are employed, which also feature prominently in the academic historiography of the time: the state, including the nation and the people; the capacity of extraordinary individuals to shape history; religion; language and racial groups; culture, especially art and science; and social and economic forces (Stöve 1982: 42; Weber 2001: 34; Raphael 2003: 76; Rothermund 2005: 14–15).

3. Where does world history take place? What is the spatial concept or horizon (*Anschauungshorizont*) of world history (Maier 1973: 86)? How are the different continents connected to each other? And in particular, how is Europe represented (Schultz 2005: 204, 208)? Who is included in the community of humanity?

These three sets of questions can be condensed into a single, overarching question: What does 'world history' actually mean in the view of these published world histories (Heuss 1976: 4; Holz 1993: 16, 24)?

The World around 1900

At the turn of the twentieth century even the most remote parts of the world became relevant to German politics and society. For the first time the world was experienced as a global whole.[9] Wilhelm II proclaimed a new world politics and Germany attempted to make itself into a colonial power, trying to control small parts of China in 1898. On the one hand the world increased in scope: there were no places anymore which could be characterized as far away and therefore of no interest. On the other hand the world decreased in the perception of the people as their consciousness of space and time changed. In particular, improved means of communication led to a convergence (Osterhammel 1994: 58–59). Moreover, there were other moments of change: the beginning of mass society, the social question, urbanization, cultural uncertainty, nervousness, restlessness, both belief in progress and worry about the future characterized as an ambivalent attitude to life (Berg and Herrmann 1991: 22; Drehsen and Sparn 1996: 12, 20; Ullrich 1999a).

Overall, global changes put all preconceptions and presumed knowledge at risk. The German middle classes felt increasingly insecure. They longed for information about these new parts of the world and wanted to strengthen their self-confidence. European dominance was questioned for the first time following the first Japanese defeat of a Western power both on land and at sea during the Russo–Japanese War of 1904/5 (Conrad and Osterhammel 2004: 10). Science in general and historiography in particular were seen as things with which people should be able to understand such contemporary phenomena and they were also expected to provide orientation for people (Bruch 1980: 22; Hübinger 1988: 150; Ullmann 1995: 16, 173, 192–96; Schröder and Höhler 2005: 31).

Popular history compendia tried to understand the globalization occuring around the year 1900. World histories were an attempt to cope with some of the phenomena of the crisis, and aimed at explaining contemporary world politics and providing a history of new big players, like the United States. The world histories intended to help the reader understand the daily news and complex changes, presenting concise information in a space-saving format. They even presented themselves as a tool to help individuals shape their own world-view and rethink the world anew. They claimed to deliver practical knowledge and aimed at shaping the personality and morality of the reader.[10]

This is why so many people around 1900 were interested in the history of the world and a boom in world histories occurred. Historians wrote new world history compendia, and publishers initiated new editions of old, already widely disseminated, world histories, adding new parts in order to include contemporary developments and the latest results of historical science. Depending on the classification one employs, about twenty popular world histories in total circulated – leaving aside the compendia published for schools and other educational purposes. They range from explicit Protestant to Catholic world histories, and from political to materialistic histories. As for authorship, they range from one journalist to a collective of mainly academic historians collaborating on large compendia (Bergenthum 2004: 21, 289–91).

Today none of these world histories is known or included in summaries of German historiography. However, around 1900 they were commonly read among the people of Germany. If one reviews contemporary bibliographies (e.g., Herre 1910), encyclopaedias and book reviews (e.g., *Historisches Jahrbuch*, *Jahresberichte der Geschichtswissenschaft*) and combines the results with the numbers of editions and copies sold of a publication, one gets an impression of the extent of dissemination, though not of reception. Of the middle-sized, exhaustive world histories the following six were particularly popular:

1. The Catholic *Annegarns Weltgeschichte* in eight volumes was popular over the entire nineteenth century, written and updated by teachers starting in 1827 (see Annegarn 1895–96).[11]
2. The patriotic *K.F. Beckers Weltgeschichte*, written and updated by teachers since 1801, was published in its third edition in twelve, cheap volumes between 1891 and 1893 (see Becker 1891–93).[12]
3. Similarly impressive is the publishing history of perhaps the most widely known work, *Fr. Chr. Schlossers Weltgeschichte für das deutsche Volk* (Schlosser 1892–93).[13] As such, a stunning fact that the liberal historian oriented at the historical pragmatism of the enlightenment was still circulating around 1900 (Hardtwig 1990a: 225).
4. The well-illustrated world history in four volumes written by Oskar Jäger was highly commended at the turn of the century (see Jäger 1887–89, 1890–94). Jäger (1830–1910) was a teacher of religion and history who became headmaster of the Friedrich-Wilhelm Gymnasium in Cologne in 1865 and later professor in Bonn (Meyer 1985: 131, 137).[14]
5. The historian and publicist Hans Ferdinand Helmolt (1865–1929) edited a nine-volume world history for the Bibliographische Institut (Helmolt 1899–1907). Because of its revolutionary take on world history it was heavily discussed even in the daily press and translations into Russian and English were prepared (Sarkowski 1976: 128; Fuchs 2001: 248; Middell 2005b: 590–600).[15] A total of thirty-six different authors wrote chapters, many of them professional historians.
6. The already mentioned historian and archivist Julius von Pflugk-Harttung published a world history in six large, well-illustrated and expensive volumes between 1907 and 1910 (Pflugk-Harttung 1907-10; see also Middell 2005b: 604–20). This undertaking built the Ullstein publisher's inter-national reputation. Despite its high price more than 50,000 copies were sold (Schwab-Felisch 1977: 182; Herz 1994: 214–29; Estermann and Füssel 2003: 282).[16] Some twenty-eight professional historians contributed in Pflugk-Harttung's work.

This short overview gives a first impression of the wide variety of ways in which a concise history of the world could be presented to the public at the turn of the twentieth century (Schulin 1974: 28).

Understanding the World and Coping with Transition

In what ways did world histories attempt to meet the expectations of their supposed audience? What did they offer the reader in terms of coping with transition? What ideas of world history and orientations were presented? In short, what kind of stories did they tell?

Unsurprisingly, in several important respects the writing of world history did not differ from the mainstream historiography of that time (Raphael 2003: 66–77). Popular world histories tried to stabilize the conventional concept of history and a specific imagination of the world.

History was perceived as a uniform entity, world history as the history of the entire human family. The course of history is optimistically and positively interpreted as progress, developing towards its height in European culture. The most optimistic view is offered by Jäger, who equates the history of humanity with the history of progress as embodied by the freedom and morality of the individual.[17]

In most of the world histories the present as the most modern and greatest time in history is stressed. The division into ancient, medieval and modern times shows this sense of self-esteem. The most extreme example is *K.F. Beckers Weltgeschichte* (Becker 1891–93), which contained eight volumes on modern times, three on antiquity and just one on the Middle Ages. The medieval period is connoted in terms of rigidity, darkness and a dull, brooding air. This portrait is shaped by events taking place in Europe, especially in Germany: medieval times start in 476 with Odoaker, and modern times with Martin Luther and his ninety-five theses in 1517. Here and elsewhere Germany features prominently in the world histories, where headlines of chapters and the structuring of the presentation emphasizes German history. This can be explained by the predominantly German readership.

However, in a worldly context other spatial dimensions are of the utmost importance. Alongside states and nations other imagined communities can be found in these world histories. Even if you find examples of patriotism and occasionally nationalistic lapses in the world histories, there is always the notion of a common Europe playing an important part – sometimes including overarching animosities between nations and states (Mütter 1992: 62; Osterhammel 1994: 64). The civilization of modern Europe is presented as a model of alliance with the attributes of freedom, individualism, statehood and nationhood. Europe as the bearer of progress and the predominant centre of world history was the image promoted. This imagining of Europe is highlighted in the presentation of the history as well as in its structure; for example, the reader reads something about the 'civilizing mission' of imperialism, which justifies the 'necessary victims' of this contact of cultures.[18] The history of non-European areas is handled after contact with Europe – namely exploration or conquest – has taken place.[19] The history of modern times is often structured in terms of European states. Most importantly, the spatial dimension of world history is characterized by a fundamental opposition between Europe and Asia at all times. European identity is constructed in opposition to the negative attributes assigned to Asia. This viewpoint can be found, for example, in the characterization of Chinese history or the presentation of the Greek–Persian wars. Regarding the latter, the powerful and forceful Athenians are described as free and equal individuals, fighting for their homeland, embodying the progress of culture and humanitarianism, founding a civilized Europe; on the other hand, the feminized Persians stand for deterioration, fainting, stagnation, moral degeneration, frivolity, effete states, and they lack any ideal character. All six world histories see this event as one of the most important caesura because the centre of world history moved from the East to the West.[20] As for the representation of Europe, it was differentiated between the 'dominant, expanding western' part, the 'irrelevant northern' part and the semi-Asiatic Eastern Europe of 'stagnating Russia'.[21]

In addition to this strong Eurocentrism, the application of the following universal factors corresponds to conventional paradigms of mainstream historiography: The state and extraordinary individuals are fundamentally important in influencing the course of history, while culture (the arts, sciences and so on) is a secondary, derived factor. Most of the world histories cover some appearances of culture in an encyclopaedic way as an appendix to historical developments. The new conceptions of culture circulating around 1900 do not matter in the popular world histories. Similarly, economic and social developments were not perceived as processes that changed history by themselves.

The importance of the state as one of the driving forces of world history can be seen in the following examples: For some of the popular world histories, 'proper' history begins with the building of states (such as Egypt) because only this form of organization allows people to act freely, to develop culturally unconstrained by the natural struggle for survival; in short, the state means progress. The state is the barrier between nature and culture, between drive and humanity. Therefore, the state remains the central precondition of history.[22] Groups organized in other ways – for example, in terms of clans – are excluded from history. In general, groups are judged according to their ability to develop statehood; the Serbs, for example, are presented as unable to build real, substantial states.[23] States without freedom and progress – such as China – are seen by most of the world histories as unworthy of inclusion (Pigulla 1996: 157).

The agency of important individuals remains a determining force in these popular world histories. In particular, the detailed presentation of individuals' lives serves to memorialize them and turn them into role models. This high regard for individuals corresponds to the liberal ideal of a free, self-determined person (Hardtwig 1990d: 110, 143, 151). The individual advances history and leads the masses, and the exploration and conquest of new areas are described in a personalized way. Several chapters are named after a particular person. In some world histories the individuals are judged in relation to their consequences for the broad masses and how they moulded and led popular developments. Jäger, for example, wants to write a bit more history of the people (*Volksgeschichte*), and a bit less history of heroes (*Heroengeschichte*).[24]

Somewhat surprisingly, far from becoming anachronistic, some old-fashioned positions of enlightenment history still circulated around 1900. Schlosser's *Weltgeschichte* (Schlosser 1892–93) is an example of an early liberal conception of world history, still influenced by the enlightenment. It reveals a moral evaluation of the free individual. History is pragmatically understood and has mainly a didactic function. History can be judged in terms of timeless moral values concerning individual behaviour. History always shows the success and failure of human behaviour in adopting these values.[25] This moral-pedagogical view of history always relates to political history as well. States also have to implement certain values, like freedom of mind and speech, equality according to the law. They have to serve all citizens.[26] Besides these more ahistorical conceptions, progress features prominently in Schlosser's world history, too. Linear, optimistic progress begins with the Greeks, and is always embodied by the striving for freedom. The enlightenment in itself is the struggle of the new, the autonomous human intellect and of human freedom in general. It is the ideal of the free bourgeois, able to evolve for themselves and develop an intellect and free mind.[27] Schlosser extensively integrates the history of literature into the presentation of world history. For him literature is a manifestation of the ethical condition of an epoch or a state. It is a motor of historical development in general, a civilizing force leading to the emancipation of the middle classes. However, the development of culture and literature is always dealt with in separate chapters.[28] So Schlosser's world history is characterized by ambivalence toward progress versus a timeless morale in history.

Another supposedly old-fashioned position is the Catholic world-view, which finds its own spokesperson in some of the world histories. The Catholic *Annegarns Weltgeschichte* sees religion as the most important principle of world history. It represents a Catholic world-view and a salvation history. History stretches from Creation to the Last Judgement, and Jesus Christ is the centre of the history of humanity. All other universal factors are derived from this religious measure of value.[29] For example, the state has only the secular function of maintaining law and order. However, the history of Ireland features with unique prominence in *Annegarns Weltgeschichte*.[30] Individuals are ahistorical examples; exemplifying religious virtues and their opposite, they serve as examples of self-improvement and they show the perishable nature of life and of God as the determining force behind the destiny of people. *Annegarns Weltgeschichte* tells the story of many saints in detail. The Middle Ages and the role of the pope are positively judged, stressing the civilizing and educational role of Christendom of the Germanic peoples. The value of art and science depends on their relation to the Catholic Church. The Spanish Inquisition is justified.[31] The continued dissemination of this world history is an example for the still existing Catholic milieu and serves as a means of distinction. Although the influence and dominance of religious thinking is declining, religion as such remains of great importance, especially the Christian religion. Even in the protestant world histories religion remains a strong normative force: it is part of European identity in opposition to Islam.[32]

So far we have seen more traditional versions of world history featuring prominently in the popular universal histories around 1900. However, there were also attempts to experiment with other more innovative models of conceptualizing and structuring world history.

One example is the concept of spatial totality in the world history edited by Helmolt (1899–1907). The spatial dimension of history was enlarged to all parts of the world at all times to cover humanity at large. To put this completeness into practice he decided to apply a geographical structure replacing the epochal or chronological structure. The following volume headings can be found:

> Preface. Preliminary History. America. The Pacific Ocean
> East Asia and Oceania. The Indian Ocean
> West Asia and Africa
> Mediterranean Countries
> South-east and East Europe
> Central and North Europe
> West Europe, Part One
> West Europe, Part Two. The Atlantic Ocean

Continents, parts of continents and oceans were thus used for the book's main structure, one which is based on Friedrich Ratzel's concept of *Völkerkreise* ('nation circles') and combines ethnographic and geographic aspects. Beside human beings, nature and land are important factors codetermining history. For example, the earth's surface, the character of the soil, and the climate, animals and plants have an enormous political importance at least for economics, trade and national security. Space and peoples are organically interlinked, and the struggle for land is a fundamental process in history. In Ratzel's theory even race, culture, power and the State are derived, secondary phenomena of land.[33] Helmolt sees the *Völkerkreis* as the proper structuring entity because all intellectual or religious tendencies are restricted to one special *Völkerkreis*.[34] However, the actual chapters of his world history make very little use of this concept. Apart from the anti-teleological programmatic statements of Helmolt, conceptions of progress remain important in many chapters of his work.

Helmolt himself acknowledges that the structure of separate *Völkerkreise* could not be consequently implemented.[35] Some regions of the world are separately treated in different volumes, like the history of Greece. Also, three different chapters on Christian Church history counteract the concept. The difference between Middle Europe and Western Europe is mainly chronological, not spatial. The first relates to medieval and the second to modern times; for example, of France, Italy and Germany. So behind the geographical framework a hidden chronological structure persists.

Apart from these contradictions the structure and the inclusion of all parts and peoples of the world are fundamentally new concepts in the writing of world history. This was an innovative and unique attempt to broaden the spatial imagination of the world in terms of history (Middell 2005c: 47–52), and chapters about the pre-Columbian America, Oceania and Africa are unique.[36] These chapters included the history of peoples which were normally characterized as 'stagnant' or 'without history' because they had no script presumably and therefore were thought to have no history (Stuchtey and Fuchs 2003: 5). Helmolt recruited anthropologists and palaeontologists to cover these topics because historical sciences did not offer any methods for dealing with the histories of these peoples (Zimmerman 2004).

Africa, for example, was not part of the historiography until 1900. Anthropology and geography had just recently started to explore these areas. The supposed lack of written sources and the lack of stable statehood led to the exclusion of Africa. This situation is true for most of the world histories around 1900. Africa was labelled 'unhistorical' and parts of Africa were simply featured as objects of European expansion. Therefore the mere existence of a large chapter – 185 pages in length – on the history of Africa in the world history edited by Helmolt is an innovation.[37] Not free from prejudices, the editor even claims to raise African peoples out of darkness and is proud not to overlook supposedly primitive people.[38] In this chapter Helmolt called in the anthropologist Heinrich Schurtz (1863–1903). Schurtz covers the pre-colonial history of Africa with questions of origin, migrations, racial mixture, slavery, tribal wars and old empires. He describes racial questions in detail including among others things the physical appearance of 'the negroes'. However, an independent history before the advent of Europeans is not conceded and the image of an ahistorical continent still prevails (no script, low cultural standard, no state and so on). In his preliminary remarks Schurtz highlights the remoteness and isolation of the continent, home to dull people who have only just started to awake in history. Indeed the contact or clash of cultures in its brutal consequences is seen and presented as the necessary course of history. The dominant perspective is that in the long run colonists brought development and civilization to primitive peoples. Colonialism is presented as the only way to pacify endless tribal wars. So though Africa is treated extensively, the appraisal is very conventional. The Eurocentric, arrogant assessment of these so-called marginal regions and peoples is similar to that in other world histories and in mainstream historiography in Germany around 1900.

One can interpret Helmolt's *Weltgeschichte* as the most inclusive historistic attempt because every culture, region and epoch was acknowledged in its selfhood and individuality. However, with the structuring of world history in geographical terms, with the treatment of even the most remote parts of the world – there are chapters about the polar areas, Armenia and Albania[39] – with the programmatic inclusion of the history of peoples hitherto considered ahistorical, with the integration of contemporary anthropology and with the inclusion of information on regions of the world featuring in the daily press, the conception of world history was adapted to the globalization in evidence around 1900. This innovation was probably only possible in this popular format (Osterhammel 1994: 56, 63–64).

Another reconceptualization concerns the notional and chronological dimensions of world history, and again the multidisciplinary integration of other sciences. To begin with the last point: Around 1900 the general authority of history declined and other sciences gained increasing influence on interpretations of the contemporary world. History lost the power to shape public opinion, to influence other disciplines and its close relationship to politics. *Nationalökonomie, Staatswissenschaften* and sociology were methodologically more innovative and had begun to study the subject matters of historical research, like economics, social structures and so on. These could not be studied with philological textual criticism and hermeneutics. Academic historians generally did not take up these new strands and remained caught in a rather narrow understanding of political history (Lenger 1992: 163–64; Raphael 2003: 70–78).

Another new discipline was geography, which informed the public about new places featuring in the daily press (colonialism); in addition, there was sinology and other philological sciences of areas outside Europe. Finally, the natural sciences gained increasing impact on the interpretation of the world. Engineers, physicians, naturalists and representatives of social Darwinism gained social prestige and influence (Schulte-Althoff 1971: 41, 43, 119, 149, 196–97; Herrmann 1991: 147–49; Ullmann 1995: 191–92; Pigulla 1996: 32–34).

A few popular world histories tried to meet this challenge. They attempted to stabilize the capacity of history in orienting the public with the integration of these trendy sciences into world history. Of particular relevance here is the world history edited by Pflugk-Harttung (1907–10). His compendium even starts with a chapter on the age of planet earth. Astrophysics precedes geology and palaeontology.[40] The concept of world history adopted by Pflugk-Harttung reminds one of the model of big history recently employed by Fred Spier (1998) and David Christian (2005). History is considerably prolonged and the history of mankind put into perspective. Together with anthropological considerations of race these new approaches increase the claim of the popular history to present a scientific view on the history of the world. Humanity and culture are seen as a part of nature, rather than its opposite, as in other popular world histories. Eventually nature determines world history and the tasks of states, peoples and persons. The Christian concept of Creation is abandoned. The origins of the planet and the human race are explained in a scientific way.[41] Actually, the zoologist Ernst Haeckel (1834–1919) presents the history of human beings as part of the natural history of species, the human descending from the animal. Research in biology and anthropology reveals the law of nature.[42] Haeckel was one of the most popular representatives of evolutionism and social Darwinism in Germany. Ernst Haeckel and other outsiders of historical sciences or controversial representatives like Karl Lamprecht (1856–1915) wrote chapters for this world history (Middell 2005b: 606–19).

This innovative multidisciplinarity can also be found in the applied categories. However, the state, the ever-important individual and religion remain significant actors of world history. Religion is most consequently historicized and fully interpreted as a secular phenomenon using arguments about mass psychology and propaganda. In contrast to other popular world histories, the role of the Catholic Church in the Middle Ages is not interpreted as a civilizing, positive influence on the Germanic peoples, and instead Germanic peoples are seen as having overcome the obstacle of Church coercion.[43] In addition, the whole structure of world history diminishes the relevance of religion.

Furthermore, in Pflugk-Harttung's work social and economic considerations feature more prominently than in other world histories, especially in the presentation and interpretation of the nineteenth century.[44] Developments during other epochs are also explained using these categories, and social and economic factors are more integrated in the presentation of history generally. However, they do not transcend the dominance of the state and do not become the fundamental factors one finds in historical materialism.

It should be pointed out that the world history edited by Pflugk-Harttung pluralized the understanding of historical development. Beside the conventional universal factors new ones are applied. The integration of these new categories is also an attempt to preserve the power to define the imagination of the world and of history. And it is also an attempt to explain world history in the most scientific way. If traditional historical sources do not exist, the results and models of other disciplines can be integrated. This also led to the almost unique application of categories coming from natural sciences, linguistics and anthropology.

Linguistic and racial groupings are extensively used. The different language families are used to classify peoples and sometimes to explain the course of history. The distinction between Aryans (Indo-Germanic), Semites and Hamites is attributed to certain sets of qualitative features. For example, only the fresh and forceful Aryans achieved progress in culture and have the power to build lasting states. Therefore the origin of the Aryan was relocated to Europe.[45]

The arguments are characterized by a mixture of concepts and no clear definition of terms. Racial, ethnological, archaeological, linguistic and historical arguments are mixed. The concept of Germanic peoples is increasingly under-stood in racial terms: tall, with blond hair, blue eyes and a special form of the skull.[46] The concept of race promised to deliver clear, physically measurable attributes for different groups of mankind. Like other modern natural sciences this concept permitted a material and empirical explanation of reality.

An introductory chapter by the then renowned anthropologist and curator Felix von Luschan (1854–1924) presents different kinds of racial classification.[47] According to von Luschan they are all deficient because they do not distinguish between mentally defined people, physically determined races and families of languages. However, this sharp division of terms is not applied in his own chapter nor elsewhere in this world history. In his overview of races of the different continents he mingles anatomical, cultural and linguistic criteria. The South African Bushman, for example, is characterized by a dwarfish, short stature and pale skin, in colour similar to a new English saddle. He notices the form of the skull (short and wide), the anatomy and form of the spine, the curly hair, the lack of an earlap, the special sound of their language and their hunting and foraging livelihood.[48]

In other chapters one can also find vitalistic, biologistic phrases, the contemporary threat of Asian peoples being just one example. Around 1900, violent racial conflict between China and Europe was expected to occur in the near future.[49] The racial argument in this popular world history continues the conventional hierarchy of different parts of the world, with Europe at the top. Throughout this world history, racial categories are most often applied in chapters to do with non-European history. Not only Pflugk-Harttung's (1907–10) world history but also in that by Helmolt (1899–1907), linguistic and racial categories feature prominently. However, they are not applied to the whole history of the world and do not replace other universal factors of history.

To summarize: On the one hand, popular world histories in Germany from around 1900 present a Eurocentric world view. Germany and Europe were spreading their civilization around the globe. Other cultures were devalued, as can be seen in the structure of books, the categories employed and the spatial structuring in general. This self-confident image should stabilize the challenged identity of European superiority. The state, the outstanding individual and religion remained the most important factors determining history, though sometimes new categories were added.

On the other hand, the then contemporary perception of globalization and increasing uncertainty led to new experiments in the writing of world history. The world histories of Helmolt and Pflugk-Harttung tried new models, they experimented with the integration of other disciplines together with their categories and methods, they provided information about hitherto unknown areas of the world, they reconceptualized world history according to contemporary global developments, and they adopted a supposedly more scientific approach to explaining history. They were products of a transitional phase, shown, for example, by the paradox that ahistorical peoples were now integrated into a world history. They attempted to direct the public in a world that had become a globe. They fought for the influence of history in the circle of disciplines.

Some Concluding Remarks

Around 1900, historiography was caught up in the following dilemma: On the one hand, historians claimed to offer direction and information in a globalizing and changing world. On the other hand, the professionalization, specialization and methodology of academic history prevented professional historians from delivering this information and offering direction (Raphael 2003: 66–77).

The public longed for a coherent and informative view of world history, something on which to base their world-view (*Weltanschauung*). Academic historians demanded the production of objective historical knowledge through methodological work with sources and declared scientific world-history writing as impossible (Drehsen and Sparn 1996: 17; Raphael 2003: 197). Contemporary attempts to modify this situation were averted, as can be seen in the *Schäfer-Gothein-Streit* and the *Lamprechtstreit*.

The differentiation of historians into medievalists, antiquarians and practitioners of other sub-disciplines, which was established at the end of the nineteenth century, did not allow one historian to be an expert in comprehensive, universal history anymore. The all-embracing composition of world history was possible only in the field of the philosophy of history, or in the popular field, or in a chronologically limited way by an academic historian, as in the conservative world histories of Theodor Lindner (1901–16) or of Dietrich Schäfer (1907).[50]

At least the solution of collaboration allowed for specialization and an intellectual division of labour. However, the lack of a common concept and of a homogeneous presentation has been criticized at all times. Even today, collective solutions are dismissed as 'botanically universal history' (Janosi 1969: 244) or as 'a chimera' (Moore 1997: 951).

The authors and editors of popular world histories saw that the time was ripe for these compendia; they declared world-history writing to be both possible and necessary. Published world histories found it necessary to justify their approach against academic accusations.[51] The realization of these works was only possible under the label popular, which freed authors from academic rigour. The label 'popular world history' opened up a space for experimentation. New forms of synthesis could be attempted and multidisciplinarity could be field-tested. They were a kind of playground where authors broadened the subjects and techniques of historiography. However, they did not leave the neo-Rankean framework of history, concentrating on the political history of Prussian Germany and neighbouring states. The authors of these world history compendia were not all teachers, but many of them acknowledged academic historians. The boundary between scientific and more popular types of historiography was fluid.

There remain a lot of questions to be asked. The adequacy of the method of study used could be discussed, and one would like to know more about changing conceptions regarding popular world histories before and after this short period covered. However, through the lens of this special historiographic source a small section of historical culture around 1900 can be glimpsed. The boom of popular world histories says a lot about the Wilhelmine society, about the fears and wishes of the people. Popular world histories tried to stabilize a conventional world-view while adapting to the challenges of contemporary globalization. New methods were adopted to justify old identities. An ambivalence toward more traditional and more innovative features can be found. Borders between disciplines were contested. The causation of history was reconceptualized. At the margins of scientific discourse other strands of historical imagination could flourish, such as Catholic historiography or the moral rigour of historiography in the tradition of the Enlightenment, as the example of Schlosser shows.

Scholarly debates about world history or new global history always reveal unsettling perceptions of globalization like, for example, the German debate after the Second World War, the fear of nuclear war and of other ecological threats, or contemporary discussion about the impacts of the internet revolution. They always centre on the question of perspective, on the theoretical question of how to write world history – for example, comparison versus transfer, interconnectivity versus entangled histories, – on changing curricula, on integrating a global perspective into the heart of academic history. At no times were these debates supported by a great number of academic historians and at no times did they demand the writing of multi-volume popular, encyclopaedic world histories (Kagan 1984; Middell 2005a: 60–61, 67, 82).

However, popular world histories did exist and do exist. They answer to the demand of the public; they offer a coherent story in a handy format. They extract information from the mass of literature produced by a fragmented, highly specialized academic scene. And perhaps they find their way into other types of media, like textbooks, historical reports in television and so on. Hopefully, there will be further studies on the relation between different medias and popular historiography. This is just the beginning of the exploration of this type of popular historiography. The research design of this study should be complemented with further studies in the material context of reception, in the history of publishing, reading and library culture.

Notes

1. I would like to express my gratitude to Sylvia Paletschek and Jane Caplan at the European Studies Centre, St Antony's College, Oxford, for their invitation and hospitality. I enjoyed the lively discussion very much. I am also very much indebted to Sandra Solan and Phil Jones. Finally I would like to thank the *Sonderforschungsbereich 'Erinnerungskulturen'* and my supervisor Winfried Speitkamp at the University of Giessen.
2. Modern comprehensive overviews of the history of German historiography do not mention popular world histories (Blanke 1991; Simon 1996; Iggers 1997; Weber 2001:

18–19, 59–65; Völkel 2006). Lutz Raphael does recognize the world history boom, but does not analyse its products (Raphael 2003: 197–208).

3. Exceptions here include Schulin (1974) and Pigulla (1996), the latter about the representation of China in German world histories from the eighteenth to the twentieth century.

4. This chapter is based on Bergenthum (2002, 2004). See also Heigl (2000) and Fuchs (2001: 245–48).

5. The cheapest were, e.g., Schlosser (1892–93), which cost 38 marks, and Becker (1891–93), 26.40 marks. In 1908 the average price of a publication in the arts and music was 9.22 marks, and in literature 2.22 marks (Hiller 1966: 115–16; Kelly 1981: 15; Wittmann 1991: 272).

6. For full references and further details, see Bergenthum (2004).

7. See, e.g., the review of the first volumes of Jäger (1887–94): 'Eine neue Weltgeschichte', *Daheim* 26 (1890): 154–58.

8. Depending on the binding the price varied between 96 and 120 marks. Compare its contradictory intentions (Pflugk-Harttung 1907–10, iv: ix-xi).

9. Even if it is disputed whether one should use the modern term 'globalization' for the nineteenth century, there was a thrust of globalization (Conrad and Osterhammel 2004: 9, 24–27; Schwentker 2005: 36–41; Conrad 2006: 7, 32–73).

10. Jäger (1887–89, i: 2); Annegarn (1895–6, i: 6); Helmolt (1899–1907, i: vi); Pflugk-Harttung (1907–10, iv: viii-xiv).

11. Subsequent editions included a second (1832–33), a fifth, compiled and updated by Heinrich Overhage (1859–60), and a sixth, updated by August Enck and Victor Huyskens (1886–92). The last two also compiled further new editions, up to the tenth (1911–12).

12. The third edition was updated by Wilhelm Müller and based on an earlier revised edition (1884–86). Fourth and fifth editions (1900–1903, 1910–11) were completed by K.H. Grotz and J. Miller and the fifth updated by Ellis Hesselmeyer.

13. The third edition (1870–84) of this work ran to 60,000 copies, and a later edition (1909) ran to 130,000 copies (Schlosser 1892–93, i: 11–12, xvi: 5). The complex publishing history is given in Bergenthum (2004: 70–72).

14. For this chapter, practical reasons have necessitated the consultation of two editions of this work: the first (Jäger 1887–89) and second (Jäger 1890–94); the latter was published in 24,000 copies. There have also been several reprints of Jäger's work: 1899, 1902–1903, 1907. A later edition (1909-12) ran to between 56,000 to 61,000 copies, and a major new edition was undertaken by Wilhelm Schäfer between 1921 and 1933.

15. The archivist Armin Tille published a major revision of this work between 1913 and 1922.

16. See Herz (1994: 229).

17. Jäger (1887–89, i: 200).

18. Pflugk-Harttung (1907–10, iv: 113).

19. Schlosser (1892–93, iv: 495–523).

20. Jäger (1887–89, i: 81–82, 115, 134, 291); Becker (1891–93, ii: 27–28, 220; iii: 346); Schlosser (1892–93, i: 15, 126, 144); Annegarn (1895–96, i: 224; iii: 309); Helmolt (1899–1907, iii: 151–52; iv: 278); Pflugk-Harttung (1907–10, i: 206, 209, 329–30, 562; iii: 44, 405).

21. Helmolt (1899–1907, vii: 3); Pflugk-Harttung (1907–10, vi: 447).

22. Jäger (1887–89, i: 2); Helmolt (1899–1907, viii: 127, 247); Pflugk-Harttung (1907–10, vi: 342).

23. Helmolt (1899–1907, v: 285).
24. Jäger (1887–89, i: 2).
25. Schlosser (1892–93, xiv: 72–74).
26. Schlosser (1892–93, vi: 542–43; viii: 4; xiv: 219–20, 305).
27. Schlosser (1892–93, i: 6–7, 144; iv: 284; viii: 449, 455–56; ix: 340, 445–46; xiv: 106).
28. Schlosser (1892–93, ii: 3–129; xiii: 368–557).
29. Annegarn (1895–96, i: 1–3, 6–7, 10–12; iii: 258–60; viii: 382–84).
30. Annegarn (1895–96, vi: 244–48; vii: 207–12; viii: 47–62).
31. Annegarn (1895–96, v: 299–301).
32. Jäger (1887–89, ii: 46–47, 207–8); Becker (1891–93, iii: 466–67); Annegarn (1895–96, v: 71, 373); Helmolt (1899–1907, iii: 388); Pflugk-Harttung (1907–10, iii: 152).
33. Helmolt (1899–1907, i: 63–103).
34. Helmolt (1899–1907, i: 18–20).
35. Helmolt (1899–1907, v: vii).
36. See Helmolt (1899–1907, i: 181–574; ii: 223–336).
37. Helmolt (1899–1907, iii: 389–574).
38. Helmolt (1899–1907, iii: vi).
39. Helmolt (1899–1907, ii: 194–96, 208; v: 196–212, 215–22).
40. Pflugk-Harttung (1907–10, i: 3–7).
41. Pflugk-Harttung (1907–10, iv: xi, xiii); cf. Pigulla (1996: 250–55).
42. Pflugk-Harttung (1907–10, i: 23–24).
43. Pflugk-Harttung (1907–10, i; 578–88, 598, 617).
44. Pflugk-Harttung (1907–10, vi: 349–62).
45. Pflugk-Harttung (1907–10, i: 139; iii: 117, 323–29, 397).
46. Pflugk-Harttung (1907–10, i: 102–4; iii : 427, 437).
47. Pflugk-Harttung (1907–10, i: 41–79).
48. Pflugk-Harttung (1907–10, i: 49–50).
49. Pflugk-Harttung (1907–10, vi: 594).
50. See also Stuchtey and Fuchs (2003: 5–7).
51. Helmolt (1899-1907, i: 3).

PART II
Popular Presentations of History in Different Medias in the Twentieth Century

5

History for Readers: Popular Historiography in Twentieth-Century Germany

Wolfgang Hardtwig

I

When addressing the public, the academic discipline of history has recently been facing unprecedented competition. Television broadcasts and series have been presenting the history of Nazi and post-war Germany in a manner appealing to a broader audience. Motion pictures tell stories from the Third Reich, the air raids and post-war life. Documentaries are in great demand. They offer an attractive combination of solid research, eyewitness interviews, a moving sound-track and contemporary photographs and filmstrips (Benz 1986; Knopp and Quandt 1988; Bösch 1999: 204–18). As demonstrated by Steven Spielberg's *Schindler's List* (1993) or by Bernd Eichinger's *The Downfall* (2004), the film business has discovered the Holocaust and the last days of Hitler's bunker to be a profitable topic. On the occasion of the sixtieth anniversary of the end of the Second World War, daily papers such as *Süddeutsche Zeitung* and weekly magazines such as *Der Spiegel* brought their readers a comprehensive series of articles on the military and social history of the war.

Meanwhile we also find a history boom in the national and international book market. Umberto Eco's novel *The Name of the Rose* (Eco 1982) initiated this increasing demand for historical novels. Usually a stirring plot is set in a historical context, thereby blurring the lines between fact and fiction, sometimes even systematically so (Heit 1994). History is degraded, at least partially, becoming an exotic background against which an easy-to-sell story of sex and crime is set. The past, as watched by an uninformed audience, is deprived of any commitment to historical veracity and reality.[1]

In comparison, any kind of historical representation meeting rigorous scholarly standards faces enormous difficulties. You do not have to be a prophet to know that an academic book will have a marginal presence in the market for depictions of the past.

However, it is not just the mass media's powers of suggestion and broad appeal that have caused this state of affairs. Today, academic historians write books on twentieth century German history and still face these difficulties – not to mention books on earlier epochs. These academic texts do not have the success of popular works of historiography that neither claim nor meet academic standards. Among these texts are Sebastian Haffner's analyses of Nazi Germany (Haffner 2000), written during his years of exile in London, and Marcel Reich-Ranicki's memoirs (Reich-Ranicki 1999). Works like these offer the perspective of an eyewitness who participated in the events described and include intense reflection and careful attention to the art of literary representation. Even to the professional historian, they occasionally offer new insights and the pure joy of reading – if the events told are not too painful.[2]

The representation of the past is increasingly dominated by the mass media. This observation may compel us to examine the history of historiography as a medium that appeals to a broader public. An analysis of audience-oriented modes of representation, of historiography as a (mass) medium, will also illuminate essential aspects of and thereby contribute to the discussion on the role that social and cultural studies play in our cultural and social environment. It would be far too easy, however, to oppose the academic discipline of history to the popularization of the past in a binary way. If we are to believe the reports from the film set, it is Heinrich Breloer, the director of a drama-documentary on Hitler's architect Albert Speer, rather than a professional historian who on the basis of solid evidence is the first to question the Speer legend that has been so effective since Speer's memoirs were published in 1969.[3] Television documentaries are usually made by professional historians advised by academic experts, the latter often interviewed in the documentary itself. The cultural sections of the large daily papers in Germany and of *Der Spiegel* offer space for history professors to comment on a variety of historical and political issues ranging from compensation for former slave labourers to the future EU membership of Turkey. Since the 1950s, the weekly magazines *Stern* and, even more so, *Der Spiegel* have devoted large sections to articles and series on history, in particular on contemporary history. Now and then even university professors find a large audience, even though their books do not deal with contemporary history.[4] In the 1980s and 1990s German academic historians indulged in waves of synthesizing, resulting in book series such as the Siedler Deutsche Geschichte or the paperback Deutsche Geschichte der Neuesten Zeit (published by dtv) with many editions and large numbers of copies printed. At the same time authors who write for non-academic readers do not necessarily write in a non-scholarly way.[5]

II

There has always been a tension between academic representations of history addressed to a scholarly community and representations of history appealing to a larger audience, although this tension seems to be even more present today. Ever since the writing of history, in the sense of a scholarly profession, became scientific, this issue has repeatedly emerged (Hardtwig 1990e). The relative success of books such as Leopold von Ranke's *History of the Popes* (Ranke 1832–36) or his *History of the Reformation in Germany* (Ranke 1839–47), Jacob Burckhardt's *The Civilization of the Renaissance in Italy* (Burckhardt 1860), or Heinrich von Treitschke's *History of Germany in the Nineteenth Century* (Treitschke 1879–96)[6] were upstaged by the actual historical bestsellers of the nineteenth-century such as Franz Kugler's well-written biography of Frederick the Great (see Hardtwig 2005a), Christoph Friedrich Schlosser's books[7] and Karl von Rotteck's *General History of the World* (Rotteck 1812–27). Written from a Catholic late-Enlightenment perspective by a liberal from the German state of Baden, Rotteck's book had a print run of more than 300,000 copies and had been translated into five languages by the time its publication was discontinued in Germany in 1872 and when the last English edition was published in New York in 1875 (see Treskow 1990). In the twentieth century Oswald Spengler's two-volume *Decline of the West* (Spengler 1918–22) was printed in forty-seven editions in the Weimar Republic alone (see Kittsteiner 2005), Emil Ludwig's *Bismarck* (Ludwig 1921–26) ran to no less than eighty-three editions with 150,000 copies printed (see Ullrich 2005). In post-war Germany Kurt W. Marek (writing as C.W. Ceram) had huge success with his archeological bestseller *Gods, Graves, and Scholars* (Ceram 1949), published for the first time in 1949 and selling 564,000 copies by 1957 (see Oels 2005).

However, German popular historiography – that is history addressing the non-professional reader – has never received adequate attention and analysis in terms of its content, form and reception. This article does not aim at a conclusive definition, description, analysis or reconstruction of the effects and the reception of this kind of historiography. Rather, a provisional exploration of the subject is intended. It is confined to the twentieth century, the era of the rising literary mass market in varying political conditions. It discusses the forms and authors of non-academic and literary historiography. The history of historiography has usually neglected the strategies and mechanisms of the effects literary historiography is producing. All of these texts share the common feature that they were not aimed at the scientific community. Rather, they were intended to appeal to a broader audience.

This kind of historiography may easily be called popular historiography, a term which is, however, somewhat problematic. In the traditional discourse of the educated classes – in the tradition of the German *Bildungsbürgertum* – there is a pejorative undertone to mention of the popular, popular culture and so on, but no such normative sense is intended when the term popular is used in these pages. Nor will scholarly works or specific features of academic historiography be excluded. Dividing lines between academic and popular history are often blurred and within one text transitions to different sorts of texts may occur. Anyway, in the case of historiography at least, terms such as scholarly or academic lack an unequivocal meaning and cannot be applied precisely. Oswald Spengler's *Decline of the West* (Spengler 1918–22) was published in large quantities, but it is not a 'popular' book. Reading Spengler requires a good deal of knowledge, even if not necessarily knowledge according to academic standards.[8] Spengler's book appealed to the semi-educated, who were smiled at by the educated bourgeoisie. And yet it also appealed to some intellectuals, who were fascinated by Spengler (see, e.g., T. Mann 1974; Adorno 1977). Golo Mann's biography of Wallenstein (Mann 1971) was subtitled 'a novel'. Nevertheless it was written by a historian who temporarily held a German professorship and declined offers of several academic chairs. Mann's biography is in fact based on meticulous research, and it requires an audience of literary connoisseurs and gourmets (Lahme and Stunz 2005). Theodor Heuss, who held a doctorate in economics but was not a historian, addresses a very limited audience with his biography of Friedrich Naumann (Heuss 1937), whereas his book on the rise of Hitler and Nazism (Heuss 1932) is more aptly called a piece of journalism.[9]

It is obvious that for our purposes 'popular history' includes a wide variety of texts. As far as content is concerned, the spectrum ranges from late or compensatory versions of an older history of philosophy, as in the case of Spengler (1918–22), to more or less well-founded biographies. The variety runs from memoir-like texts, such as Golo Mann's *Erinnerungen und Gedanken* (Mann 1986),[10] to highly interpretive works like Sebastian Haffner's study of the 'meaning' of Hitler (Haffner 1978). Popular history also comprises early examples of modern war reporting, for in addition to biographies war has by far been the favourite subject of historically interested readers from the 1920s to the 1950s, if not beyond, notwithstanding changes in political and educational conditions (Daniel 2005). The field of research ranges from books spanning the centuries and explicitly conceived in opposition to academic historiography, such as Egon Friedell's *Cultural History of the Modern Age* (Friedell 1925–27),[11] to historical non-fiction by authors like Paul Ceram (see Oels 2005) and memoirs of the world wars, prisoner of war camps, bombing raids and the Russian occupation of Berlin (Hardtwig 2005b; Hermann 2005; Schütz 2005). It also includes a very specific historiography pertinent to certain socio-political milieux and ideological sectors of German society (Kössler 2005; Puschner 2005; Weichlein 2005).

Much has to be omitted, such as works combining popular historiography and fictional historical narrative which have been pivotal in the post-war literature of the two German states (Hardtwig 2002a). The period of investigation is confined to the twentieth century. This decision need not be accounted for, but two reasons may be more than obvious. Firstly, the years around 1900 constitute a clear break: after the *fin de siècle* non-academic historiography differentiated itself ever further and increasingly gained momentum in the literary market. Secondly, in this period the still-ongoing and pressing discussion of how academic historiography should respond to the challenge posed by the booming culture of memory began. From the perspective of academic historiography I will next outline some aspects and problems that can serve as a kind of introduction to popular historiography. I will look at the origins, reception and effects, as well as the ideological intentions and literary techniques of, and the qualities, limitations, and public functions specific to, popular historiography.

III

A good example of the success of non-academic historiography is Sebastian Haffner. Born Raimund Pretzel in 1907, Haffner's youth was overshadowed by the First World War and the German revolution of 1918. The son of a liberal Berlin family, he went in exile to Great Britain in 1938, and it was after arriving in London that Haffner assumed his new name so as not to imperil his German relatives. He became an editor of the weekly newspaper the *Observer*, for whom he returned to Germany as a correspondent in 1954. In 1961 he again took up permanent residence in Germany and during the next decade he gained fame as a columnist of the German weekly *Stern* while he continued to contribute essays and book reviews to intellectual magazines such as *konkret* and *Merkur*. In 1975 he gave up journalism to focus on writing books on history and politics (see esp. Haffner 1968, 1978, 1979, 1987). Most of his books have been translated into English, and *Anmerkungen zu Hitler* (Haffner 1978) was published in ten editions. Haffner's biggest success, however, came with the posthumous publication of his memoirs, an account of his youth written in 1939 and found in his papers after his death (Haffner 2000). This book created a bitter controversy. Two critics in particular accused Haffner of fabricating his recollections and retrospectively changing his opinions. Critics reproached Haffner for adopting the role of an astute analyst whose (allegedly inauthentic) prophecies claimed to foretell the German catastrophe even prior to the beginning of the war in 1939.[12]

The escalation of this controversy was obviously due to the fact that Haffner – as a newspaper columnist, television commentator and author – was a polarizing figure. His beginnings were distinctly anti-communist; in the 1960s he sympathized with the student movement; later he became a staunch advocate of Willy Brandt's *Neue Ostpolitik* and even seriously discussed the limitations and prospects of a republic of councils (Haffner 1982: 67ff.). He showed an odd sense of historical symmetry which is reminiscent of the arguments of some nostalgic accounts of East German history (Mittenzwei 2001) when Haffner compared Adenauer and Ulbricht. In 1966 he called Ulbricht a 'great politician'

(Haffner 1982: 123). On the other hand he complained about the 'many Germans who after Hitler have no longer dared to be patriots' (Haffner 1978: 204). He drew a sharp distinction between 'regular' war crimes which ought to be overlooked – without exculpating the German military – and Hitler's mass killings (ibid.: 171). Nazi fantasies of a German hegemony over a united Europe in 1938 were comprehensible to him (ibid.: 131), whereas he treated the terms 'Marxism' and 'Hitlerism' as equals. By 'Hitlerism' he meant a synthesis of Hitler's specific anti-Semitic theory and elements of *völkisch* ideology both of which constituted Hitler's ideological syndrome (ibid.: 109). Haffner liked the pointed formulation. He was able to change his opinions abruptly, and he was an energetic simplifier of complex problems. Haffner's intellectual passion was guided by an element of play as much as by his inclination to sharp polemic, corresponding to his self-conception as a journalist. The very same self-conception is also expressed in his books: 'I have never been interested in scholarship' (Haffner 1982: 197). Nevertheless he called contemporary history the 'best kind of history' for he thought a distance of ten or twenty years from the events to be the 'ideal distance of the historian' (ibid.: 12). He coined the postulate that historiography 'first and foremost is an art ... but also a kind of scholarship'. He declared omissions to be the main feature of this art of historiography (ibid.: 9). Haffner, with his opinions and literary strategies, was enormously successful in the book market. As Haffner explained, he was interested in the past because of 'the ethical problems and the aesthetic appeal of human life' (ibid.: 197). Hundreds of thousands of readers obviously shared the same interest, an interest rarely satisfied by conventional academic historiography.

IV

It would be a mistake if the term 'popular historiography' was understood as meaning a mere popularization of academic knowledge.[13] Popular historiography usually lays claim to special originality, occasionally even to being better than scholarship. Oswald Spengler repeatedly criticized established historiography, whereas Emil Ludwig got involved in a controversy about the best method of writing history.[14] Many authors show a distinct awareness of being unconventional and of having to confront the audience with neglected or tabooed persons and subjects.[15] They emphatically claim to be the first to deal with the 'amoral' side of history, they pretend to destroy legends or to know it all, as expressed in the rhetorical formula 'it has often been said ... but this is not true' (Haffner 1978: 41).[16] Indeed the bestselling authors among writers of popular historiography often succeed in dramatizing historical subjects and in drawing them to the attention of a public interested in literature.

With virtuosity they employ literary techniques discredited as non-scholarly in academic historiography, though academic historiography has never been ignorant of such techniques of representation – such as making the scene of the action vivid and dramatizing chronological sequences.[17] Some of the most successful historical non-fiction books in the second half of the twentieth century have been travelogues of actual or imagined journeys.[18] Not only can the archeological past become the subject of travel literature, for so too can the historical landscapes of early modern or modern history. For example, Christian Graf von Krockow (1991) deploys historical and art historical depictions of places and objects in his attempt to bring to life the history of Prussia from its beginnings to the postcommunist era.[19] This vivid spatial depiction corresponds to the intensification of temporal constellations and the rhetoric of turning points and decision-making. Haffner artfully stages Churchill's resignation from the office of the First Lord of the Admiralty in May 1915 (Haffner 1967: 63ff). In Stefan Zweig's biography of Fouché, the 'world historical day' of the Eighth Thermidor is similarly evoked (Zweig 2000: 91). By way of artistic techniques of representation, distance from the past is often diminished, its difference relativized and its immediate relevance to the present emphasized. In popular historiography the reader rarely encounters the alterity of the past. It is thus an exception when authors create a sense of 'otherness' by invoking the melancholic and sometimes fatal attraction of the antiquated, the lost or the perishing, as in the work of Golo Mann. In his biography of Wallenstein (Mann 1971) he resorts to long quotations from early modern sources, thus creating these effects. The same holds true for his artistic and appealing descriptions of historical endings; for example, of Napoleonic family history in the nineteenth-century, of the last margraves of Ansbach and of the last grand duke of Hessen-Darmstadt, the great patron of the arts Ernst Ludwig (Mann 1982: 7–29, 43–97).[20]

In contrast to academic historians, the authors of popular historiography can introduce and even present themselves as part of their narrative by using a whole arsenal of techniques. Some adopt formulations like 'but it happened quite differently' or 'No, what Churchill did, was …' (Haffner 1967: 63, 139), or the Socratic 'You never know' (Zweig 2000: 59). Others intensify their message by expressing their own feelings – 'the idea of dying at Sanssouci conveys an aura which makes me shudder' (Krockow 1991: 91) – or by sensitive and subjective depictions of nature, such as those of Golo Mann, who discreetly intertwined his own experience of exile and the Napoleonic refuge of Arenenberg Castle in Switzerland (Mann 1982: 7).

Whatever the narrators think is wrong, they can adjust. They may rhetorically take the reader by the hand, 'for the sake of avoiding confusion' (Haffner 1967: 8), or they may ascend to the lofty level of generalizing state-ments on human nature. These utterances of wisdom usually involve emphatic references to the irreducible contingency of history, to the inability of people to master their own lives fully, and to the all-embracing, irrational impulses driving both individual and collective action. One thus reads that 'the age' demands a certain kind of action, or that 'fate, a greater genius than all poets ever could be, brings its decisive importance to bear', or that a 'demonic elementary power' or a 'strategic demon and genius' is driving the hero (see, respectively, Mann 1982: 59; Zweig 2000: 90; Haffner 1967: 56, 29).

Expressions like these, however, do not mean that their authors are incapable of outlining structures. Again Golo Mann succeeds in skillfully summarizing the complex system of absolutism in a few sentences (Mann 1982: 47–48). Haffner's lucid analysis of the expectations of a charismatic leader in early twentieth-century Germany comprises but a few words. Usually a comparative glance at other countries, societies and persons is also included in the repertoire of this mode of historiography (Haffner 1967: 12; 1978; Krockow 1991: 68). Whereas academic authors have to restrict themselves to a seemingly objective language, the popular author is free to sound drastic or polemic or sarcastic. When discussing the memoirs of Heinrich Brüning and the 'permanent shaking hands and masculine vows', Haffner cannot help but call this funny in a cruel way (Haffner 1982: 87). Haffner also mocks the education of British aristocrats (Haffner 1967: 18), while Krockow takes aim at the hunting passion of Wilhelm II and the whole milieu of the East-Elbian aristocracy: 'Four years later, according to a press release by the Prussian *Hofjagdamt* [Royal Hunting Office] dated October 31, 1902, the Emperor had shot 47,443 items of game' (Krockow 1991: 244). The author of popular historiography has all dimensions of life at his disposal, from the private life of Fouché to the sexual ambivalences of the Prince of Eulenburg to the messy life of the aged Frederick II (Zweig 2000: 12; Krockow 1991: 92, 220ff).

Most of the aforementioned literary possibilities and techniques are applied only in the biographical genre. Thus they are linked to only one field of popular historiography, albeit one which, in addition to war, is the most important field. As is well known, before their renaissance in the early 1980s, biographies had been generally neglected by post-war academic historiography. The present boom in biography therefore points to popular historiography – to the conditions of its origins, effects and reception, to its intentions as well as to its inherently limited insights. Some of these general features of popular historiography will be addressed next.

V

Let me set out a number of relevant points to the study of popular historiography. Firstly, there is the history of the literary market and the increasingly important history of the media in general. Around 1900, expansion and internal differentiation in the culture industry reached a peak, one widely recognized even then. In 1912, Helmut von Steinen introduced the idea of a split between the 'cultural book' and the 'mass book' (Wittmann 1991: 277–284). On the one hand, a tendency to convergence was observed – as can be seen, for example, with Kröner's union of German publishers (*Union deutsche Verlagsgesellschaft*). On the other hand, an increase in the differentiation of fields and in the division of labour among publishers or within one publishing house occurred. Only then were editorial departments in the modern sense established, while program-matically ambitious or ideologically committed 'cultural' or 'individual' publishers, as they were called, started to develop strategies which set out how to transform the 'cultural book' into a 'mass book', so that demanding literature attracted a broader audience. Samuel Fischer, for example, specialized in the mass market for literary classics, old and new, from Goethe to Thomas Mann and Hermann Hesse; Eugen Diederichs made his publishing house into an organ for the cultural-religious 'life-reform' (*Lebensreform*) movement (Hübinger 1996). The Langewiesche brothers, Karl, Robert and Wilhelm, put their money on 'distinguished mass products', relatively inexpensive books on aspects of national culture, such as the so-called 'Blue Books' which sold in their millions, and they responded to the popular demand for belles-lettres. This trend continued in the Weimar Republic, though according to research on reading habits, it had to compete with an increasing hunger for novelties (Wittmann 1991: 323). In addition to, as well as overlapping with belletrist fiction, the reworking of the immediate, contemporary past was dominant in the Weimar Republic, with Emil Ludwig's biography of Wilhelm II (Ludwig 1925), Erich Maria Remarque's *All Quiet on the Western Front* (Remarque 1929), which sold one million copies in 1929–30, Werner Beumelburg's *Sperrfeuer um Deutschland* (Beumelberg 1929), which sold 120,000 copies, and finally Thomas Mann's *Der Zauberberg* (Mann 1924).[21] The publisher Ernst Rowohlt subjected himself to market forces by publishing books with a democratic and republican tendency – among them an anthology of expressionism (Pinthus 1920), Kurt Tucholsky's satires, and Emil Ludwig's books – without refusing to publish books by right-wing authors, if economically necessary (Wittmann 1991: 310).[22] Since then, the trend of the market has continued towards the mass book, notwithstanding the political and economic catastrophes of the century – although in the 1960s still only four to five per cent of the population were considered to be regular book buyers, and although today the democratization of the book seems to have peaked due to electronic information and communication (ibid.: 392, 397). Meanwhile, readers' demand for books on the most recent war remained unchanged after the Second World War. There were respectively 450,000 and 780,000 copies sold of book editions of serialized novels by Hans Hellmut Kirst and Joseph Martin Bauer – not to mention the success of Konsalik (ibid.: 392).[23] From today's perspective, some of the representations of the Second World War in magazines and serialized novels in the 1950s even qualify as an early contribution to the gradual formation of a critical constituent within the historical culture of the young West Germany (Füßmann 1994; Grütter 1994; Rüsen 1994a; Hardtwig 2002b; Knoch 2005).

There are, consequently, a variety of fields to be examined by social, economic, cultural and educational history: the interaction of supply and demand; the relevance of individual publishers and editors and their publishing houses to authors and their books. Of importance with regard to the latter are

Thomas and Golo Mann's publisher Fischer, the work of Marek (alias Ceram) as editor and author at Rowohlt publishers, Hans Magnus Enzenberger's *Andere Bibliothek* and the rediscovery of lost or forgotten texts, the groundbreaking role played by the Social Democratic member of the Reichstag, Hermann Dietz, as publisher, and Wolf Jobst Siedler, who had been an editor at the Ullstein publishing house before he started his own press, Siedler-Verlag, in 1980.[24]

Secondly, there is a specific social habitus of the writer or, to resort to a wider concept, of the intellectual with their typically twentieth-century characteristics. Recently, the intellectual has received intense scholarly attention. From 1882 to 1892, the number of writers and journalists in Imperial Germany rose to about 5,000, an increase of more than 50 per cent.[25] The dynamic expansion and diversification of the literary market enabled writers to considerably increase their influence on the market as well as their interpretive power and domination of opinion in society – this being the case across the whole political spectrum, from Thomas to Heinrich Mann, from Houston Stewart Chamberlain to Ludwig Renn, from Ernst Jünger to Erich Maria Remarque (Hertfelder and Hübinger 2000). The new market situation also opened a space for representations of the past beyond the rather narrowly confined realm of traditional, liberal, scholarly politics and publications. Once introduced, these new modes of writing history exerted influence on the market. They deliberately dissociated themselves from academic historiography, sometimes by criticizing it or by claiming to represent the true method of historiography (Hardtwig 2005c). Cases in point are Spengler and Ernst Ludwig. Even Ernst Kantorowicz's biography of the Hohenstaufen emperor Frederick II (Kantorowicz 1927), which has recently received much scholarly attention, has to be put in the context of a historiography which claimed to produce new and widely received effects ultimately aimed at 'action'.[26] Also in need of examination is the self-conception of authors as well as the material basis of their existence, their specific lifestyle and their habitus. With assertiveness and an undertone of self-mockery, Christian Graf von Krockow has described life and conditions of the freelance author – this 'entrepreneur of word and text'. A certain degree of financial independence is desirable. The name authors make for themselves, their reputation, is one of their most important means of production. Indispensable to them are good health, high productivity, knowing their job, and discipline. Krockow even counts the number of keystrokes in a certain unit of time. Only a few weeks of distraction, so he asserts, will result in 'being considerably out of training and in a drop in performance' (Krockow 2000: 251, 245–60). Also important is an 'efficient sales organization connecting high quality work to serial production' – a subject is variously used for broadcasts, lectures, papers and book chapters, which again result in more talks and lectures (ibid.: 258).

Thirdly, the forms as well as the political and ideological stances and intentions of popular historiography have to be related to the specific developments of twentieth-century German history. As self-evident and trivial as it may sound, at least one aspect in this regard should be highlighted. According to scholarly discussion, the political and cultural segmentation of German society – inherited from Imperial Germany, continued in the Weimar Republic, ideologically bridged in the Third Reich, gradually eroding in the Federal Republic – was a major roadblock on the way to a functioning republican and democratic system. Thus it is necessary that an investigation includes the traditional historiography of different social milieux, such as political Catholicism or the socialist labour movement. Did this kind of historiography reproduce, reinforce or rather qualify the political-cultural boundaries of their respective milieux? Did it incorporate or rather neglect scholarly methods of historiography? Did it respond to Protestant or Jewish bourgeois discourses? Did it reinforce or rather contribute to overcoming tensions and divisions within its respective milieu? To frame these questions in a more general conceptual way: Research should focus on the contribution of popular historiography to the formation of and change in historical-political awareness in Germany, as well as on the problem of whether popular historiography can be seen as a useful source for the analysis of these historical processes (Weichlein 2005; Kössler 2005).

Fourthly, a historical examination of popular historiography has to avoid the pitfall of social or political reductionism. The historian in this case deals with texts – with their historical potential for explanation and interpretation as well as with the related forms of representation and narrative. These are textual artefacts whose literary complexity (or non-complexity), relative autonomy vis-à-vis political and social contexts, and specific development of modes of interpretation and representation have to be taken into account. The task is, then, to bring together the social demand for an interpretation of the world, specific cultural traditions and changes, the potential of ideas popular historiography has in store, and the forms of representation to each other in a plausible and verifiable way. In each historical case, without neglecting the intrinsic importance of each aspect, the exact combination of these factors needs to be reconstructed as accurately as possible. A worthwhile additional assignment, not to be undertaken here, would be a closer investigation of the globalization of the market for popular historiography and historical non-fiction books in general. There has, for example, been a remarkable number of translations of books into German written in the tradition of the French *Annales* school and these have contributed to the reception of everyday history by German audiences.[27] In this case in particular, the importance of certain publishers, such as Klett-Cotta and Wagenbach, and of their editors and consultants can hardly be over-estimated.

Fifth: It seems beneficial to recall the initial constellation of this endeavour – it started from the vantage point of intellectual and cultural history. The boom in popular historiography in the twentieth century needs to be conceptualized as a result of two fundamental divisions taking shape during the emergence of modernity. History as an academic discipline had to dissociate itself simultaneously both from the philosophy of history and from literature. The founding fathers of historicism deliberated on and discussed both processes of dissociation. In perhaps the most tangible way, Ranke discussed the claim to autonomy laid down by the newborn academic discipline of history and derived his own methods and narratives from a historically specific literary constellation of problems. It was, however, equally important to the formation of his methods and narratives to fight off the Hegelian philosophy of history. The history of historiography has for a long time concentrated on the processes of professionalization and academicization of history (Hardtwig 1998). Recently, more attention has been devoted to the need, prevalent in the late nineteenth and early twentieth century, for interpretations of the past which were deeply rooted in the philosophy of history: the desire for a holistic notion of universal history, for a theologically structured history, for categories somehow related to transcendence, and for a mode of knowledge by way of which historical phenomena could be explained fundamentally and without consideration for individual origins and forms (Kittsteiner 1998; Heinßen 2003: 23ff). In the course of the 'linguistic turn', the way was paved, at least sporadically, for an awareness of the literary nature of texts, including those written in a strictly scholarly way (Hardtwig 1990b). Undisputedly the modern distinction between factual and fictive narratives has been more and more reinforced. Consequently, and possibly by way of compensation, there has been and still is an increase in the desire for deliberately literary and narrative presentations of the past without the burdens of academic requirements.

Sixth: All popular historiography is exposed to the fundamental tension between academic history and memory. Recently, this tension has been more and more discussed. Time and again, heated controversies about the politics of memory have been fought out, from the historians' debate (the *Historikerstreit*) in 1986 to the exhibition of German military crimes during the Second World War (the *Wehrmachtsausstellung*, 1995–99, fundamentally revised in 2000), from the boom of memory in audiovisual media to the globalization of Holocaust remembrance. As far as scholarly debate is concerned, these processes correspond to the rise of the paradigm of memory culture.[28] This binary way of approaching the past, however, needs to be itself historicized. There is no twentieth-century publication on the World Wars, on the Third Reich or on German history that escapes this tension. The distinction drawn between history and memory remains the most productive effort to conceptualize this binary approach. Collective memory has been described as the totality of non-scholarly modes of memory (Hockerts 2002: esp. 63). Its inherent tendency points toward simplification, the reduction of complexity and the bridging of the distance between past and present. Academic history, by contrast, aims at recording as accurately as possible the concrete conditions of events and processes, at reconstructing interrelations in all their complexity, and at de-emotionalizing memory as much as possible. As demonstrated by some contributions on Holocaust remembrance, a narrower focus might differentiate between the appraisal of memory on the one hand and the process of learning and understanding on the other (Schatzker 1988). The former primarily appeals to emotions whereas the latter strives for a rational and sober analysis as well as for a methodically informed explanation of the complexity of history. In the background of distinctions like these there is always the experience of the 1930s and 1940s, in particular the Holocaust. In principle, however, this tension has effects: they can be seen in, for example, Theodor Heuss's writing on Friedrich Naumann (Heuss 1937); in fact they can be seen in every kind of memory or report of wars, bombing raids, war captivity, the experience of violence in concentration camps or the experiences of the population when the Red Army was advancing. With increasing nervousness, academic history postulates a clear-cut dichotomy between history and memory. Academic historians claim to have priority over contemporary witnesses. The academic discipline of history has a point if it feels threatened by the boom of collective memory – though simultaneously academic historians welcome, profit from and are involved in the intense interest in the past and the intensity of debates on the politics of memory.

Lastly: More and more members of society are included – and there is a general tendency to include everyone – in the processes of producing, communicating and using knowledge, as a result of the formation of the knowledge and information society in the twentieth century. The relationship between history and memory needs to be conceptualized in this context. Modern information society originates from the educational expansion of the nineteenth century, succeeded by the advance of, firstly, print media, then audiovisual media, and finally the digitalization and globalization of knowledge. Thus popular historiography has to be contextualized within the development of the modern knowledge society (Szöllösi-Janze 2004). Not only has this development resulted in a quantitative rise in the audience, but it also changed ways of processing and receiving information. From the beginning of the twentieth century, at the latest, it has been joined time and again to criticism of the traditional idea of a cultural antagonism between scholarly experts and a lay audience. There seems to be a socio-cultural process that is partially opposed to the progressive specialization and differentiation of the spheres of life and knowledge under modernity. This tendency has been expressed as much by authors of nationalist and racist historiography, who claim to meet true scholarly standards, as well as by authors like Spengler or Emil Ludwig, who explicitly distanced themselves from scholarly historiography. Egon Friedell and other modern authors of historical non-fiction but also journalists and writers such as Sebastian Haffner, all systematically break down the wall between the academic expert and the non-academic layperson, whereas academic history necessarily reinforces the dividing line. Scholarly authors wishing to participate in the blurring of this division usually comply with their editors' demand for simplification. It is difficult to arrive at a clear judgment in this regard. What seems to be a loss of competence and respectability to some is considered by others to contribute to the democratization and wider circulation of knowledge. An appraisal of old and new historical bestsellers can hardly avoid being shaped by these ambivalences. The future public role of academic history may depend upon its willingness to account for these developments and to find well-reasoned responses to the problems discussed in this essay.

Notes

1. According to its German publisher, Ken Follett's *Säulen der Erde* (Follett 1990) – originally published in English as *The Pillars of the Earth* – remained at the top of the German bestseller lists for six consecutive years. In 2004 a poll carried out by the public-service television channel ZDF which asked Germans for their favourite books, Follett's book ranked third after J.R.R. Tolkien's *The Lord of the Rings* and the Bible. In April 2005, the number one bestseller according to *Der Spiegel* was Dan Brown's *Sakrileg* (Brown 2004), the German translation of *The Da Vinci Code*.

2. An early example of this genre is Wolfgang Leonhard's *Die Revolution entläßt ihre Kinder*, first published in 1955; the sixteenth edition, with 271,000 copies printed, appeared in 1978 (Leonhard 1978). In August 2001 the seventh edition of Sebastian Haffner's *Geschichte eines Deutschen* (Haffner 2000) was published, selling 320,000 copies. Memoirs or eyewitness accounts of the expulsion of Germans from the East are: Lehndorff (1961) and the account of Lehndorff's sister Libussa (Krockow 1988). When the third paperback edition of the latter was published, more than 60,000 copies had already been sold. Libussa's story made Krockow a bestselling author; previously he had been an author of historical non-fiction for more than twenty years. The last two examples show the absurdity of the claims of some German newspapers, especially in their cultural sections, according to which Germans have only recently begun to deal with their own history of expulsion. See also Schütz (2005).

3. The most recent paperpack edition of Speer's memoirs (Speer 1969) appeared in March 2005. According to the publishers, 500,000 copies and foreign rights for twenty countries have been sold so far. On Speer, see Fest (1999).

4. See Meier (1982) and Nipperdey (1983).

5. See some of the examples from the *Kleine Geschichte* series: Schulze (1996) and Demandt (2003).

6. On Ranke, see Muhlack (1997); on Burckhardt, see Hardtwig (1997); and on Treitschke, see Hübinger (1997).

7. See Schlosser (1815–41, 1823, 1843–57). The latter was published in further revised editions.

8. See Felken (1988) and Demandt and Farrenkopf (1994).

9. On Heuss, see Kössler (2005), Puschner (2005) and Weichlein (2005). Heuss's *Hitlers Weg* (Heuss 1932) was reprinted eight times in its first year of publication. His *Deutsche Gestalten* (Heuss 1951), which sold over 10,000 copies, was originally written as a series of biographical essays for the *Frankfurter Zeitung* between 1938 and 1943; it appealed to a broader audience and was republished after the war, in part due to Heuss's prominence as President of West Germany (see Becker 2005).

10. On Mann's work, see Jonas and Stunz (2004) and Lahme and Stunz (2005).

11. On Friedell, see Rutschky (2005).

12. On Haffners biography, see Ullrich (1999b) and Soukup (2001). For criticism of Haffner, see Paul and Köhler (2001) and the rebuttal by Haffner's son (Pretzel 2001); see

      also Mohr (2000) and Mohr et al. (2001). On the international success of Haffner's memoirs, see Altwegg (2003).

13. On the conception of popular science, see the recent survey by Kretschmann (2003).

14. On Spengler's relationship to academic scholarship, see Demandt and Farrenkopf (1994); on Emil Ludwig, see Ullrich (2001, 2005).

15. Indeed, non-academic historiography was sometimes the first to tackle subjects which academic history did not dare deal with or which had been neglected within academia. Some of these books by non-academics (who nevertheless complied with academic standards of research) were astonishingly successful. The most important example is, of course, Joachim Fest's *Hitler* (Fest 1973), which so far has sold 800,000 copies. Less successful due to a less spectacular subject, but equally innovative, is Schivelbusch (1977).

16. See also Zweig (2000: 12).

17. Still valuable, but comprising only the German debate before the 'linguistic turn', is Koselleck and Lutz (1982); see also Kocka and Nipperdey (1979) and Hardtwig (1979, 1982). On the literary dimension of nineteenth-century German historiography, see Fulda (1996); despite its exaggerated conclusions and polarizations, see also Süssmann (2000).

18. See, e.g., Bamm (1955). In its first year, twelve editions of this book were published and 120,000 copies printed; a 1960 special edition marked 230,000 copies printed, and in 1977 the eighteenth edition was published; from 1964 onward, a paperback edition was also available. On archeological bestsellers, see Oels (2005).

19. Krockow's vivid presentation is made more so through his use of depictions from Theodor Fontane's *Wanderungen durch die Mark Brandenburg* (Fontane 1862–88); see Krockow (1991: 73 ff). In the tradition of Walter Benjamin's *Städtebilder* (Benjamin 1927–29) a new genre of historically informed, topographic, political and cultural depictions of places was established, see, e.g., Schlögel (1988) and Willms (1988); for a journalistic version in this, see Schlögel (2001). On the spatial turn of historiography, see Osterhammel (1998, 2000) and Schlögel (2003).

20. It should be noted, however, that the collection of Mann's essays, originally published in high culture reviews (Mann 1982), was not enormously successful in sales terms.

21. On these, see Wittmann (1991: 125) and Ullrich (2005).

22. On the crisis of publishers and booksellers and resulting new strategies, see Grieser (1999).

23. Hans Hellmut Kirst's three *08/15* novels (Kirst 1954a, 1954b, 1955) were first published in 1954–55 as serialized stories in magazines. Josef Martin Bauer's *So weit die Füße tragen* (Bauer 1955) meanwhile sold more than a million copies; after the novel was made into a film in 2001 (directed by Hardy Martin), two new paperback editions were published in 2002.

24. The importance of a good editor is emphasized by Krockow (2000: 316).

25. See Hübinger and Mommsen (1993), Hübinger (1994) and Charle (1997: 108ff).

26. On Kantorowicz, see Benson and Fried (1997); see also Grünewald (1982), Fuhrmann (1996b) and Oexle (1996). On the theory of history of the George circle, see also Schlak (2001).

27. See, e.g., Le Roy Ladurie (1982, 1983) and Muchembled (1984, 1990); for other works popular with audiences, see Ariès (1994) and Corbin (1990). Even rather sophisticated reflections on the profession of historiography have been translated, see: e.g., Bloch (1985), Ariès (1988) and Febvre (1988). For an introduction to the most important

paradigms of historiography in the twentieth-century from an international perspective, see Iggers (1996) and Raphael (2003).

28. For a selection of the literature, see Assmann (1995b, 1999) and Welzer (2001). For some German examples, see: Augstein et al. (1987), Reichel (1995), Frei (1996), Wolfrum (1999) and Niethammer (1999). For a survey, see Jarausch (2002) and Jarausch and Sabrow (2002).

6

Between Political Coercion and Popular Expectations: Contemporary History on the Radio in the German Democratic Republic

Christoph Classen

From today's viewpoint it might not seem an obvious choice to include an essay on East German radio in a volume on popular historiography. There is currently a boom in history, and contemporary history in particular, on TV, in museums and exhibitions and lately on the internet. If we take this as a starting point, then we can assume it to be a phenomenon of the last thirty years. That means, of course, that the German Democratic Republic (GDR), or East Germany as it is also known, was only touched by this boom in its last decade. Even more important is the fact that this boom seems to be linked to two other phenomena in particular: on the one hand, evolving consumer culture after 1945, including the media; and on the other, the transition to what is often called second modernity or postmodernity – the leaving behind of classic industrial society and its telos of modernization and ever-increasing growth. The current high visibility of history seems to be due to contemporary media which has led to an increase in individualization, pluralization and denormalization and, consequently, resulted in a sense of an insecure future; this phenomenon in turn makes people demand an increasing amount of orientation and assurance, which they seek in history (Rödder 2004). As we all know, the socialist leadership of the GDR had difficulty with consumer culture as well as the farewell to classic modernity, and on an abstract level it could be assumed that the end of the GDR might have been a result of its inability to adapt to these developments.

In the case of radio, these matters seem no less complex. Undoubtedly radio has had its share in the media saturation of the twentieth century; likewise, the medium is still much in use today and hence very popular. Yet with the rise of television and the widespread availability of records and tapes since the 1960s, the use of radio has changed fundamentally. Radio has become a casual background medium that accompanies our daily life and supplies us mainly with music, interrupted by brief snippets of news and service features presented in specific journals (Jenke 1999). But it hardly plays a role when it comes to conveying history, not even in a popular form.[1] If radio does focus on history, it is only on some non-commercial stations addressing target audiences of low numbers of listeners.

Thus it seems sensible to focus on that period in which radio was the dominant medium in the GDR; that is, the period from the end of the Second World War to the mid 1960s when TV began to take over. In the 1970s and 1980s even GDR radio increasingly developed towards the up-to-date medium we know today and, consequently, lost its political impact (Geserick 2004). As a result, history became only a marginal topic on radio programmes and was mostly left to cinema and television to address it (Beutelschmidt and Steinlein 2004; Schwab 2007).

That, however, does not answer the question of whether or not it makes sense to analyse a particular form of popular culture in the GDR. If one compares this to the major part of academic literature on media in the GDR, this question could clearly be answered negatively: there the mass media are mainly described as instruments of political propaganda that were supposed to cement the claim to power of the dictatorship. Concessions to the audience's taste were merely owed as a response to competing Western media.[2] Nevertheless there can be no doubt that references to history, and contemporary history in particular, had their impact on the East Germany's culture of history. In fact history – and not only on the radio – was so omnipresent that one might be tempted to talk about an obsession with it. This obsession obviously had little to do with the phenomena mentioned above: a second modernity – followed by an increasing demand for direction – did not emerge in the Germany of the 1950s and 1960s, nor did the GDR show any commercial structures that might have served such a demand. Thus there seems to have been a different form of popular history whose character will now be analysed.

I would like to begin with some remarks that will provide a context for radio as a medium and the general impact of entertainment and popular culture in the GDR against the background of the cold war. In the second part of the chapter I will draw upon examples from typical historical features presented on East German radio. Finally, I would like to formulate some general remarks on the relationship between acquiring and popularizing history in East Germany under the Socialist Unity Party of Germany (SED) and how society responded to this.

Radio and Popular Culture in the GDR

In 1950, a point in time when the cold war had reached its first high, the editor-in-chief of *Neues Deutschland* explained that his paper was not meant 'to entertain people' or 'to make money'; rather, the *Neues Deutschland* was published to lead a political struggle. He saw the paper as a 'political institution that appeared to be a paper for reasons of expedience instead of being a paper that dealt with politics for reasons of expedience'.[3] This quote describes very well what kind of press was supposed to emerge in the newly created GDR; namely, one defined by its sole and unconditioned obligation to the political aims of the Communist Party. To a certain extent this was the reversal of Marshall McLuhan's famous saying (see McLuhan and Fiore 1967): for the *Neues Deutschland* the message was the medium.

What *Neues Deutschland*'s editor Herrnstadt said about his paper could be said about radio of that period. The age of high Stalinism was characterized by a media concept which saw radio foremost as an instrument of implementing the claim to political power and reformation. This was linked to a devaluation of its entertainment function (Classen 2005). The devaluation was not a newly emerging process in 1950, but had already gone parallel to the process of socialization according to Georg Simmel – that is, the growing involvement of ever-increasing parts of the population in political processes and social discourse. The social elites, who had refused to accept anything popular since the nineteenth century, were however confronted – starting at the same time – by the fast-growing range and efficiency of exactly such offers (Stein 1984: 244–46). An increase in literacy among the population and improved methods of printing and distribution had contributed to a rapid growth in the supply of and demand for entertainment literature and theatre. This trend of extending the offer of popular forms of entertainment against the background of commercializing the public continued with the arrival of new audio-visual media in the twentieth century and gained additional momentum.

Thus, after its initially military use, radio soon developed into a public medium addressing a mass audience after the First World War. Moreover, its increased availability and the improved quality of transmission led to the development of audience preferences between the wars: beside information, entertainment caught on (Dussel 2002: 153–64). Admittedly, programme makers in Germany, where broadcasting was under state control yet masked by a façade of private enterprise, hardly gave in to this demand. Because of conservative fears of a culture dominated by the masses, radio programming in the Weimar Republic mainly focused on high culture and education (Berking 1984).

Only during the era of National Socialism did the people responsible give in to demands for easily consumable forms of more or less apolitical entertainment, though this did not only happen in broadcasting (Pater 1998; Dussel 2002: 176–243). Of course, this trend was linked with the pursuit of conveying the right politics and ideology to the body of the German people, be that subliminally or openly by broadcasting copious speeches, commentaries, newsreels and special messages. Parallel to this, in its need to legitimize itself the regime took care, especially during the Second Word Ward, that even in a state-controlled medium like radio the claim to high culture – as had been the case in the Weimar Republic – was almost totally abandoned in favour of programmes structured to meet the demand for entertainment of the majority of the population. Entertainment, as propaganda minister Goebbels put it, was important for the war 'as it offered recreation and relief of front and home'.[4] Thus the point of departure in 1945 may be sketched as follows: whereas traditional bourgeois resentment against popular, mass culture in Germany continued to exist, a practice had emerged in the meantime that met the demand for this kind of output. This popularization first happened in the privately run media due to commercial interests; later, under the Nazis, state-controlled broadcasting also followed suit mainly for reasons of legitimizing the government.

Regarding the requests listeners had concerning radio as a medium, the end of the war and the fall of Germany in 1945 were only a partial rupture. Facing living conditions full of want and austerity, the desire for popular formats of entertainment that allowed people to leave the hardship of everyday life behind – at least for a while – had not lost its intensity.

The listeners' preferences described above, which had emerged with the rise of the medium in the 1920s, were in obvious contrast to the concept of the SED leadership cited above, a concept which primarily saw all mass media – according to Lenin's classic axiom – primarily as an instrument of political reformation. Here the media were regarded as an 'organ of democratic education of the masses' that should take into account the 'fast-growing awareness of the masses' by an 'in-depth conveying of ideological problems'. 'Work, work – education, educating oneself and educating the people' was the role of all journalists, as Hermann Axen, the member of the Central Committee in charge of the media, announced at a congress in May 1950.[5] Moreover, popular formats and preferences became generally suspicious in the GDR's attempt to distinguish itself from West Germany. Typically, anything popular was identified with America and thus with an apparently soulless non-culture. A similar interpretation could already be found in the 1920s and 1930s when – during the crisis of the Weimar Republic – America became associated with the negative impact of modernity and a field onto which were projected relevant fears; this happened even in the workers' movement (Peukert 1989: 187–89; Saldern 1996: 213–45; Maase 1997: 163–65). In the GDR of the 1950s, the traditional rejection of popular culture and outdated cultural chauvinism quite often coalesced with the increasing importance of the Soviet Union as a role model, including in the field of cultural politics, and the revolutionary pathos of socialist revolution to a very peculiar melange.[6] Only after the regime had nearly been overturned in June 1953 did it change its attitude to popular entertainment. This change could be seen in changed attitudes toward the function of radio. The observation made in the West, however, was that the new measures had been introduced in order to stabilize the system, and this held a certain truth. Nevertheless the stronger orientation towards entertainment and Western-style programmes in broadcasting remained a controversial subject in the years to come (Agde 2000).

The GDR and History

What then led to the obsession with history I mentioned above, an obsession that dominated state-sanctioned culture in the GDR over its forty years of existence? In order to understand this it is necessary to return once more to the nineteenth century and the process of socialization already referred to, a process that resulted – amongst others things – in the emergence of new dynamic public spheres and an intensification of strategies of persuasion and legitimization. This went hand in hand with a radically changed interpretation of history as a category that had already begun with the French Revolution and which was itself a result of the Enlightenment (Koselleck 1989). In fact there had been, as Assmann informs us, memory cultures in the Middle Ages and early modern era which were able to create identities and which had a stately superstructure (Assmann 1997), but only now could history become an ontological category that would include not only the past but its reflexive interpretation as well (Koselleck 1997: 89–90). In modernity, given the divergence of the 'horizon of experience and expectations' (ibid.), history became a universal leitmotif in which experience and expectations, past and future, could merge; that is, which was characterized by its dimension of historical philosophy which distinguished it from previous interpretations. History itself now gained the status of an omnipotent transcendental power; or, to use Foucault's words, history constituted its own discourse.

The adoption of an affirmative historical philosophy, of the idea of a process that can be traced back to apparently clear laws, can already be found in Kant, Hegel and Fichte, on whose writings, as is commonly known, Marx and Engels based their historical materialism. Therefore Marx's and Engels's break from the idealistic tradition does not lie in a fundamental understanding of history as an ontological process that follows fixed laws. On the contrary: what has been exchanged are merely the principles which seem to push the process of history forwards. Instead of ideas or the 'spirit' of the world – as Hegel has it – now economic conditions become the driving forces of law-bound historic processes. The dialectics of the struggle of distributing material resources, the class struggle, seem to abolish the drivers of history: 'The history of all societies so far is the history of class struggle' (Marx and Engels 1959: 462). Here we might add the dialectic relation of the lawful course of history on the one hand and contingency on the other: even though the development of history requires several stages of development to lead from an original society to a classless communist one, actual actors are needed in order to actively promote this process. According to Marxism-Leninism, the communists will become the carriers of an objective historic process. What becomes obvious here is the transition from an affirmative historical philosophy to a political agenda, something that is characteristic of communism.

It stands to reason that the idea of history as a law-bound category defining the past as well as the future cannot emerge without processes of secularization and an increasing awareness of the contingency within modernity. Thus history gained the function of compensating for a loss of metaphysical assurance due to an ideology that saw itself to be rationally scientific but also atheist. This function leads to a particular way of interpreting history: 'By knowing the orderly course and destination of history, the conscience is able to reassure the reason of the world. The pathos of historical philosophy lies particularly in the fact that it can oppose the current awareness of not being reconciled, of a world marked by powerlessness and suffering' (Angehrn 1991: 106). Looking at the social upheavals of the nineteenth century and the disastrous experience of the twentieth century, the attractiveness of an interpretation of the world that allows one to reduce complexity, to establish reason and to provide direction seems to be quite obvious.

It stood to reason, then, that even the communists in the GDR relied on the explanatory model of historical materialism, a historical philosophy that had been phrased by Marx and Engels and sharpened by Lenin for the purpose of action: in the end it provided a key element of communist ideology. Yet at the same time, the case of the GDR is a special one as the 'partial' state founded in 1949 had to fight for its legitimacy from the very beginning. Firstly, there was the problem of being a partial state; indeed, the unpopular division of Germany into two states – East and West –was a problem for both Germanies. Secondly, the SED regime owed its origins to the very unpopular Soviet victors of the war rather than a proletarian revolution. Thirdly, the head of state produced massive resistance through an initially enforced course of radical social restructuring which did not take into account the social interest and condition of the majority of the population.

Against this background political instability, the effort to anchor the young state in history – that is, to give it a line of historic continuity in the sense of an 'invented tradition' (Hobsbawm and Ranger 1992) – was a matter of great importance from the foundation of the state onward. Thus in the 1950s a master narrative was coined that served the purpose of establishing a myth of foundation that was interpreted by the GDR as a (preliminary) end to class struggle, one might say a communist version of the eschatological narrative of the end of history. By establishing the first socialist state on German soil and following the transfer of the means of production into the hands of the proletariat, Germany – like the Soviet Union – enjoyed the chance of becoming a society devoid of contradictions and for the first time humankind could look forward to thoroughly harmonious and happy future . Of course, here, too, the rule applied that the lawful victory of socialism was not in itself a reason to lay back and leave the future course of history to its own devices. Not only did it become important to overcome the residues of the old order in one's own country, especially the quite persistent reactionary conscience found among some, for the struggle was only half won: the Western world – and especially the western part of Germany, the Federal Republic – was, from this point of view, still stuck in a social order of bourgeois capitalism from which it had to be liberated.

From the beginning, therefore, history in the GDR was not only influenced by communist historical philosophy; to a large extent it was directly claimed by the SED regime as part of Soviet hegemony. Thus it was in large part subject to political influences and needs that did not always serve the purpose of affecting the general public.

Contemporary History on the Radio

A special emphasis of radio history programmes broadcast on the radio in the GDR was the recent past, particularly the era of the Nazi regime and fights between communists and Nazis preceding that era. Indeed these fights were understood as a dramatic culmination of class struggle, a fight for life and death, in which communism came to be victorious in the end, though there were many casualties. In the first two decades following the Second World War nearly the whole German population suffered from the dramatic impact the war had on their lives and could still vividly remember those who had played an important role. This existential experience of war shaped people's memories and perception of the then present, especially as many issues – such as prisoners of war – remained pertinent in both parts of Germany for a long time. Undoubtedly the recent past was a most suitable subject for radio programming, and tapped into a wellspring of emotion.

Quite a few radio programmes on the political situation were thus related to the experience of war and tried to utilize this collective context of experience for a productive reinterpretation of the present. One of the focal points of memory and myth was the Battle of Stalingrad and the fall of the German Sixth Army at the beginning of 1943. This battle had already been stylized by Nazi propaganda as an event of great importance, especially in the shape of myths of heroes and victims.[7] After the war Stalingrad managed to maintain its mythical status but had now became a symbol of the lost war in general. The misery of the closed-in soldiers, weakened by cold and hunger and deserted by their own leaders, intensified the German self-perception of themselves as victims of war and the Nazi regime (Kumpfmüller 1995). What additionally made Stalingrad an emotive issue was the fact that many people were personally affected: many families mourned relatives who had fallen in the battle for the city, yet due to the high number of soldiers missing in action and prisoners of war many families still hoped for a return of their relatives – a hope, however, that only rarely materialized.[8] In the post-war era the myth of Stalingrad amalgamated the collective, national tale of suffering and doom with individual mourning of the dead or uncertainty concerning the fate of missing people.

In the early years of the GDR the Battle of Stalingrad marked a mythical rupture of huge impact. There was constant reference to this mighty myth up to at least the 1960s.[9] However, the focus lay less on the German victims than on an interpretation of Stalingrad as not only the turning point of the war but also the beginning of a new era in history, proving socialism's superiority over capitalism (Fischer 2001). This attitude can be demonstrated with the example of a feature broadcast in 1950 on the seventh anniversary of the Sixth Army's capitulation. Here the speaker, a former army doctor, reveals himself to be a member of the German community united by fate, and he tells of the moment when he himself was captured: his arrest, he told his audience, took place in 'one of the numerous bombed out basements' that were 'filled with wounded, exhausted soldiers, starved and frozen to death'.[10] Going on from this, however, he reverses this national tale of doom and sacrifice and represents it as a 'victory' which 'demonstrated the military, political and moral superiority of the Soviet people'.[11] In order to explain this change of perspective, the narrator styles his moment of capture and first encounter with a Soviet soldier as a moment of individual epiphany that initiated a process of recognition and change. Walking into Soviet imprisonment was described as a 'path into life' and as a moment of 'wonderful encouragement and power'.[12] Here we are faced with an attempt to replace the German myth of Stalingrad – one of doom and sacrifice – by a Soviet version, the national victory in the Great Fatherland War. The narrative of sacrifice becomes one of victory. Thus, the motif of individual change in the broadcast is also typical of public debate concerning the war in the first two decades of the GDR (Heimann 2000). The medium of individual biography – focusing on a personal change – served the purpose of resolving the contradictions between past and present in a harmonious manner.

Nevertheless, considerable doubt remains regarding the question of how many listeners were able to identify with this interpretation, which meant the adoption of the Soviet narrative of Stalingrad. To do so would have meant an upheaval in previous perceptions and interpretations in Germany: the defeat of Stalingrad had to be seen as a victory; the former enemies, the Soviets, would have to be seen as saviours and friends; and listeners would have had to accept the narrator's representation of his experiences. In this spirit the way into Soviet prison camps was described as a 'path into life' and as a moment of a 'wonderful encouragement and power' which 'even though it might sound rather strange … even caught us, the beaten, defeated and totally demoralised remnants of soldiers'.[13] This kind of interpretation did not meet with a kind reception in the general public since the deep anti-Slavic and anti-communist resentments of the German population were not overcome by the end of the war. Soldiers returning from Soviet prison camps must have been largely alienated by the view painted in this broadcast.

Similar to the way in which Stalingrad became a cipher for the war and the suffering of front-line soldiers, the experience of the air battle in the GDR became condensed around the bombing of Dresden in February 1945. As with the case of Stalingrad, Dresden mainly represented the German victims: '40,000 people' had been 'murdered', '180,000 flats [were] destroyed' and '47 hospitals [and] 21 churches over 12 square kilometres had been razed to the ground'. This was the wording in a radio feature on the ninth anniversary of the bombardment in 1954.[14] The portrayal of 'meaningless and helpless victims' seemed to be self-evidently true given a city crowded by refugees and the dubious military worth of the attack 'at a point in time when the outcome of World War II had already been decided'.[15] The outstanding role Dresden played in public memory when compared to other bombed-out cities was due to the factors mentioned, but also to the city's image as the town 'of art and culture of the Baroque age', an image that was also mythically enhanced: 'The *Frauenkirche* no longer stood, no *Hofkirche* and no *Zwinger*; Dresden and its centuries of culture seemed to have been wiped out'.[16] What cannot be ignored is the nationalist undertone that more or less directly emphasized the cultural superiority of Germany.

The presumed connection between inhumanity and lack of culture among the 'Anglo-American' enemies – enemies both during and after the war – became an oft-used representation, and one which was repeated with each anniversary. This representation used old-fashioned anti-American stereotypes from the period between the wars and from the Nazi era and transferred them to the post-war American leadership of the capitalist West (Saldern 1996; Gassert 1997). The chauvinist argument about a 'lack of culture' among the 'American occupation forces' that revealed itself in murder and terror as well as in cultural ignorance seamlessly fits into the explicitly nationalist campaigns with which the SED attempted to underline its claim to the whole of Germany and to get rid of its image as a 'Russian party' (Lemke 2000). If one were to believe the propaganda of the time, the Americans did not shy away from defiling national symbols and were even prepared to blow up the rock of the *Lorelei*: 'People all over the world have only one enemy: the Anglo-American war parties and their agents. They threaten our fatherland, they destroy our beautiful nature, they annihilate the soil that is our home', the deputy general manager of the *Deutschlandsender* announced on the radio in 1950.[17] Facing such appeals to patriotic feeling, Dresden functioned as a key symbol in narratives about the deliberate destruction of German cultural values and, eventually, about the anti-German politics of the West. Meanwhile, the GDR was stylized as a guarantor of universal peace in a world yet to come.

At the time the attempt to use emotionally charged myths such as Stalingrad or Dresden was not limited to the medium of radio but could also be found in the press. Due to the high degree of state control and the political norms set, especially for political features, the topics discussed and the modes of addressing them resembled each other quite strongly across different media. What was a particular feature of radio, however, was the fact that it could (seemingly) give a mode of individual address: the speaker's or writer's person could be experienced in a more sensual way because of their voice provided a higher degree of immediacy than would be possible in a written and printed text. Not only could the speaker communicate feelings by directly talking to their audience, they were less pushed into the background by the text and its content. This could lead to a certain suggestive potential, something that the Nazis, for example, attempted to utilize in their emotional enactments of a people's community and the *Führer* (Marßoleck 2001).

Many writers met the potential of the medium of radio by enriching their features with personal experiences and memories. Thus they did not only legitimate themselves as members of the German community of sacrifice and suffering, but also tried to give their accounts a special degree of credibility and validity. For example, on one anniversary of Dresden bombing one editor impressively describes how she herself experienced the bombing: searching for 'my relatives, I encountered children crying for their mothers; mothers searching for their children and fathers who, fatigued and with grimy faces … carried away the charcoaled bodies on stretchers'.[18] The woman was not only able to deliver a credible description of things ten years after the bombing; besides her account carried particular veracity because the event was part of her biography. Similar to today's TV documentaries, historical argumentation was used for present purposes and autobiographical evidence had a special credence in history programming on the radio. It granted the speaker authority and invited the listener to identify with the victims of the events described (and with the speaker themselves). It brought the past vividly into the present.

Despite the use of such stylistic devices as autobiographical evidence that utilized the potential of the radio medium, there remain considerable doubts about how effective the interpretations of history put forward were on the audience. A reason for their failure could be the political overdetermination of mass media communication: this made it necessary to constantly align popular patterns of interpretation and myths of the immediate past to current political issues, even if such a link was not possible without ruptures or reversals of commonly held views.

In the end this resulted in a 'historical presentism'; that is, a connection of past and future in which the past is always interpreted and cited regarding its usefulness for the current political situation (Sabrow 2001: 410). The omni-presence of historic references – what I earlier referred to as the obsession with history – went hand in hand with the near total devaluation of history as something belonging to an era in its own right, something we might expect as this is already immanent in the teleology of historical materialism. The recourse to collectively shared experience, however, restricted the usefulness of revisionist or innovative interpretations of history. Sometimes it was simply not possible to weave narratives and interpretations that would serve relevant political situations.

Additionally it was mostly current issues – sometimes only current on that very day – which tended to dominate the use of historical references and analogies. This can be seen in the campaign against President Theodor Heuss when he ran for office a second time in 1954. Not only was Heuss's approval of the so-called *Ermächtigungsgesetz* ('enabling act') while a member of parliament in 1933 brought up,[19] Heuss himself was branded a new version of Hindenburg – a part of the bourgeois façade fascism had needed as camouflage from the beginning.[20] Likewise, as soon as he had won the election in 1948, the French president Charles de Gaulle was dubbed a 'fascist dictator' and an American

Gauleiter (Nazi governor).[21] Consequently the practice of military intervention in the so-called proxy wars offered numerous reasons to accuse the 'motherland of capitalism', the West, of fascist tendencies. In 1952, for example, one broadcast claimed that 'American imperialism is adapting all features of fascism – from manipulating and terrorizing elections and the extermination of prisoners of war and inhabitants in occupied countries like Korea to establishing a kind of Gestapo and concentration camps'.[22] Quite noticeably the historical analogies drawn and the labels employed both follow the bipolar logic of the cold war.

The epithets were not only quite arbitrary, they could also change quite rapidly depending on the state of things. This was particularly the case for authors who worked on radio dramas rather than journalistic features, who suffered because it was not easy to rewrite a play at short notice so as to take into account the day's political events. Radio plays, along with musical programmes, were very popular and occupied a cultural space similar to that of the dramas, soaps and series shown on contemporary television: they offered opportunities for emotional identification with others without listeners having to leave their homes (something they had to do when going to the cinema). This was also true of historical topics: radio plays allowed for the re-witnessing of history, and radio plays with historical topics were immensely popular during the heyday of radio between the 1930s and the 1950s. However, those in charge of radio programming in the GDR were unsympathetic to the genre, and they saw drama departments as residues of bourgeois unprogressiveness because of the difficulty of aligning artistic production to political requirements at short notice. Consequently the people working in such departments were not treated with kid gloves (Wagner 1997: 41–42). Vice versa, history – and in particular contemporary history – was regarded by most authors as a political minefield due to the copious uncertainties it entailed. Indeed the archives are full of programmes that were shelved for political reasons. As a result, the GDR did not succeed in producing interesting and popular historical radio plays for a long time despite the fact that the genre enjoyed a high popularity.

Conclusion: Four Theses about the Impact of Radio in the GDR

I want to conclude by making the following four observations. Firstly, in the GDR contemporary history was a highly politicized field in which, to adopt a modern term, politically correct representations were possible. But what was broadcast was shaped less by social moods than political themes: these included the idea of the Soviet Union as the German's big friend, the rise and superiority of socialism, and such like. The content of these broadcasts could be called abstract counter-narratives that were hardly aligned with traditional and popular interpretations and narratives. In other words: the political over-determination prevented that any conveyance could be easily achieved between real-life experience and traditional interpretation on the one hand and the new interpretations on the other.

Secondly, these new interpretations were closely related to the fact that the culture of time in the early years of the GDR was highly oriented to the future. References to history primarily served the purpose of confirming the teleological narrative of the progress of historical materialism. History was brought up time and again, but always fulfilled a functional relation to the present. As Walter Ulbricht said in 1955, without any hint of irony, 'Our historians are still far too infatuated with the past' (cited in Sabrow 2000: 227). The master narrative in the GDR up to the mid 1960s was that of the end of history, of the salvation of humankind by socialism and the GDR. As a result, the past had to be disposable, and interpretations of the past were continually adjusted to fit current political requirements. Nevertheless, this meaningful and teleological connection of past and present – a historical philosophy – bore the potential of identifying with the state.

Thirdly, it seems that those in charge lacked sensitivity and understanding of radio as a medium. In the post-war period of austerity, radio faced demands mostly for entertainment and relaxation. Listeners' letters that have been archived clearly show that the majority were not fond of political indoctrination and verbose programmes. However, according to those responsible for radio programming, that was exactly the task of the mass media: to educate and to overcome so-called 'unprogressive conscience'. Even the most popular form of historical programme, the radio play, suffered from the political climate, and it was often impossible to combine writers' creative potential and a successful narrative structure with the expectations of politics. Thus, the crucial suggestive potential radio had in the field of history - enabling listeners to re-witness historical situations by offering them exciting dramatic adaptations – was often undermined.

Fourthly, contemporary history can, following Hans Rothfels's classic definition, be seen as the epoch of contemporaries (see Rothfels 1953). That means that it is much less negotiable than, say, medieval history. People nowadays did not live through that epoch, and so it is not part of their experience. Therefore this period of time is open for multiple interpretations and diverse appropriations. The case of contemporary history is a different one: it is, to use Jan Assmann's terminology, a part of 'communicative memory' (Assmann 1997: 50–51); it remains of a time which society permanently debates and discusses because nearly everyone has their own personal memories and subjective view of things. Correspondingly it becomes very difficult to establish canonical interpretations of that time. In the controlled public sphere of the GDR, however, official and canonical narratives of history ruled in order to certify the meaningfulness of the political order.

Notes

1. Some radio stations are trying to participate in the history boom, typically by broadcasting short features on anniversaries of important events of contemporary history or on the birthdays of important people of more recent history.
2. For a similar argument, see Holzweißig (2002).
3. 'Unsere Presse – die schärfste Waffe der Partei. Referate und Diskussionsreden auf der Pressekonferenz des Parteivorstandes der SED vom 9.–10. Februar 1950 in Berlin', cited in Herrmann (1963: 39).
4. Directive on restructuring the broadcasting programme, dated 15 February 1942, cited in Klingler (1983: 70).
5. Minutes of the Broadcasting Congress held on the fifth anniversary of the founding of German Democratic Broadcasting at the press office in Berlin, 11–12 May 1950; German Broadcasting Archive Potsdam (DRA), Historisches Archiv, Bestand Schriftgut Hörfunk 1945–1952, F 201–00–00/0001: 440.
6. For the so-called debate on formalism at the fifth plenary of the Central Committee, see Jäger (1994: 34–36).
7. For example Hermann Göring, in his speech on the tenth anniversary of the capture of the German military command on 30 January 1943, made the comparison between the closed-in soldiers and heroes of Germanic mythology.
8. On the prisoners of war – of whom only 6,000 out of a total 90,000 survived – see Lehmann (1992).
9. For example, every anniversary of the capitulation (2 February) Stalingrad was a topic on the radio until the mid 1960s; whether things changed after that cannot be said as archivists mostly stopped filing programme scripts in the German Broadcasting Archive after that time.
10. Programme script for 'Tageskommentar' (author: Dr Rudolf Pallas), Berliner Rundfunk, 1 February 1950; DRA Potsdam, Historisches Archiv, Bestand Hörfunk, B 204–02–01/0511. Pallas became a prisoner of war of the Soviets in 1943 and became a member of the communist organization Nationalkomitee Freies Deutschland (NKFD). In 1949 he was manager of youth radio with the Mitteldeutsche Rundfunk, Leipzig; later he held the same post Berliner Rundfunk.
11. Programme script, 'Tageskommentar' (see n.10).
12. Programme script, 'Tageskommentar'
13. Programme script 'Tageskommentar' (see n.10).
14. Programme script, 'Mit dem Stadtreporter unterwegs' (author: Susanne Drechsler), Deutschlandsender, 13 February 1954; DRA Potsdam, Historisches Archiv, Bestand Hörfunk, DS 54/231.
15. Programme script, 'Kommentar des Tages' (author: Manfred Klein), Berliner Rundfunk und Radio DDR, 13 February 1956; DRA Potsdam, Historisches Archiv, Bestand Hörfunk, BR 56/122.
16. Programme script, 'Mit dem Stadtreporter unterwegs' (see n.15).
17. Programme script, 'Kommentar des Deutschlandsenders' (author: Hermann Zilles), Deutschlandsender, 25 June 1950; DRA Potsdam, Historisches Archiv, Bestand Hörfunk, B 204-02-01/0005.
18. Programme script, 'Mit dem Stadtreporter unterwegs' (see n.15).
19. Programme script, 'Aus Deutschlands Hauptstadt' (author: Alois Landherr),

Deutschlandsender, 17 July 1954; DRA Potsdam, Historisches Archiv, Bestand Hörfunk, DS 54/1469.

20. Programme script, 'Tageskommentar' (author: Erich Selbmann), Deutschlandsender, 17 July 1954; DRA Potsdam, Historisches Archiv, Bestand Hörfunk DS 54/1472. For a similar argument, see Holzweißig (1996: S.75–106).

21. Programme script, 'Kommentar: Frisierte Demokratie' (author: Hans Hagen), Berliner Rundfunk, 10 November 1948; DRA Potsdam, Historisches Archiv, Bestand Hörfunk, B 204-02-02/0165.

22. Programme script 'Kommentar des Tages' (author: Karl-Eduard von Schnitzler), Berlin I, II und III, 8 October 1952; DRA Potsdam, Historisches Archiv, Bestand Hörfunk, B 095-00-01/0112.

7

Moving History: Film and the Nazi Past in Germany since the Late 1970s

Frank Bösch

In summer 2007, the German public discussed the film *Valkyrie*, about Claus Schenk Graf von Stauffenberg and the attempted assassination of Hitler in July 1944. Although filming had only just started, numerous newspapers carried out detailed debates about this piece of popular historiography. An investigative journalist of the *Süddeutsche Zeitung* even managed to get access to the screenplay and compared its designated historical facts to academic books and previous films.[1] Famous historians, journalists and relatives of the historical characters explained Stauffenberg's resistance to Hitler and discussed whether a Hollywood production and an actor like Tom Cruise would be adequate for such a theme.

Such debates even before the release of historical films are not uncommon. They prove that audiovisual historiography about the Third Reich is seen as a key element in assuring oneself about historical and national identity. Even in the case of a film which no one has seen yet, the public updates its relation to the historical past and considers the status of filmic representations of the past. Furthermore, nervous debates about new historical films prove the great relevance of collective memory, whose importance is ascribed to popular historiographies.

The relevance of audiovisual popular historiography has increased in the last decades. One might assume that this development was unforeseeable some decades ago, when television was first established. Especially during the late 1960s and early 1970s, historical fiction seemed to lose its significant public role. While movies about the Second World War had their great success in the 1950s (Wegmann 1980), political TV news magazines like *Panorama* were significant for the following decade (Hodenberg 2006: 302–22). They presented history as news – as in the case of the Eichmann and Auschwitz trials – but in public debate the social sciences became more influential than historical arguments. In general, analyses of contemporary questions seemed to replace popular historiography. However, this trend enjoyed no longevity. Only a decade later, historical movies, series and documentaries began to prosper. In particular, the worldwide success of the American series *Holocaust* in 1978/9 demonstrated the impact which audiovisual forms of popular history could have.

This comeback of audiovisual popular history since the late 1970s is of course not easy to explain. One might interpret it as a result of the growing chronological distance from the Nazi Past and the Second World War, with a declining interest in politics or with the rise of crises which have increased the need for historical identification in a secular age. The rise of conservative governments in the 1980s, which tried to find a new national identity, additionally led to public disputes about contemporary history. One might also argue that history offered a rich source for a mixture of entertainment and education in the media, and in particular in television.

All these reasons might explain why successful popular historiography has mainly focussed on the period of the Third Reich (1933–1945). Guido Knopp's documentaries for the channel Zweites Deutsches Fernsehen (ZDF), for example, quite often reached about six million viewers and were sold world wide. Their contents have been analysed and criticised by many historians in recent years (Bösch 1999; Keilbach 2002; Loewy 2002; Kansteiner 2003). At the same time, numerous German movies dealing with the Nazi past had great success – for example, *Aimée und Jaguar* (1999), *The Downfall* (2004), *Napola* (2004), *Speer und Er* (2005), *Sophie Scholl* (2005) and *Rosenstraße* (2003). The majority of these films were either ignored or fiercely criticized by German historians. They regarded them as simplified and too emotional, and censured them for mistakes in their historical content.

However, I would like to argue that historians should treat even fictional historical films and TV series in a more scientific way. After all, these movies offer certain modes of historical remembrance which themselves have their own history. The collective acceptance of these historical portraits is negotiated by the public when the audience decides if the product should be noticed or ignored (Kaes 1987: 207). Furthermore, these movies shape the individual remembrance of the past. Many veterans, for example, remember their individual war experience according to the images presented in war movies (Welzer 2002: 178–92). In addition, such movies can be regarded as historical actors, which enhance collective actions in the present (Lagny 1997: 468).

The series *Holocaust*, which was broadcast in 1978/9 in more than fifty countries, is generally seen as a turning point in the discussion of the German past. Especially in Germany the enormous impact of *Holocaust* showed how great the influence of a TV programme on the public and academic conceptions of history could be.[2] Therefore this chapter will take *Holocaust* as a starting point to discuss the changing role of historical representations of National Socialism in fictional films and TV productions. Firstly, I will ask how the depiction of history in movies and TV series has changed since *Holocaust* was originally broadcast. In this regard I will analyse the transformation of the media culture of remembrance. I will point out three phases since the late 1970s in which the German audiovisual culture of remembrance changed significantly. In order to do so, I will draw on my analyses of about forty German movies and TV series dealing with the Nazi past and public debates about them. Non-German productions will also be considered if they had a great impact on German audiences and debates.[3]

Secondly, I will ask how the relationship between academic history and popular historiography in film developed. In doing this, I do not want to examine the historical accuracy of each film or series. For obvious reasons, movies never follow historical sources as exactly as scientific books do. Therefore, it seems to be more productive to compare common elements of those movies to trends of historical research in each decade. Here I would like to argue that though movies do not necessarily draw in depth on the results of historical research they nevertheless refer to contemporary historians' work.

The Impact of *Holocaust* on Movies and Research in the 1980s

It is well known that the broadcasting of the American docudrama *Holocaust* in 1978/9 led to a great and emotional debate about the past in German society.[4] More than twenty million Germans watched the series, which described how a single Jewish family from Berlin suffered during the Third Reich and participated in all the tragic events of the destruction of the European Jews. But even more important than the great number of viewers was the fact that the majority of viewers discussed the series with friends and colleagues and that tens of thousands of German viewers wrote to the TV channel or tried to call its hotline. It is true that a number of people insulted the channel with anti-Semitic comments. However, more viewers expressed their sympathy and described their personal experience of the Holocaust, and many of these letters were quickly published (see Knilli and Zielinksi 1983; for Austria, see Diem 1979: 577). Opinion polls found that anti-Semitic attitudes and sympathies for the Third Reich changed after the broadcast of the docudrama (Bergmann 1997). Another effect of the reception of *Holocaust* was that the German parliament finally abolished the statutory period of limitation concerning murder, after years of postponing a decision about it. This law mainly concerned murder committed during the Third Reich.

The impact of *Holocaust* on historical research is also obvious. The programme actually helped establish this area of research in Germany and in the world and gave a field of historical research its name. Many in the media asked why German historians had failed to research these questions or to inform the public about this period of German history. The news magazine *Der Spiegel*, for instance, gave as its headline 'A Black Day for Historians' (*Ein schwarzer Tag für Historiker*). Famous contemporary historians like Martin Broszat tried to excuse themselves by arguing that the Holocaust had already been well researched in

many studies, but this was not really true. However, the historians admitted that
there was an obvious need for other, more popular and emotional forms of
imparting knowledge about the Holocaust and the Third Reich to a broader
public (Broszat 1979; Scheffler 1979).

How can one explain the enormous impact of this docudrama? On a closer
look, one can see that in the year before it was broadcast public discussion about
the Holocaust had already increased. On the fortieth anniversary of the
Reichspogromnacht in 1978 the number of commemoration ceremonies went up
significantly (Schmid 2001: 325–93). Public reports about it also increased in
1978 due to the debate about the Nazi past of Hans Filbinger, Minister-
President of Baden-Württemberg from 1966 to 1978, and the trial of the staff
of the Majdanek concentration camp (Horn 2002). The number of TV
programmes about the Holocaust also increased in Germany in 1978. Examples
of this are TV productions like *Dr. W.– Ein SS-Arzt in Auschwitz* (1978),
Manager des Terrors (1977) about Reinhard Heydrich, and *Aus einem deutschen
Leben* (1976) about the commandant of Ausschwitz, Rudolf Höß (Wolfgram
2002: 24). Statistical surveys also show an increase in the number of documentaries around 1978 (Kansteiner 2003: 264). Only this general trend can
explain why the media reported at such length about *Holocaust*, even before it
was broadcasted.

The impact of *Holocaust* was generally welcomed, and it served as a stimulus
for new discussions. On the other hand, the content of the series was less
accepted. It was widely criticized as too emotional and not authentic enough.
However, the content of *Holocaust* influenced the growing number of movies
and docudramas about National Socialism in the 1980s. A great deal of
Holocaust's emotional impact was due to scenes showing the deaths and woes of
women and children. This had an effect on the movies of the 1980s. Stories of
saved children were the topic of successive films – such as *Regentropfen* (1981),
Stern ohne Himmel (1981), *Ein Stück Himmel* (1982) and *Hitlerjunge Salomon*
(1990). Meanwhile, the life of Anne Frank was portrayed three times in the
1980s and, following *Holocaust*, several movies about Jewish families were
produced in Germany. In addition, there were also films which were based on
true stories, such as *Die Geschwister Oppermann* (1983) and *Die Bertinis* (1988).
Through these and other productions history became emotionally moving.[5]
Political and social history was connected to the history of everyday life, and
personalized narratives focused attention on the history of the victims,
something which had not been developed by historiography at that time.

However, the historical images which were shown in these and other films in
the 1980s were not unproblematic. The Jews presented in these movies were, like
those in *Holocaust*, mainly rich, assimilated members of the educated middle and
upper class. They were often married to Christian Germans and fought for their
honour. Other typical elements of Jewish history in Germany were rarely
presented: anti-Semitic conflicts before 1933, poverty and Jewish traditions were
left out of the German films, even more so than in the American TV series.

Unlike *Holocaust*, German movies rarely showed the Holocaust and the extreme violence which was enacted against the Jews. This was partly due to the fact that the German films mostly concentrated on the early years of Hitler's dictatorship and on the western parts of Germany. Auschwitz and the gas chambers, which were shown in *Holocaust*, remained on the margins of representation in the 1980s. This is similar to the open-air mass shootings that *Holocaust* vividly showed from the perspective of eyewitnesses and with the use of documentary material. Films like the French survival story *Schrei nach Leben* (1985), which showed murders in the ghettos and concentration camps, were condemned as kitschy adventure movies in the German papers.[6] Therefore, one could conclude that *Holocaust* led to a broad public examination of the anti-Jewish culture of the 1930s, but not of the genocide itself.

Unlike their depiction in *Holocaust*, 'Aryan' Germans were presented as faceless followers of the Nazi regime in the German movies of the 1980s but seldom as violent racists. Furthermore, the films quite often showed examples of people offering help to Jews in everyday life. In *Die Geschwister Oppermann*, for example, pupils support a Jewish classmate, while in *Regentropfen* the wife of a lieutenant demonstratively shops in a Jewish store during the April boycott of 1933. And in *Die Bertinis*, the eponymous family finds help in spite of the anti-Semitism around them. Often the authorities show tolerant clemency until they succumb to the pressure of certain National Socialists in a bid to save their own position.

Of course these films showed Nazis who oppressed Jews. However, they were presented as anonymous persons, who had absolute power thanks to being members of the Nazi Party or had personal motives for enriching themselves at the expense of, or avenging themselves against, Jews. Unlike those of the victims, the offenders' biographies were almost irrelevant. Likewise violence against Jews was frequently anonymous, represented by stones thrown at the windows of Jewish families by a nameless mob. The stones and broken windows can be seen as a symbol that more or less replaced the mass killings by a riotous but mostly harmless form of anti-Semitism.

In *Holocaust* there was one character that had an exceptional career as a National Socialist: a lawyer and member of the Schutzstaffel (SS) called Dorf. Unemployment, want of success and his wife's desire for prestige were the central motives for his opportunistic rise in the SS. That career chances were a crucial impetus for the functioning of the Third Reich was also shown in German films like *Lili Marleen* (1981) and in the adaptation of Klaus Mann's novel *Mephisto* (1981). At the same time these German movies offered several moments of relief by showing resistance. Lili Marleen, for instance, secretly helps her Jewish lover and smuggles photos of the extermination camps into Switzerland.

However, the depiction of the Nazis and their beneficiaries produced the most urgent questions in the public debate – which included historians – about the historical accuracy of these films. The series *Väter und Söhne: Eine deutsche*

Tragödie (1986), for instance, provoked a debate about whether IG Farben anticipated the availability of forced labourers when they established their factory at Auschwitz, and several academic studies on the company were published in the following years (e.g., Plumpe 1990). Likewise the television play *Die Wannseekonferenz* (1984) started a discussion about how far the extermination of the Jews was decided at the famous meeting after which the programme was named.[7] But while the victimhood of the Jews was accepted in films and public debate, the question of German guilt was still fought over.

At the same time, there was an increase in depictions of opposition to the Nazis from the bottom of German society. In the early 1980s two films were made about the Weiße Rose, the most important student opposition group, whose members paid for their opposition with their lives. The movie *Die weiße Rose* (1982) showed a broad opposition of students and a professor, but the majority of the supporters of the regime were left out. The TV production *Fünf letzte Tage* (1982), about the last days of Sophie Scholl in her detainment, showed several prison officers commiserating with her plight. Furthermore, Klaus Maria Brandauer filmed the solitary Munich assassination attempt of Hitler by Georg Elser (*Georg Elser: Einer aus Deutschland*, 1989).

As well as these heroic examples many German films showed everyday opposition. Various films and TV series were produced in the 1980s which focused on the period from a rural perspective – like the series *Heimat* (1984), *Wallers letzter Gang* (1989) and *Herbstmilch* (1988). In these, National Socialism was seen as something that came from outside, from the cities, and which repeatedly rubbed up against the stoicism of rural inhabitants. National Socialism was also portrayed as a phenomenon that somehow lost its importance in everyday life. This is especially true for the series *Heimat*, which understood itself as a direct German counterpart to *Holocaust* (Reitz 1984: 100).

Many of the attributes of German films and TV series from the 1980s mentioned above corresponded to the historical research from these years. After the emphasis on Hitler in the 1970s, films unmistakably joined historiography in a turn toward social history, micro-history and oral history. Media trends and those of historical research seem to have mutually influenced each other. The intensive research of small towns and rural areas during the era of National Socialism also seems to be connected to the movies of the 1980s (Noakes 1996). Just as films did, historical research took a closer look at the everyday resistance which was missed in a focus on great political events. Another parallel can be seen in the fact that the Holocaust was only made a major topic of German historical research from 1982 onwards (Herbert 1998). One can at least assume that increased media coverage of Jewish victims of the Nazis helped to bring about this change in historiography.

Media depiction of resistance to the Nazis also corresponds with the perspectives in academic historical research. Immediately after the movies concerning the Weiße Rose appeared, scientific studies and editions of their letters were published (Jens 1984; Blaha 2003). This is even more the case for the failed assassination of Hitler by Georg Elser, which had been rarely noticed by historical research. Even books about opposition towards Hitler in the 1990s neglected Elser's well planned attempt to kill the dictator (Fest 1994; Steinbach and Tuchel 1994).

The movies about resistance also show how films can become catalysts of the culture of remembrance. Brandauer's film about Georg Elser, for instance, ended by stating that he was executed at the concentration camp in Dachau, and that no monument of him existed. Consequently, memorials to Elser were erected in different places over the following years. Similarly, the movie *Die Weiße Rose* stated at the end that the judgements against the group had not been subsequently repealed; the German parliament reacted by annulling them in 1985.

The Critical Turn since the Late 1980s

Since the late 1980s one can see changes in the depiction of National Socialism in films that are part of a new phase in audiovisual history. These later films reconstruct the past much more often from the perspective of the present. Memory culture and the connection between the past and the present became central themes in many recent German films. As early as 1988, *Land der Väter, Land der Söhne* (1988) told the story of a young journalist investigating his father's National Socialist past. A year later, *Abraham's Gold* (1989) showed the conflict between two members of the '68 generation and their fathers and grandfathers about their past. In 1990 the director Michael Verhoeven was honoured for *Das schreckliche Mädchen* (1990), depicting the problems of a young student from Passau investigating the National Socialist past of her hometown. And in the same year the star-studded movie *Rosengarten* (1990) came out, which showed a Jew returning to contemporary Germany to find out more about the history of his sister, who had been killed in the SS child murders in Hamburg in 1945.

These movies ventured beyond the time limit of 1945 and positioned National Socialism in a rather tense relation to the present. The continuity of anti-Semitism and National Socialist values were important elements in these films. The crimes of National Socialism were connected to the process of coming to terms with the past and the acquittals of the jurisdiction of West Germany. This change in perspective again corresponded to shifts in relation to methodical questions as well as shifts in the thematic range of research on National Socialism. The culture of remembrance and the process of coming to terms with the past in general became more central to historical research in these years (Diner 1987; Assmann 1988). Historians also started to interpret National Socialism in relation to the experience of the Federal Republic. The *Historikerstreit* – the great debate among historians about the origins of the Holocaust – particularly underlined the fact that the interpretation of National Socialism was, even among historians, a contested matter and deeply connected to the present.

The historical narratives of films showed significant changes, too. The countryside and the fates of individuals were still central topics in many films. But while in the 1980s the countryside was something of a hideaway from National Socialism, the movies of the 1990s often showed rural victims, offenders and followers together in moments of decision. The anti-Semitic persecution of Jews played an important role here. In *Leni muss fort* (1994), for instance, a Bavarian village decides to let a Jewish foundling, who had been raised by a farmer's family, be taken off. The TV drama *Drei Tage im April* (1995) is set in a small Swabian village in April 1945, shortly before the end of the war. There, three cattle cars of dying Jewish concentration camp prisoners are ignored and denied any help. Instead, the people of the village move the wagon into the next valley to get rid of the problem.

This new focus on the violence in everyday life also matched a new trend of historical research on National Socialism. The earlier assumption of a top-down dissemination of orders was dropped and sociological models of explanation, like group-pressure and regional dynamics, moved to the centre of interest (Browning 1992). It is also noticeable that since the late 1980s the fate of other groups of victims – such as Polish forced labourers and Russian prisoners of war – has been acknowledged, such as in *Der Polenweiher* (1986) and *Das Heimweh des Walerjan Wrobel* (1991). This focus on Eastern European victims of National Socialism can also be found in historical studies. Since the end of the Cold War the crimes committed on Eastern European and Soviet prisoners of war and forced labourers have received more attention in historical research.

In the late 1980s the relationship between cinematic and historical reality changed too. Since 1945 almost all films and series about National Socialism have been related to real historical events. However, they have seldom been claimed to be a direct historical reconstruction. In *Holocaust* this rather tense connection between history and fiction was addressed in the opening credits: 'It is only a story. But it really happened'. The characters were fictional, but they acted in known events. The use of documentary material also proved the historical reality of the Holocaust. However, since the early 1990s there has been a trend toward using historically authentic stories rather than famous historical events with fictional characters. The emotional impact of these movies is due to the fact that they show true stories and reconstruct known fates. In doing so, these films adopt the standards of historians, analysing sources and talking to eyewitnesses.

There are several reasons for the increasing use of historically authentic stories. The films using these are part of a new culture of remembrance. The rise of extreme right-wing parties in Germany has also supported the need for true stories, which can educate the younger generations. Furthermore, TV documentaries about National Socialism since the 1990s, which were shown in increasing numbers, established new expectations to which docudramas and films responded. In general the trend towards reality TV that became evident in the 1990s influenced the watching habits and expectations of film and TV viewers.

This trend toward authenticity was especially evident in *Schindler's List* (1993), which was by far the most influential movie about National Socialism in the 1990s. The famous black and white aesthetics of the movie, the use of the moving camera and the filming of photographic icons enhanced the authentic impression of the movie (Korte 1999; Schulz 2002). The accuracy of its content also led to its positive critical reception among historians.[8] The impression was created that this fictional movie depicted a historical reality that had not yet been captured in the numerous TV documentaries about National Socialism.

The cinematic change of perspective that is marked by *Schindler's List* is again reflected in historical research in the mid 1990s. At this time historians started to look at the Holocaust in terms of regional elites and events in the occupied territories of Poland and Eastern Europe, the latter becoming easier after files from Eastern European archives became available (Aly 1995; Pohl 1996). Not only were the connections between atrocities, enrichment and corruption within these territories analysed by historians but also the smooth transition between profiteers and heroes (Sandkühler 1996).

The public debate about *Schindler's List* made it clear that the depicted crimes were accepted as part of Germany's own past. Conversely, the question of whether a German could be depicted as a rescuer was also discussed.[9] The question concerning guilt had thus shifted. A too-positive depiction of a German during the time of National Socialism now appeared to be problematic. Not only the movie, but also the reception of it in the media created a new way of dealing with the past.

Schindler's List also showed how the debate about the representation of the Holocaust changed. Claude Lanzmann, the director of *Shoa* (1985) demanded once again a ban on any film showing the Holocaust.[10] This issue stayed at the centre of almost all articles on the feature pages, but Lanzmann's position became more and more opposed. The majority stressed that *Schindler's List* had set a new limit to representation by making the gassing of the Jews a topic without showing it in the movie. Thus *Schindler's List* marked an end to the long discussion of whether or not to show Nazi murders in movies. The directness of *Holocaust* was taken for granted.

The majority of films concerning the Nazi past in the last decade have followed the realistic approach established in the late 1980s and have attempted to tell 'true stories'. But the debate concerning norms of representation of Nazi crimes that surrounded *Schindler's List* was followed by other films that went a step further and presented humorous stories in the context of these otherwise tragic events. Although comedies about the Nazis had a long tradition, Roberto Benigni's film *La vita è bella* (1997) set new standards.[11] This comedy not only focused on deportation, forced labour and the brutal eviction of a concentration camp, it also contained a clever twist by refusing to reconstruct the Holocaust with an aura of authenticity in the manner of, for example, *Schindler's List*. The story of a father who refuses to tell his son the official version of the Nazis can also be seen as a protest against the official pictures and stories produced by the National Socialists. The refusal of reality becomes a way to survive.

Several other comedies followed in the next few years, like *Der Zug des Lebens* (2000), *Chicken Run* (2000), *Goebbels und Geduldig* (2002) and *Mein Führer* (2006). They were proof of a new easiness in dealing with the Nazi time, which became possible in connection with the serious examinations done in the years before. A humorous way of dealing with dictatorship also became the dominant narrative frame of films about the former German Democratic Republic (GDR, or East Germany), such as *Sonnenallee* (1998), *Helden wie wir* (1999), *Good Bye Lenin* (2003) and *NVA* (2005). These films supported the public view that the GDR was simply a grotesque regime in which protest within everyday life dominated. *Das Leben der Anderen* (2006) – the celebrated movie about the Stasi that was awarded an Oscar – is rather an exception here. However, it also takes up the issue of resistance, which is also typical of most of the films about National Socialism.

Berlin under Fire: Recent Trends

Since the late 1990s, German movies about the Nazi past have become even more numerous and successful. Like the various TV series in the 1980s that were produced as German responses to the success of *Holocaust*, the success of *Schindler's List* and several TV documentaries had a similar effect on the German movie industry. The historical narratives of these more recent films also changed. First of all, if we look at their content we can see that the focus of them shifted from the provincial areas to the big cities. Berlin has become the focus of many films since then, such as *Comedian Harmonists* (1997), *Aimée und Jaguar* (1999), *Rosenstraße* (2003), *The Downfall* (2004) and *Speer und Er* (2005). One could explain this in terms of the Berlin boom that has occurred since the seat of government moved there after German reunification. Other successful films about different periods in German history also take place in Berlin and have shown problems of urban life.[12] In general, the culture of remembrance has started to concentrate on the capital of the 'Berlin Republic', and mixed new symbols of remembrance with new national myths (Kirsch 2003).

The cinematic focus on the capital has led to a different interpretation of the past. National Socialism and the war appear as destroyers of a nostalgically transfigured urban culture (Koepnick 2002: 79). The tension between decadent urban life and danger of death has become a central topic. Although Jewish victims are often central figures in these movies, the depiction of brute violence and concentration camps has somehow disappeared. Instead, the urban inhabitants are shown as victims of bombing raids and dictatorial force. This tendency is also evident in the public debate about the publication of Jörg Friedrich's *Der Brand* (Brand 2002). The Germans have become victims again.

After the dominance of the history of everyday life in the 1980s, these recent movies have concentrated more often on the elite and the persecution of the Jews. If one takes a look at groundbreaking publications on National Socialism over the last few years similar trends are visible. On the one hand, elites have received more attention since the second half of the 1990s (Herbert 1996; Kershaw 1998–2000; Wildt 2002). On the other hand, there have also been groundbreaking publications about the destructive violence within and on the edge of the Third Reich in the last few years. However, it is obvious that most of the recent important studies of the Holocaust were not written by Germans but by American historians (Friedlaender 2006). Similarly, the majority of recent movies that centred on the topic of the Holocaust were once again non-German or international productions, such as *The Pianist* (2002), about arbitrary force in the Warsaw ghetto; *The Grey Zone* (2001), about Jews forced to work in the crematoria of Auschwitz; and *Fateless* (2005), about everyday life in Auschwitz-Birkenau. An exception here is the German production *Der neunte Tag* (2004), which presented scenes from the Dachau concentration camp. However, this movie focuses on the German resistance and German victimhood once again.

The German movies of the last few years have a number of different themes. The question of individual moral responsibility during the era of National Socialism is one of these. Characters with a lot of potential for identification had to confront temptation and moral dilemmas during the dictatorship. This could be the young boxer at an elite school in *Napola* (2004), the aristocratic wife confronting the Gestapo in *Rosenstraße* (2003), a priest or a student during an interrogation in *Der neunte Tag* (2004) and Sophie Scholl: *Die letzten Tage* (2005), a Nazi housewife in love with a lesbian Jew in *Aimée und Jaguar* (1999), or the secretary in Hitler's bunker in *The Downfall* (2004). Here, the National Socialists are characters without a biography who offer temptations to leading characters. These characters show great resistance in most of the films. The boxer who sets his career aside, the aristocratic wife who demonstrates against the arrest of her husband, the general who contradicts Hitler, and the priest who refuses to cooperate and is sent to a concentration camp – all of these cases create an image of national socialist society that makes exceptional cases a rule. Of course, movies do not have to depict a statistically correct representation of history. But together they leave the impression that current German films offer a generous moral rehabilitation.

Consequently, not only have the settings of movies narrowed but also the time period of many plots. The movies and TV series of the 1980s had shown long-term developments and biographies. More recent films, however, do not discuss why many Germans became National Socialists, and neither do they question how and why they turned into democrats after 1945.

The connection claimed between these later films and historical truth is a close one. The majority of these movies understand themselves as part of a reconstruction of history on the basis of sources. In many cases they make their sources public and claim to be historically accurate, just as historians do. The legitimacy of the representations in *Sophie Scholl*, for example, lies in the use of new files about the examination and trial, the contents of which were accurately taken into the screenplay.[13] Likewise, the producers of *The Downfall* stressed that their film was strictly based on documents and followed the known facts (Fest and Eichinger 2004). Meanwhile, *Speer und Er* was advertised as drawing on new historical results; *The Grey Zone* (2001), *The Pianist* (2002) and *Edelweiß-piraten* (2004) utilized reports which were written by the victims right after the war; and *Rosenstraße* and *Aimée und Jaguar* were based on true stories and accounts from witnesses (Wende 2002). In this way, the movies changed their relation to the reality beyond the film. In Niklas Luhmann's terms, the movies claimed to work with the functional criteria of the scientific world (false/true), although they still operated with the major function of the media system (entertaining/boring). Furthermore, the film-makers employed an understanding of historiography which has become a bit old-fashioned among historians: an accurate reproduction of sources should not be taken for a historical interpretation.

These films also mixed fictional and historical material more than before. A number of them show scenes that look like bits of National Socialist newsreels and which were familiar to the audience from documentaries. Scenes from Hitler's last public appearance on 20 April 1945, when he decorated child soldiers (*The Downfall*), Eva Braun's private films on the Obersalzberg (*Speer und Er*) or the famous pictures of the Warsaw ghetto (*The Pianist*) were used as the basis of certain scenes to enhance a film's authenticity. Conversely, the press treated these staged sequences like historical material, and it was sometimes unclear if Hitler himself or the actor Bruno Ganz was shown in the newspaper photographs (Wildt 2002).

Many historians criticized those movies with harsh words in the press. However, the effect of using staged scenes from the past was that historians discussed these films much more often as historical reconstructions than they had done in the 1980s. Movies like *Rosenstraße*, dealing with the protests of German women in 1943, led to a scientific debate about the events in the Rosenstraße, marriages between Jewish and non-Jewish people in Nazi Germany and the possibilities of resistance (Meyer 2004).[14] Many of those movies focused attention on the results of historical research. Historians who were experts on the issues covered in them profited from those movies because their books were recommended together with their expertise. The movies also drew attention to the work of historians and to questions concerning popular history in cinema and TV. The majority of viewers in cinemas were not affected as much by these movies as they had been by *Holocaust* in 1979. But at least these movies increased the interest in contemporary history.

Many of these recent films claim to break taboos about the past, addressing issues which have so far been overlooked by popular and academic history. *The Downfall* and *Speer und Er* in particular were advertised with articles and interviews which claimed that Hitler was for the first time presented as a human being and not as a caricature or within a pedagogic setting. The right-wing press in particular interpreted such movies as a 'sign of emancipation' and the beginning of a more relaxed way of dealing with the past in Germany.[15] Other movies, which showed Hitler in an even more private context, appeared at the same time. British and German TV showed the melodramatic movie *Uncle Adolf* (2004), which presented Hitler as a charming man, and *Hitler: The Rise of Evil* (2003), which also focused on private elements of his biography like his relation to his niece.

In fact, such movies were not that new. The plot and even several scenes of *The Downfall* (2004) had already been presented in a similar way in *Der letzte Akt* (1955), which also described the last days of Hitler and was also based on witnesses' reports, such as those of Hitler's secretary, Traudl Junge. The popular presentation of Hitler in *The Downfall* was also reminiscent of the way in which his private life and the Nazi elite had been portrayed in many TV documentaries since the 1990s. *The Downfall* showed spectacular pictures of Hitler, ones which were not transmitted by Eva Braun's camera: Hitler showing his emotions, crying, laughing and even marrying. Indeed, the camera moved closer to Hitler's face than ever before. Obviously, the main focus here lies rather on emotionalizing and personalizing aspects than on explanations and background information.

From this perspective, these movies represented a step back from the research which had been done over the past few decades. Although the movies relied much more on historical facts than ever before, they turned away from historical interpretations of the Nazi past. The TV series *Holocaust* was fictional and contained several historical mistakes or implausible elements. However, it had tried to give an interpretation of the Third Reich. In this regard it was more closely connected to academic history than many of the films made nowadays.

Conclusions

This chapter has focused on two major issues of the treatment of history in feature films and TV productions since the late 1970s. Firstly, it looked at how audiovisual representations of the National Socialist period have changed since the late 1970s. The analysis has revealed some significant developments. First of all it is clear that the success of the American TV series *Holocaust* had a major influence on German movies and TV series in the 1980s. Although the content of the series was criticized in many aspects, numerous German productions have used similar narratives. This example shows how the worldwide media industry invented transnational popular historiographies. However, one should not speak of a simple transfer of American interpretations. Furthermore, German productions changed the narrative of harried families, put them in different settings and constructed different popular historiographies. They left out stories about those responsible for the crimes and scenes in the extermination camps of Eastern Europe. Instead, the resistance of famous persons or ordinary people in rural areas was presented.

These narratives changed at the end of the 1980s. Since then, many feature films have claimed authenticity and connected their stories to the present. The innocence of rural life was transformed into a sphere where collective guilt was crucial. Compared to earlier decades, movies made since the late 1980s have started to discuss the Nazi past critically. Since the late 1990s, another turning point has become obvious. Movies have tended to concentrate on major cities in which German protagonists have had to face temptations and moral dilemmas. As in the movies of the early Cold War, the protagonists manage to resist these offers. Although these later films are historically more accurate than before, they also avoid broader historical interpretations. To sum up, the development from the late 1970s to the present constitutes a change from long-term historical developments to condensed situations of decision; from the fates of Jewish families to the tribulations of German urban citizens; and from fictional stories with moral issues to the depiction of a historical truth.

The second issue this chapter has discussed is the development of the relationship between academic history and popular historiography in feature films. The analysis shows that historical research and film are more closely connected to each other than seems to be the case at first sight. While historians may criticize the historical content of films, historians and films often share the same perspective on National Socialism. Just as films and TV series did in the 1980s, scholars exploring National Socialism at the time preferred social and micro-historical approaches and analysed the regions. A change of focus to resistance in everyday life came about in the 1990s, when the mass murder of different groups of victims moved to the centre. In recent years, the renaissance of biographical studies and the academic interest in urban life can be seen to have parallels in the content of recent movies.

As the perspectives of film and textual historiography greatly overlap, one can assume a mutual influence. The chicken-and-egg question can hardly be answered. However, it is clear that historical research is not necessarily providing the impulse for popular history. In this respect, one should reconsider the term 'popularization' because it is always based on the assumption that scientific truths are first produced by researchers and then simplified by the media. Instead, the approaches of feature films and historiography often go hand in hand.

This chapter has also analysed the content of films, public debates about them and their relationship with the contemporary historiography. What we do not know precisely is how cinema audiences and television viewers reacted to these films and how they shaped their ideas about the past. Therefore one should be careful when speaking of certain forms of collective memory just because certain types of films have had great success. The reception of those films depends not only on the content of the film and the public debate about it, but also on the individual cultural background of viewers. Although popular historiographies are less sophisticated than academic books, films might offer very different ideas of the past. While academic history tries to find clear but differentiated answers, films are always more ambiguous. Consequently, films like *Valkyrie* might be seen as an act of patriotic resistance, as a disloyal breach of military obedience or as a general justification of assassinations. Finally, neither historians nor journalists decide how such films are understood; rather, interpretation is in the hands of the audience.

Notes

1. *Süddeutsche Zeitung*, 9 August 2007.
2. See the articles on the impact of *Holocaust* in the journal *Historical Social Research/Historische Sozialforschung* 30(2005): 4–154.
3. For a more detailed version of the arguments in this chapter and a broader view of the research project of which it is a part, see Bösch (2007).
4. See Märthesheimer and Frenzel (1979).
5. For movies up to the 1980s, see esp. Insdorf (1989).
6. E.g., *Süddeutsche Zeitung*, 21 November 1986; *Frankfurter Allgemeine Zeitung*, 21 November 1986.
7. See *Der Spiegel*, 17 December 1984; *Süddeutsche Zeitung*, 19 December 1984; *Frankfurter Allgemeine Zeitung*, 21 December 1984.
8. See Loewy (1995), Wildt (1995) and Eley and Grossmann (1997).
9. See Weiss (1995).
10. *Frankfurter Allgemeine Zeitung*, 5 March 1994.
11. Benigni's film may be better known to readers by its English title: *Life is Beautiful*. On Benigni's film, see Bleicher (2002) and Fröhlich and Loewy (2003).
12. It is remarkable that many of these contemporary films deal with the problems of the younger generations living in Berlin. Compare, e.g., *Sonnenallee* (1998), *Lola rennt* (1998), *Good Bye Lenin* (2003), *Herr Lehmann* (2003), *Die fetten Jahre sind vorbei* (2004) and *Was nützt die Liebe in Gedanken* (2004).
13. *Die Welt*, 24 February 2005.
14. Essays by historians about the film *Rosenstraße* can be found on a 2004 discussion forum at: http://www.h-net.org/~german/discuss/Rosenstrasse/Rosenstrasse_index.htm. Retrieved 20 July 2008.
15. *Die Welt* 12 August 2004; see also Ian Kershaw in *Frankfurter Allgemeine Zeitung*, 17 September 2004.

PART III

Memory Culture and Popular Historiographies: Case Studies

8

Memory History and the Standardization of History

Dieter Langewiesche

'Periods of Remembrance'

'Memory history' (*Erinnerungsgeschichte*) is found at the start of every process of historical transmission.[1] As a theoretically grounded approach in the methodological arsenal of historical studies, however, it is a relatively new branch of historical inquiry, albeit one that is rapidly growing. The catastrophic experiences of the first half of the twentieth century contributed considerably to this. They created, according to Dan Diner in his European-oriented, universal-historical attempt to understand this period, a separate 'time of remembrance', whose 'negative telos' overlaid other experiences and taught us to view history differently (Diner 2000: 17). The remembrance of this period, together with an institutionalization of remembrance and the universalization of Holocaust memory, was central in defining memory cultures, at least in some parts of the world (Cornelißen et al. 2003).

It was for this reason that Pierre Nora, the French doyen of memory studies whose celebrated multi-volume work *Les Lieux de Mémoire* (Nora 1984–1992) became the model for numerous similar books on the sites of memory of other states and nations, referred to our time as the 'epoch of remembrance'. France was, according to Nora:

> arguably the first country to enter this period of passionate, conflict-laden, almost compulsive remembrance. Then, after the fall of the Berlin wall and the disappearance of the Soviet Union, the 'rediscovered remembrance' of Eastern Europe resurfaced. And finally, with the fall of the Latin American dictatorships, and with the end of Apartheid in South Africa and the Truth and Reconciliation Commission, the symbols of a real globalization of remembrance were put into place, and numerous varying but comparable forms of coming to terms with the past emerged. (Nora 2002)

The worldwide commemoration of the Holocaust also belongs to this globalization of memory, in which a hitherto unseen phenomenon is becoming apparent. We are witnessing a new development in which, for the first time, the responsibility for history is being internationalized. This subject has not yet been researched, so I will begin with some general observations.

On the Internationalization of the Responsibility for History

A process is emerging in memory cultures which can also be seen in the political sphere: the internationalization of responsibility. In powerful global institutions – such as the UN, World Bank, International Monetary Fund and World Trade Organization – decisions are being made which are binding for member states. In Europe, this form of internationalization has reached a level that is being referred to as permeable statehood (*offene Staatlichkeit*) or the integrated state. In many spheres of activity, member states relinquish their sovereignty to the institutions of the European Union which has at its disposal a means of implementing laws that take precedence over national law (Häberle 1997; Scharpf 1999; Wahl 2003; Puntscher Riekmann 2004).

Admittedly, responsibility for history is not included in the treaties that codify the internationalization and 'Europeanization of the state and the legal system' (Wahl 2003: 22), but the internationality of memory cultures also engenders a sphere of responsibility which is no longer limited to the nation-state. Let me specify some examples of this unprecedented development.

If a place of remembrance for the history of forced migration in the twentieth century were to be set up in Germany, it would soon become a theme common to all Europe and result in discussions and even state intervention outside Germany, even if this was not the original intention of the German organizers. Turkey, equally, cannot prevent its policy toward the history of the mass deportation of Armenians during the First World War from being the subject of public debate abroad and being condemned by foreign state institutions.

The French National Assembly has voted through a draft bill, which – should it pass through all the stages of the legislative process – would make the denial of the genocide of Armenians in the Ottoman Empire a punishable offence. Things have not reached this stage yet in Germany but parliamentary factions have demanded in a number of motions that Turkey allow public discussion and unhindered academic research into the 'crime against the Armenian people', as it is referred to in one parliamentary motion. The motion continues: 'the states of the European Union distinguish themselves in that they take responsibility for their colonial past and the dark side of their national history'. Unanimously passed by the Bundestag, the text of the motion speaks of 'a European culture of memory', which 'includes the public discussion of the dark side of particular national histories'.[2]

A willingness to concede that what was done to the Armenians in the Ottoman Empire during the First World War was genocide, and to encourage public debate on the subject, has thus become a criterion for Turkish membership of the EU. Here, the EU states grant themselves joint responsibility for the history of their members: the forum of the EU becomes a historical space for which Europeans lay claim to a collective responsibility. This transnational policy towards history – the idea that the politics of memory is a European collective task, with sanctions against people and states who contravene it – is a new phenomenon, a historical-political innovation of our time, the 'epoch of remembrance'.

Today, as such examples attest, state policy towards history has to be justified on the international stage, and not just within the European Union. History has become a sphere of responsibility which internationalizes historical meaning and provides the power to impose political sanctions. States apologize publicly for the facts of their past (Lübbe 2001) and those in power can be held to account for their country's policies before the International Court of Justice in The Hague. Thus, the responsibility for history becomes actionable, either before a court or before a public which grants the victims of a past occurrence the moral right to be vindicated before history and, potentially, to be financially compensated in the present.

The recognition of historical guilt through state apology and compensation: this form of the democratization of historical responsibility increases the value of memory history since it assigns everyone the right and the ability to take part in deciding how a society should deal with its own history and the history of others. Memory history is not produced as professional history, the writing of history by experts: anyone who has memories of the past or historical opinions of any kind can participate in it. This can be conceived of as democratization, but it is also a form of the deprofessionalization of history: memory history comes into existence as lay history, as historical interpretation by lay persons. This can lead to problems, which will be addressed later.

The State Regulation of History

The internationalization of historical responsibility is clearly accompanied by the attempt of many states to bring historical remembrance under state regulation. Recently, on 12 December 2005, numerous historians in France protested publicly such a move when a new law made it a legal requirement that the school curriculum treat, in the words of the law, 'the positive role of the French presence overseas, especially in North Africa' (Franzke 2007). In opposition to the state's law about what and how history was to be taught, they advanced a burning declaration in favour of 'liberty for history'.[3] The outcome was successful: the aforementioned law was overturned by prime-ministerial decree after a decision by the constitutional court. These historians were not, however, merely protesting against the official attempt to regulate the remembrance of French colonial history. They demanded, moreover, that all legal prescriptions of this kind be overturned because they considered them unbefitting of a democratic country. A democracy, namely, is to be identified by the fact that, among other things, it can tolerate different historical interpretations and create the latitude for competition between conflicting memories of the past.

This is easily said, and in theory it sounds utterly convincing, but it can lead to the need to tolerate, in the name of democracy, versions of the past which are for good reason considered politically dangerous. The French historians called for this tolerance. It was not only the image of French colonial history taught in schools that was to be deregulated. They were also against three other laws which they saw as legal attempts to regulate history. This included two laws of 2001 – one in which France recognized the European slave trade as a crime against humanity, and another which referred to events in Turkey in 1915 as 'the Armenian genocide' – though contravention of these laws was not a punishable offence at that time. Thirdly, in the name of democracy the French historians turned against the law of 1990 that made the denial of the Jewish genocide during the Second World War punishable by imprisonment or a fine.

This has nothing to do with Holocaust denial. For these historians it was more a matter of defending – in the land, and in the spirit, of Voltaire – the right to express one's opinion against all state intervention. Here, historical beliefs are assigned without ifs and buts to the human right to freedom of opinion, including historical opinions which are demonstrably false and which could be politically dangerous. It is for this reason that the denial of the Holocaust is not a punishable offence under Anglo-American legal systems. It is energetically fought against in the public sphere but not punished by the state. In the name of protecting democracy all historical opinions are considered valid, even objectively false ones which have been rejected by experts. As a result, any attempt at state regulation of history is rejected, even if it is well-meaning and has historical fact on its side. Memory history needs this freedom to a particularly large degree because every memory stems from a subjective perspective and proposes history from this narrow viewpoint. Memory history is also, therefore, constantly subject to competition with other memory histories, at least in democratic societies. Let me cite some examples.

In France, for a long time it was impossible to reach any consensus regarding the Algerian war of independence since the experiences of this war, and the ways society dealt with it afterwards, differed greatly (Kohser-Spohn and Renken 2006). As the actors on the stage of memory changed, the memory of the Algerian war became more open and critical. This was even seen in the use of language: a 1999 French law stipulated that the Algerian war be referred to as such in official texts, and no longer as the 'events in North Africa' or by other euphemistic formulations. The official effort to commemorate this war reached a peak in 2002 when President Jacques Chirac inaugurated a memorial in the centre of Paris in honour of the soldiers who fell in Algeria, Morocco and Tunisia, and spoke of the 'duty to remember' (*devoir de mémoire*).

Commemorative remembrance sought out additional, officially unforeseen paths, as befits a democratic society (Hüser 2006; Gilzmer 2007). Minorities developed their own memories and brought them into the public eye, with different symbols of remembrance and sites of memory. Even the French rap scene took on the theme of the Algerian war, broadening the remembrance of it to other colonial experiences and seeking to connect it with xenophobic phenomena in the present. Thus, memory history can develop imaginative forms and follow unforeseen paths, quite independently of and untouched by academic history writing. And because it is lay history, memory history is inherently popular, as some German examples also demonstrate.

The Politics of History and the Diplomacy of Memory

Memory history is booming. In Germany, research groups have been set up dedicated to exploring the significance of memory within the subject we know as history.[4] It is even dealt with in exhibitions, which sometimes meet with great approval, lead to considerable differences of opinion and mobilize a wide public among whom debates are carried out. Let us consider, for instance, the exhibition of the Hamburg Institute for Social Research (Hamburger Institut für Sozialforschung) on the Second World War as a war of extermination. Many people saw this touring exhibition; some agreed with it while others accused it of being scandalous, before it was withdrawn and replaced by a less provocative version (Hamburger Institut für Sozialforschung 1996, 1998a, 1998b, 1999, 2002).

It is clear that, even today, highly differing memories of the war are present within German society, hence the bitter public debate aroused by this exhibition which, in its very title, aligned itself unmistakeably with one of these competing historical memories: 'The Crimes of the Wehrmacht'. This memory is not shared by everyone.[5] Here, a conflict can be observed between two mutually exclusive memories. Since the historical events being remembered concern present individuals and institutions, whether as historical actors themselves or as their descendents, this period of history still has wide contemporary relevance in society. Conflicting memories of this period lead to mutual accusations of historical misrepresentation. The history of forced expulsion, a violence-laden issue of twentieth-century history, offers a further example of the conflict of historical memory and of the political explosiveness of a situation in which the state attempts to establish which memories are acceptable and which ones are not. The Turkish state, for instance, forbids the description of the mass deaths of deported Armenians in the First World War as genocide while the Armenian state does the opposite. The question as to which of these assessments is factually more valid is the subject of lively debate.[6] States which intervene in the politics of history, by defining which particular memories are acceptable and by threatening those that do not accept these memories with punishment, are attempting to prevent historical debate because they fear that it could damage their historically grounded self-image and their moral standing in the present. The internationalization of the responsibility for history, however, limits the effects of these national attempts to regulate historical interpretation.

As the national boundaries of memories of the past are dissolved, we can understand the fears that have been expressed in Poland and the Czech Republic regarding the founding of the Berlin 'Centre against expulsion' ('Zentrum gegen Vertreibung'). The expulsion exhibition in the 'House of the history of the German Federal Republic' ('Haus der Geschichte der Bundesrepublik Deutschland') from December 2005 to April 2006, on the other hand, managed to present this contested topic in such a way that a conflict of memory was avoided (Petersen 2005; Stiftung Haus der Geschichte der BRD 2005). Why this exhibition had no knock-on effect in society is difficult to judge. Presumably, conflict was avoided in this case because different memories were presented alongside each other without establishing firm causal relationships between them – a presentation of memories that considered the events from different viewpoints without making the expulsions subject to value judgements regarding respon-sibility and guilt. Thus, every memory retains its own authority and everyone finds their own suffering documented, even if the events being remembered separately and displayed along side each other were, at the time they happened, causally linked to each other with a clear sense of before and after, of cause and effect.

Just how far perceptions and assessments of this exhibition can differ is shown by the press reaction.[7] Newspaper editorials sought to use the titles of articles to set out the core message to be drawn from the exhibition. Thus, when the exhibition opened in December 2005, the text of an article which appeared in largely identical form in numerous newspapers (with some variations in length) was able to convey widely different messages when one newspaper entitled the article 'The Germans Were Victims', while another used the heading 'Wooden Carts and Barracks in the Museum: An Exhibition Informs Us about the Expulsion'.[8] Other newspapers, which purchased this article attached titles to it which prepared the reader for the emotiveness of the memories treated by the exhibition.[9] Many newspapers focused their reports on the Germans expelled and the difficulties of their integration, while others saw in the exhibition 'a visible symbol against all forced expulsions'.[10] Furthermore, it was clearly a relief that this theme, a potentially explosive one regarding the relationship between Germany and its eastern neighbours, could be represented in a way that was 'not nationally egotistical' by demonstrating a 'curiosity for the small things, tactfulness and a willingness to treat experiences of suffering on equal terms'.[11] Even Poland's ambassador, who was initially 'on the lookout for the offensive' in the exhibition, left it 'in a reconciliatory mood'.[12]

That the exhibition managed to be a 'benchmark of diplomacy' without being sparing of the important facts was attributed to the fact that it centred on the 'words of the eyewitnesses'[13] without, at the same time, rolling out a 'German *Sonderweg* [literally: 'special path'] of memory'.[14] Yet the causal connections between the European expulsions during and after the Second World War did not have to be written in to the memories of eyewitnesses and their descendents. The Bonn exhibition entrusted the visitor with the task of 'making a picture for oneself by drawing together the different threads of the narrative'.[15] Confronting the visitor in an overt way with these contradictory threads of memories would surely have provoked conflict over the remembered past. Presenting them side by side, with equal validity, helped avoid conflict between the different communities of memory but it also prevented possible insights into the events which individual memory had not retained or had even, moreover, shut out. This particular form of memory history could have an exclusionary effect, shutting out other memories and communities of memory. Memory, although based on communication – for it only fulfils its purpose if it is passed on – would then only be communicative within a single community of remembrance; in relation to the outside world it would act as a means of both exclusion and self-defence. One's own view of history would be defended and contrasted with competing versions of history, the latter even branded as untrue. In extreme cases, insofar as the state interferes in the remembrance of history, expressing these opposing views could be a punishable offence.

What is Memory History?

In a stimulating essay elucidating the theoretical concept of 'memory cultures' (*Erinnerungskulturen*), the focus of a special research group at the University of Giessen, Günter Lottes (2005) develops a nuanced set of concepts relating to memory history. He speaks of 'memory interests' (*Erinnerungsinteressen*) and 'memory work' (*Erinnerungsarbeit*), of the 'subject of memory' (*Erinnerungs-subjekt*) and the 'artefacts of memory' (*Erinnerungsgegenstand*), of 'communities of memory' (*Erinnerungsgemeinschaften*) and 'masters of memory' (*Erinnerungsherren*), of the 'conflict of memories' (*Erinnerungskonkurrenz*) and of the 'hegemony of memories' (*Erinnerungshegemonien*) within 'realms of memory' (*Erinnerungsräume*), of the 'adaptation of memory' (*Erinnerungsanpassung*) and the 'fate of memory' (*Erinnerungsschicksal*), and of 'individual memories' (*Individualerinnerungen*), 'main memories' (*Leiterinnerung*) and 'core memories' (*Erinnerungskernen*). This conceptual arsenal implies that historical memories do not come into existence on their own, that they are produced and disputed, and that they can succeed but also fail. Furthermore, it is not experts who decide whether historical memories will emerge, gain acceptance or fail. Memory history is not the creation of historians; it has many stewards, emerges as lay history in many cases, and endures so long as it remains alive among the population.

Historians are a contributory factor on both sides: on the side of those who produce memory and on the side of those who aim to prove that certain memories are incorrect and thus aim to reduce their social effect. But historians are no more than a contributory factor. It is society that decides whether it will accept expert interpretations – which are far from unanimous after all – or follow other, possibly contradictory, historical ideas. This is true of every form of historical knowledge but especially true of memory history since it emerges from lived experience and only gains social significance when individual memories are shared by many people and thus become the collective memory of a group.

Memory history emerges as a social construct developed by many people including historians, though the latter by no means hold a position of pre-eminence. The writing of history by experts for experts would have no chance of becoming memory history. This could only occur if it left the circle of experts and became recognized as the voice of a community of memory. This is perfectly possible, as was especially visible in the influence of national histories in the last two centuries. Nations are, as Ernest Renan (1947[1882]) recognized, always communities of memory. Here, we are dealing with a conception of history which stretches far beyond the time span of an individual's recollections and which needs to be transmitted to be accepted. This is where one needs historians, but by no means only, or even primarily, historians. Literature, all forms of media, festivals (once of great importance), sports and all the other phenomena to which Michael Billig (1995) ascribed the term 'banal nationalism' – from the flag on a house and the daily weather map on the television to the social security provisions of a nation-state for its members – all contribute, without the help of historical experts, to making national histories believable and anchoring them in the daily lives of individuals.

Günther Lottes thus conceives of the nation as an abstract community of memory, spanning a large historical period and encompassing the whole of society, in contrast to the two other types of community of memory which he identifies. One is the 'experience-rich community of memory' which can only exist within a generation of contemporaries. A third group is a community of memory within milieux or groups whose historical experiences stretch beyond the lifetime of a single generation but are not shared by the whole of society. This includes, for example, confessional groups, whose world-view is bound up with a particular version of history, different from that of other confessional groups: one need only consider the Catholic national pantheon which, even within the same nation-state, is populated very differently from its Protestant counterpart (Haupt and Langewiesche 2001; Buschmann and Langewiesche 2003; Altermatt 2005). For a long time, the national homogenization of historical views came up against confessional boundaries. Catholic versions of the past were able to resist the pressure to homogenize, which emanated from the dominant national memory in a state under Protestant hegemony, because the experience of being a Catholic in a society with a Protestant majority repeatedly reinforced the historical views transmitted within the Catholic milieu. Socio-moral milieux (Lepsius 1993) usually also acted as historical milieux (*Geschichtsmilieus*). By looking at history in a different way to others, the ties of the milieu were strengthened.

The fact that historical views are held in the present which are no longer within the reach of individual memory links memory history (as contemporary history) with a form of history which goes beyond individual recollection and which can only be experienced in an abstract way. On this threshold of lived experience, Maurice Halbwachs (1950) claims that collective memory becomes history. This history which one has not experienced oneself can, however, cross over into memory history when transmitted history and lived experience are in harmony, insofar as they express the same experiences, thus allowing a continuity of meaning to emerge between the realm of lived experience and that which came before it.

If one follows these reflections, memory history can be conceptualized in three stages of increasing abstraction:

- historical views which are bound to the experience of a generation;
- historical views that go beyond the lifetime of the individual but only belong to certain groups within a society (for example, a confessional or ethnic group);
- historical views which lay claim to validity for the whole of society across many periods.

On none of these three levels does one find uniform perceptions of history. They are always the result of competition, but the possibility of this competition, in which historical views are formed and modified, varies greatly (Wolfrum 2001; Bernecker and Brinkmann 2006). This can be observed in some examples that reveal the conditions for the social production of memory and how they relate to the professional writing of history.

Plurality not Particularism: A Problem Fundamental to Every Memory History

The first point is that the ability to tolerate conflicting historical views and protect them against intervention by authority is only found in sufficiently pluralistic, open societies. Unhindered historical competition is linked to pluralism of social values and requires a state which is prepared to protect this pluralism. Democracy could therefore be defined, as far as memory history is concerned, as the readiness not only to reluctantly allow contests over memory but also to encourage them consciously. Democracies can thus be recognized by their support for a diversity of historical views and by their approval of conflicts over historical interpretation. However, even in long-established democracies, it is a matter of debate whether this diversity can, in fact, exist without a commonly undisputed core.

In the U.S.A. this debate led, only relatively recently, to the founding of the

Historical Society in 1998.[16] This organization grouped together those academic historians, including some very prominent ones, who were concerned that 'cultural wars' (Ribuffo 1999: 162) in the historical sciences resulting from postmodernism could cause the historical foundations of American identity to collapse. Admittedly, memory history is not a term these dissident historians use, but the accusation of particularistic multiculturalism which they level against postmodern historical writing targets a fundamental problem of one of these forms of memory history: that history is put forward from the particularistic viewpoint of a community of memory, like the perspective of a confessional or ethnic group, yet when seen from this perspective alone there is no possibility of adding one's own historical view, in a relativist way, to the overall picture. This, of course, is something that the hard-line advocates of this trend would not want. In this extreme form, history appears as a kaleidoscope of recounted remembrances. At each turn of the kaleidoscope a new picture emerges, isolated from those before and after, because the principle of the kaleidoscope's construction allows no overall, complete picture to be seen (Langewiesche 2003).

The opponents of such a radical relativism write in their programme of the danger of a 'Balkanization' of historical writing and of the whole of intellectual life in U.S. society (Lasch-Quinn 1999: 33). The standards of academic inquiry, they claim, are dissolving into arbitrariness and there is no longer a method for reaching any consensus regarding what is important in the past and what is not.

This loss of common criteria for judgement, it is claimed, is the reason why American society is interested in history but not in academic historical writing. In becoming a mere projection of identity for individual groups in society, historical writing has lost its power to perceive history as 'knowledge of human diversity' (Kors 1999: 17). This means, with regard to the issue of memory history, that by focusing exclusively on the history of a single community of memory, that community alone is offered the chance to assure itself of its own historically based identity, and not the nation as a whole. History would thus lack a core common to all and the power to promote integration. For a society of immigrants, this would be especially awkward, which explains why this issue is the subject of particularly weighty discussion in the U.S. Even in Europe, however, where one still tends to accept the fiction of homogenous nation-states, this problem will, in spite of all empiricism, rear itself in the future. It is, one might say, a historical topic with a future. And it can quickly become explosive if, for instance, Turkish immigrants and their descendents ask about their own history in German schools and universities, because they hope to find their identity in the history of their forefathers rather than in German history.

What role will memory history play in this? This question shall be considered from three perspectives: firstly, by recourse to a theoretical work from the eighteenth century by Johann Martin Chladenius; secondly, by examining the British historian Sir John Harold Plumb's fulminating historical criticism, and finally by turning to the German historian Reinhart Koselleck and the French philosopher Paul Ricoeur, whom we have to thank for a incisive discussion of the relationship between memory and history.

Memory History as the History of Partial Eyewitnesses: Johann Martin Chladenius

In his great *Allgemeine Geschichtswissenschaft* (Chladenius 1985[1752]), which offsets much of what has been written about the subject ever since, Johann Martin Chladenius was not yet familiar with 'memory history' as a concept. Yet he thought intensely about this phenomenon since history, in Chladenius's view, is always something that is observed. History for him is always the contemporary history of witnesses and it could never be perceived in a uniform way. He explains why this is the case in his unsurpassed theory of 'viewpoints' (Sehepunkte). He did not yet know the temporal viewpoint, that is, the distance in time from an event which becomes history. As a result there could be no memory history which went beyond the lifespan of those who lived through it. All historical knowledge in his theory stems from what the individual observes and remembers, what they talk about with others, whose observations and memories they, in turn, listen to. It is in this realm of memory – the space which Maurice Halbwachs (1950) termed collective memory, though today one speaks mostly of communicative memory (A. Assmann 1993, 1999, 2006; J. Assmann 2005) – that historical knowledge originates. For Chladenius, this emerges as something multivocal and never uniform, but also as something which later generations cannot change, because Chladenius was not familiar with the retrospective rewriting of history as an act of innovation.

The truth of historical transmission, which Chladenius recognizes as something limited due to the ever-subjective viewpoint of the individual, emerges for him from the eyewitness. Likewise, Reinhart Koselleck speaks of the importance of eyewitness authenticity. When this no longer exists, 'ancient history' (*alte Geschichte*) begins for Chladenius. He asks what it is, in fact, 'that actually makes a history ancient. We answer: the nature of historical knowledge changes when all witnesses have died out; in such a way that one henceforth has to learn of it from those who retell it second-hand' (Chladenius 1985: 353).

Then he makes a distinction within the group of second-hand storytellers. Do they repeat what they have heard from actual eyewitnesses or is it a purely second-hand story? When 'none of the first generation of second-hand storytellers is alive' the time of ancient history has come: 'when nobody remains who would have been informed of the events by listening to his forebears, so that one henceforth has to stick solely to the monuments' (ibid.: 353). In our time, in the middle of the eighteenth century according to Chladenius, history becomes 'ancient' at a faster rate than before because one no longer tells the history one experiences to the young but writes it down instead. Chladenius does not give memory a specific place in the arsenal of different approaches to history. For him, rather, all historical knowledge, insofar as it is authentic, emanates from memory history. It rests on eyewitness accounts either directly, if one experiences the event oneself, or indirectly, if one hears it reported by an eyewitness. In both cases it has the status of an authentic historical account. Beyond this threshold 'ancient history' begins, based on second-hand accounts without the authenticity of eyewitnesses.

Every memory history is characterized by eyewitness authenticity but always, unavoidably, restricted by partiality. Chladenius was aware of this, and his profound reflections on the subject are unsurpassed to this day. Historical writing from an individual viewpoint, such as a confessional viewpoint, can never claim to represent a 'true' version of history. Historical writing is to be understood, and Chladenius was the first to clarify this so precisely, as a chain of approximations on past occurrences, viewed from different perspectives.

Memory History as an Act of Innovation: John Herald Plumb and Reinhart Koselleck

In Chladenius's view of things the significance of temporal distance for the perception of history was touched upon but he did not yet recognize the full extent of its importance. Nevertheless, he belonged to those, who, in the terms of the British historian J.H. Plumb, paved the way for his slim yet weighty volume, *The Death of the Past* (Plumb 1969). For the 1971 German edition, the title was translated as *Die Zukunft der Geschichte: Vergangenheit ohne Mythos* ('The future of history: the past without myth'). This title seems to be contrary to the spirit of the original but actually identifies the author's meaning rather successfully. Plumb makes a sharp distinction between 'the past' and 'history'. He uses the term 'the past' for everything historical which is mobilized for a particular purpose – the normal form of social interaction with history from the earliest times to the present day. People use the past to 'explain the origins and the purpose of human life, to sanctify institutions of government, to give validity to class structure, to provide moral example, to vivify [their] cultural and educational processes, to interpret the future and to invest both the individual human life or a nation's with a sense of destiny' (ibid.: 11). In short, the task of the past was always, and still is, to connect the meaning of the past with the meaning of the future.

History, on the other hand, is quite different: a creation of scientific inquiry, an intellectual process. Plumb sees history-as-science as fundamentally destructive. It demystifies, and thereby destroys, the system of poetic meanings that people have constructed with the help of the past.

The true task of the historian as scientist, Plumb claimed, was to free the history of humanity from the tyranny of the past, to destroy the tyranny that lay in the use of the past for the purpose of lending cohesion to the present: the business of academic history defined in biting terms. Can, and should, memory history contribute something to this? In order to attempt to answer this question, it is perhaps first necessary to locate memory history within the general typology of historical writing which we owe to Reinhart Koselleck. Koselleck (2003) identifies three categories of historical writing, into which all forms of history can be grouped: 'writing down' (*Aufschreiben*), 'amending' (*Fortschreiben*) and 'rewriting' (*Umschreiben*). Koselleck couples these three categories with the three temporal frameworks of historical experience which have endured unchanged from the works of Herodotus and Thucydides to the present day: short-, medium- and long-term experiences. Eyewitness history, as Chladenius knew it, a history which belongs exclusively to collective or communicative memory, is distributed across all three categories, though it entirely monopolizes the first type: the writing-down stage. Only that which contemporaries pass on about an event remains, at least potentially, at the disposal of later generations.

Memory history, the first stage of contemporary historical information and the point of departure for all that follows it, is an innovative form of historical narration, or historical writing, because writing down itself is an act of innovation. When historical science turned away from the study of events to the analysis of long-term structures – and this, for a while, was the dominant trend worldwide – it abstained from this form of innovation without giving an account of why this was the case (Langewiesche 2008b). Memory history, booming at present, has contributed to the redressing of this shortfall, largely without giving the appearance of doing so.

Memory history also plays a part in the two other categories of historical writing, 'amending' and 'rewriting'. Amending is the normal business of the historian. The great majority of historians are amenders, which is lucky for them and for their contemporaries for they would otherwise be living in a time of profound upheaval. Amending implies historical continuity or, to put it more precisely, that those in the present are conscious of a strong continuity from the world of their forebears.[17] Such a sense of continuity calls for a historical narrative which is compatible with amendment. Only when this sense of continuity is broken does the time come for rewriting, the highest form of innovation of which historical writing is capable. But this is not a self-referential innovation from within the mind of the historian; it is rather their innovative answer to the upheavals of their time. And only when the two come together – social upheaval and the rewriting of history – only at this time of crisis does a new vision of the past come into being which is accepted by society. Society accepts it because its new experiences call for a new vision of history. An experience of upheaval and an upheaval of collective historical views are thus conditional upon each other.

As far as memory history is concerned, if it emerges under the conditions of social upheaval, it creates a new conception of the past. This is not the tyranny of the past of which Plumb writes and which he identifies as the main form of narration about the past. It is not the past which puts the present in chains; it is rather the past seen with new eyes due to a changed experience in the present. This viewpoint, which Chladenius did not yet know, is certainly innovative but it always contains the danger of exchanging one tyranny for another, above all when a tyrannical present tries to adapt the past to fit into its own chain of meaning.

Plumb attempts to avert this danger by bringing academic history writing into play, which, he argues, first became possible in the twentieth century. Indeed, he was familiar with numerous examples of academic historical writing from earlier centuries but argues that it was not until the twentieth century that society became receptive to it. This is because, he claimed, industrial society became adjusted to permanent flux in a new way, and therefore no longer needed history in the sense of the past, or needed it only as a place for nostalgia and sentimentality.

The opposite argument, however, is empirically more plausible: profound change actually reinforces the desire to locate oneself firmly in the past. This is visible in two examples. As the successor states of the former Yugoslavia began to establish their territorial claims, they turned to long-trusted historical myths in order to regain, in the tumultuous present, a perspective on the future (Stråth 2000; Sundhaussen 2003). Another example, in Germany, is the success of Heinrich August Winkler's *Der lange Weg nach Westen* (Winkler 2000) which sought to endow the newly united Germany with a new version of its past: the definitive end to *Sonderweg* of modern Germany. Winkler conceives of this *Sonderweg* in three parts and all paths, he claims, have now come to an end: Germany, having arrived in the value-system of the West, is offered a national narrative which promises security in the future to both Germany and her neighbours through an awareness of the past. This, too, is a rewriting of history after an experience of upheaval in the present. This rewriting is accepted by society because it is in harmony with individual memory history and lends it legitimacy and meaning.

On the Reconciliation of History and Memory: Paul Ricoeur

Whether it is historical writing in the sense of the past or of history that is paramount in Winkler's vision of the path of German history will not be debated here (see Langewiesche 2008e). Instead, I want to return for a moment to Plumb's provocative, universal-historical view of historical writing through the ages. It is not the supposed distancing of industrial society from its history that allows for the social success of historical writing that is critical of tradition: the destructive work of science, to paraphrase Plumb. A process, rather, is taking place which could be described as the democratization of the way history is dealt with. A contributing factor in this is a form of historical writing which Plumb would have regarded as unscientific and thus categorized as history in the sense of 'the past': historical writing under the spell of the nation.

In the nineteenth century, across the world, a new force made its way to the centre of political events and the social value system: the people (*Volk*) or the nation. The democratically conceived concept of the nation offered a promise for the future as well as a new programme of meanings for the past. It constructed a new perspective on history, through which all of history could be painted in national colours. This rewriting of history took up the founding myths of the nation and reproduced them. Historians participated wholeheartedly in this enterprise, yet during the same century of nation building and the construction of national historical myths, history developed into a science. History and the past, between which Plumb draws a sharp distinction, do not therefore have to be seen as opposites. To be more precise, it was only due to the fact that the two developed without this sharp distinction between them that the new historical viewpoint could become so extraordinarily effective in society. History rose to become one of the decisive factors in the process of nation building, in the emergence of nation-states and in the nationalization of daily life. It was not until the nineteenth century that historical writing achieved this position of strength. This was possible because it engaged people (as 'the past') and simultaneously gave the new vision of history a scientific authenticity (as 'history'). This elevation to the level of a science was vital for history since faith in science had become the new cult of the nineteenth century. This interplay between history and the past has been sensitively thought through by Paul Ricoeur (1998), who sees no sharp distinction between them, but rather a reciprocal relationship. They are dependent on each other. He writes of the 'instruction of history by memory' (ibid.: 126), without history giving up its critical function. Yet only if history engages with memory, he argues, can critical historical writing hope to be heard by society and to have an effect on it. Ricoeur calls this effect therapeutic: memory history as historical therapy.

What does this mean? Paul Ricoeur in no way advocates the kind of historical writing that adjusts the pasts to such a degree that it serves to confirm the present. In fact, he turns decisively against 'historical determinism' in the hope, instead, of 'retrospectively introducing contingence into history'. He understands contingence as a barrier against a 'retrospective illusion of disaster' from which a 'compulsion to repeat' could derive, as if from a trauma. He therefore argues in favour of narrating history as 'a cemetery of un-kept promises'. Such a way of telling history, he claims, would have a therapeutic effect (ibid.: 127–30).

For this to happen, however, memory and history would have to be brought into discussion with each other in order to reconcile the 'rupture between history and the discourse of memory' (ibid.: 114). This is only possible, he argues, if history takes pre-scientific memory seriously, including the memory history of non-historians, while simultaneously subjecting it to critical inquiry. The possibility of historical writing having an effect on society depends on its ability to make the connection between 'faithfulness to memory' and 'historical truth'. By engaging the population, historical awareness shapes imaginations of the future. To paraphrase Koselleck (1989), futures past give shape to that which is to come. This is only possible, however, if historical writing puts forward a view of the past which is accessible to the experience of contemporaries. Thus, the web of causal connections between memory history as the work of many and historical science as the business of experts is outlined. However much the two methods differ, there is no sharp distinction between them of the kind that Plumb wants to read into all historical thought across the ages, and nor should there be. Otherwise, historical writing would be depriving itself of its chance to have an effect in society. And, moreover, it would also be running the risk of missing innovative insights into history which occur only when new experiences in society allow for a new perspective on history. Fortunately, this experience is not granted to every generation (I say 'fortunately' because this experience is bound up with profound and often violent upheaval). But should such a phenomenon occur, if it does not want to become antiquated then historical writing, including memory history, cannot merely stick to the task of writing down and adapting history. At this point the time has come to rewrite history.

I should add, in conclusion and to avoid misunderstanding, that here I am not referring to the stimuli of new, or supposedly new, methodological approaches which promise to remodel the social and philosophical sciences, the many 'turns' that are proclaimed and which follow each other in increasingly quick succession. These attempts at innovation for experts by experts will have to be put down to the demands of increased competition in a globalized academic market. They serve to attract attention in an increasingly confusing academic market and to mark out fields of research in which new products can be introduced. An intrinsic part of academia, they by all means allow for changed perspectives on history. It still holds true, however, that beyond the boundaries of these specialist markets a new view of history will only have an effect if society is receptive to it. And that again is not something that professional historians will decide. This decision rests with society itself.

Memory history is more closely linked to this decision than any other form of history because it draws no systematic boundaries between experts and lay persons, between science and real life. Thus, memory history leads right to the heart of the conflicts of the present. This accounts for its appeal but it is also where its dangers lie. The two go hand in hand.

Notes

1. Translated by Tom Williams. A German version of this chapter appeared in Langewiesche (2008a). For a detailed discussion of 'memory history' (*Erinnerungsgeschichte*), see the section entitled 'What is Memory History', below. Memory history is understood as a popular historical narrative which is constructed by lay historians and occasionally by professional academic historians but without giving the latter priority.
2. Motion by the faction SPD, CDU/CSU, Bündnis 90/Die Grünen und FDP, German Bundestag, 15th legislative period, published paper 15/5689, 15 June 2005. See also the

motion by the CDU/CSU, Bundestag published paper 15/4933, 22 February 2005; and 'Ansprache des Bundestagspräsidenten Dr. Norbert Lammert anläßlich des Gedenktages für die Opfer des Genozids an den Armeniern am 24. April 2007 in Berlin'. Retrieved 15 August 2008 from: http://www.bundestag.de/parlament/praesidium/reden/2007.

3. The text of this declaration is as follows:

> *Liberté pour l'Histoire!*
>
> *Emus par les interventions politiques de plus en plus fréquentes dans l'appréciation des événements du passé et par les procédures judiciaires touchant des historiens et des penseurs, nous tenons à rappeler les principes suivants:*
>
> *L'histoire n'est pas une religion. L'historien n'accepte aucun dogme, ne respecte aucun interdit, ne connaît pas de tabous. Il peut être dérangeant.*
>
> *L'histoire n'est pas la morale. L'historien n'a pas pour rôle d'exalter ou de condamner, il explique.*
>
> *L'histoire n'est pas l'esclave de l'actualité. L'historien ne plaque pas sur le passé des schémas idéologiques contemporains et n'introduit pas dans les événements d'autrefois la sensibilité d'aujourd'hui.*
>
> *L'histoire n'est pas la mémoire. L'historien, dans une démarche scientifique, recueille les souvenirs des hommes, les compare entre eux, les confronte aux documents, aux objets, aux traces, et établit les faits. L'histoire tient compte de la mémoire, elle ne s'y réduit pas.*
>
> *L'histoire n'est pas un objet juridique. Dans un Etat libre, il n'appartient ni au Parlement ni à l'autorité judiciaire de définir la vérité historique. La politique de l'Etat, même animée des meilleures intentions, n'est pas la politique de l'histoire.*
>
> *C'est en violation de ces principes que des articles de lois successives – notamment lois du 13 juillet 1990, du 29 janvier 2001, du 21 mai 2001, du 23 février 2005 – ont restreint la liberté de l'historien, lui ont dit, sous peine de sanctions, ce qu'il doit chercher et ce qu'il doit trouver, lui ont prescrit des méthodes et posé des limites.*
>
> *Nous demandons l'abrogation de ces dispositions législatives indignes d'un régime démocratique.*

The declaration is signed by Jean-Pierre Azéma, Elisabeth Badinter, Jean-Jacques Becker, Françoise Chandernagor, Alain Decaux, Marc Ferro, Jacques Julliard, Jean Leclant, Pierre Milza, Pierre Nora, Mona Ozouf, Jean-Claude Perrot, Antoine Prost, René Rémond, Maurice Vaïsse, Jean-Pierre Vernant, Paul Veyne, Pierre Vidal-Naquet et Michel Winock. A further 600 historians put their names to the petition. The delaration can be found at: http://www.rfi.fr/actufr/articles/072/article_40466.asp. Retrieved 16 August 2008.

4. As in the case of the research groups funded by the Deutsche Forschungsgemeinschaft at Gießen (researching *Erinnerungskulturen*, 'memory cultures') and Tübingen (researching *Kriegserfahrungen*, 'war experiences').

5. Hartmann (2004) recognizes the way these different memories can be explained beyond accusations of expulsion and claims that they are unteachable. He proposes a typology for war crimes on the Eastern front which categorizes the crimes by particular areas and then asks who was deployed in these areas and when. Hartmann does not mention that these spaces may have given rise to different memories, which can only be connected to each other if those who pass on these memories are prepared to take on board the memories of others.

6. Salt (2003) and Lewy (2005a, 2005b) argue that this matter cannot be considered resolved on the basis of previous research. The controversial literature is evaluated by Schaller (2004). The politicised term 'genocide' is considered academically unusable by one comparative study (Gerlach 2003).

7. The following results are based on the extensive collection of press articles that were made available to me by the organization.

8. The article was written by Edgar Bauer. It appeared in several newspapers and must have had a marked effect on the public perception of the exhibition. The 'victims' title appeared in *Schwarzwälder Bote*, 3 December 2005, and *Oberbadisches Volksblatt*, 3 December 2005, the other title in the *Cellesche Zeitung*, 3 December 2005.

9. 'Emotionale Zeitreise – Flucht und Vertreibung. Bonn: Erste offizielle Ausstellung in Bonn/Gratwanderung zwischen Wahrheiten', *Recklinghauser Zeitung*, 3 December 2005; 'Ausstellung auf schmalem Grat. Haus der Geschichte in Bonn schlägt mit der Schau "Flucht, Vertreibung, Integration" eins der brisantesten Kapitel jüngerer deutscher Geschichte auf', *Aachener Zeitung*, 3 December 2005; 'Gratwanderung zwischen den Wahrheiten. Das Bonner Haus der Geschichte wagt sich an das Thema Flucht und Vertreibung. Millionen Menschen waren davon betroffen', *Westdeutsche Zeitung*, 5 December 2005. The image of the tightrope walk (*Gratwanderung*), taken from Bauer's article, was used by a number of other newspapers including *Die Glocke* (Beckum), the *Vlothoer Anzeiger* and the *Mindener Tageblatt*, all on 3 December 2005; 'Kommunions-kleid aus Mullbinden. Ausstellung dokumentiert Leid der Vertriebenen aus den Ostgebieten', *Badisches Tagblatt*, 3 December 2005; 'Einzelschicksale und Hintergründe', *Stuttgarter Nachrichten*, 3 December 2005; 'Flucht und Vertreibung: Heikles Thema der Geschichte', *Waldeckische Landeszeitung*, 28 November 2005; and 'Ein hochsensibles und politisch brisantes Thema', *Wiesbadener Kurier*, 3 December 2005.

10. Article by Helmut Herles, *General Anzeiger*, 3 December 2005.

11. Thomas Schmid, 'Koffer, Mullbinden, Ausweisungsbescheide. Die Ausstellung "Flucht, Vertreibung, Integration" beweist Taktgefühl im Umgang mit einem schwierigen Kapitel deutscher Geschichte', *Frankfurter Allgemeine Sonntagszeitung*, 4 December 2005.

12. According to Hans Michael Kloth, 'Reise in düstere Zeiten', *Der Spiegel Online*, 3 December 2005. Retrieved 17 August 2008 from: http://www.spiegel.de/kultur/gesellschaft/0,1518,388409,00.html. Adam Krzemiński suggested in his account that the exhibition should also be shown in Warsaw: *Polityka*, 18 December 2005.

13. Franziska Augstein, 'Auf dem Leiterwagen', *Süddeutsche Zeitung*, 3–4 December 2005.

14. Michael Kohler, 'Kein deutscher Sonderweg. Die Ausstellung "Flucht, Vertreibung, Integration" im Bonner Haus der Geschichte', *Frankfurter Rundschau*, 6 December 2005.

15. Jörg Lau, 'Ein deutscher Abschied. Heimat II. Wie der Vertreibung aus dem Osten gedenken? Ohne Selbstmitleid. Eine Ausstellung im Bonner Haus der Geschichte', *Die Zeit*, 8 December 2005.

16. Information is available on the homepage of the Historical Society – http://www.bu.edu/historic – and above all in their periodicals: *Journal of the Historical Society* and *Historically Speaking: The Bulletin of the Historical Society*. Every two years the society holds a large specialist convention. On their homepage their programme reads:

> The Historical Society invites you to participate in an effort to revitalize the study and teaching of history by reorienting the historical profession toward an accessible, integrated history free from fragmentation and over-specialization. The

Society promotes frank debate in an atmosphere of civility, mutual respect, and common courtesy. All we require is that participants lay down plausible premises, reason logically, appeal to evidence, and prepare for exchanges with those who hold different points of view. The Historical Society conducts activities that are intellectually profitable, providing a forum where economic, political, intellectual, social, and other historians can exchange ideas and contribute to each other's work. Our goal is also to promote a scholarly history that is accessible to the public.

17. An excellent analysis of this process was produced by Richard Koebner between 1941 and 1943, based on conscious realization of the threat to his own existence on account of being a Jew at the time of National Socialist rule. See Langewiesche (2008c).

9

The Second World War in the Popular Culture of Memory in Norway

Claudia Lenz

As in all countries which were occupied by Germany during the Second World War, the German Occupation in Norway was met by resistance. This resistance was not only carried out by organized military groups but also by parts of the civilian population. Though it took very different forms and developed in different ways, resistance became an elementary component in the national self-image of Norway after 1945. Memory of the resistance in the post-war period was mostly shaped by the circulation of popular stories about 'resistance heroes' and their actions – such as in the extensive 'experience' literature. Individual participants in the resistance also played a major role in the emergence of official rituals of commemoration and in the creation of symbols within the sphere of public memory. In Norway, this culminated in the creation of the Norges Hjemmefrontmuseum in 1970, a museum dedicated to the resistance with exhibits that are almost exclusively shaped by the narratives of resistance veterans. Many memorials are connected to events of resistance and/or persecution, such as the memorial grove at Akershus Castle in Oslo which commemorates the murder of members of the resistance movement which took place there in March 1945. This memory of the resistance, personified by some outstanding figures and materialized in symbols, places and practices of commemoration became a kind of 'collective property' during the first decades after the war (Larsen 1999: 20). This resulted in common narratives of the kind 'everybody took part' in (or at least supported) the resistance in some way or another. Cultural representations of the resistance condensed into a national master narrative about the Occupation, organized by an extremely schematic opposition between 'We, the patriots' and 'The others/enemies', a discursive pattern which also organized individual memories and private stories (Lenz 2007) or, in Michel Foucault's terms, regulated what could be thought and said about the past (Foucault 1978).

Those who 'took part' in the resistance could demand a high degree of political authority after 1945, and many politicians and representatives in public organizations in post-war Norway were veterans. There was a clear connection between the authority to define the past and the authority to define present-day politics. But the 'master narrative' of the resistance, which claimed to cover the experiences of the broad majority of citizens and with which everyone apparently could identify, contained lacunae. In particular, though they had contributed to the resistance, women were largely invisible or at least subordinated to 'male' resistance heroes. Thus, though everyone participated, women's contributions were regarded as a matter of their daily duties rather than a matter of political agency, not to speak of heroism, and they were rarely seen as being worthy of mention. With a closer look, however, dimensions of everyday life under Occupation and the activities of the resistance become visible, and they clearly contradict this male-dominated view. The notion of gendered roles within Norwegian society during the Occupation in general, and more specifically within the field of resistance, becomes more differentiated the closer one looks. On the one hand, typically 'female' spheres of everyday life were politicized and coupled with resistance activities, such as hiding persecuted people and supplying them with food and other things necessary for survival in a time of shortage. On the other hand, women became involved in the organized resistance movement and some of them also in its military branch Milorg. But although the traditional boundaries of gender roles were exceeded, post-war memories gave the opposite impression: that of a traditional order of the sexes which was the patriotic order of things. Thus, women's resistance remained the blind spot in public memories for a long time. This is the starting point of the questions that underlie this chapter: In what ways has the exclusively male representation of the resistance been represented in popular memory culture in Norway? And: Why, when and in which ways did this system of cultural representation change?

This chapter is based on the assumption that within narratives about the resistance both national and gendered identities are represented and reproduced. Legends of heroes not only display pictures of real patriotic conviction and 'true' affiliation to the nation, and they do not only call upon nationalized norms and values, for they also map the positions of men and women within the national order. It is worth analysing the gendered structure of representations of the resistance during the Occupation in all their variety, from everyday stories to official rituals of commemoration, because they contain what can be called the 'affective glue' of social groups and in their simplicity they serve up gendered role models for the present day. The questions to be asked are thus: Can such thing as a 'gendered order' of the resistance be observed in popular memories? Do memories about the Second World War which are handed down by the media confirm, provoke or even exceed gender conceptions? What roles do gendered identifications in national resistance discourses play? Nation, gender, resistance: these are the core concepts of this chapter and their dynamic 'order' from 1945 onwards will be examined here. First, I want to give a short outline of the Occupation in Norway.

Occupation History and its Remembrance: An Outline

The German invasion of Norway on 9 April 1940 was just the first step of what was experienced as a national mortification. The invasion came unexpectedly and Norwegian troops could not defend the country. However, King Haakon VII and the government escaped from Oslo and fled into exile in Britain in June. In September 1940 the Germans installed a puppet regime under the leader of the fascist Nasjonal Samling, Vidkun Quisling. This attempt to put the country under Nazi rule launched a whole range of protests, civil disobedience and resistance actions in which many Norwegians participated. The slogan *holdningskamp* ('resistance through attitude') sums up the fight to hold the country against the policy of nazification which polarized society into those who were against the Germans and those who were willing to collaborate. But things weren't that simple. Even if the Nasjonal Samling never had more than 50,000 members (out of a population of 3 million) there were other conditions that made *holdningskamp* difficult.[1] The Germans were one of the largest – and best paying – employers in Norway, and more than 150,000 Norwegians worked for the occupation forces.[2] Moreover, German soldiers lived in many Norwegian places, sometimes as long-term residents in the houses of the native population. Thus, social relations developed on an everyday level between ordinary German soldiers and the Norwegians. So, where did 'arrangements' with the enemy end and where did voluntary support begin? This is a crucial question and is related to sexual and love affairs between Norwegian women and German soldiers. Seen in the context of this situation it becomes understandable that sexual relations between Norwegian women and German soldiers were a 'normal result' of the cohabitation of Norwegians and Germans. In fact, they occurred in the tens of thousands: about 9,000 children resulting from these relations are documented in the archives of the SS organization Lebensborn. On the other hand, these relations were regarded as a provocation if not national treason in the light of a politicized climate knowing just for or against the Germans. As well-known from other cases where national identities are contested and national sovereignties are threatened, women's sexuality can become a symbolic borderline. This is exactly what occurred in Norway, where that order was drawn between patriots and *Quislingers*, between correct attitudes and treason.

The dominant version of national historiography which emerged after 1945 represents an extremely enduring and effective interpretive framework in Norwegian memory culture. National 'basic narratives' concerning the Second World War have been analysed in the case of Norway by Anne Eriksen (1995) and that of Denmark by Claus Bryld and Anette Warring (1998), and they argue that these narratives are the outcome of an analysis of the public cultures of memory and commemoration in both countries. Despite the different course of events in Denmark and Norway, the structure of the dominant versions of their respective histories of occupation resemble each other. In both post-war Denmark and Norway, references to the Second World War and the German occupation played a central role in constructing national identities and values. The basic narrative of the five years of occupation was built upon the idea of a resistance movement gradually supported by every 'real' Dane or Norwegian.

The time of the Occupation is seen as a mythically loaded state of emergency in national history, a time in which the people of a small state stood united against a powerful enemy, gathered around their deepest values. In this way the nation and the national community is symbolically and morally recreated. The dominant idea is of a homogeneous national community without any political and social differences. The price of this integrative tale of 'the nation in resistance' has firstly been the immense and lasting stigmatization and exclusion of anyone branded a traitor. And the second consequence has been the suppression of existing political and social conflicts and differences before, during and after the occupation in order to maintain the image of a united nation.

When analysing how the discursive patterns of private and public memories are intertwined, it becomes obvious that the construction of memories is part of the creation, distribution and struggle over power.

Memory and the Gendered Regulation of Authority and Power

How do stories which are considered worth remembering emerge in public and private contexts? And how do those who are regarded as valuable narrators gain their authority to tell about and interpret the past? Before investigating these questions with regard to examples taken from my empirical material I want to introduce a theoretical concept which, from my point of view, allows for a better understanding of the regulating mechanisms related to speaking about the past: Michel Foucault's analysis of power/knowledge systems (see Foucault 1974).

The images and stories about the past circulating in any society are parts of a 'contested' past, which means that they are elements in negotiations and struggles about the distribution of material and symbolic resources within society. Foucault's basic assumption is that everything considered to be 'true' and 'meaningful' is the effect of discursive practices. As Stuart Hall sums Foucault's view:

> Discourse … constructs the topic. It defines and produces the objects of our knowledge. It governs the way that a topic can meaningfully be talked and reasoned about. It also influences how ideas are put into practice and used to regulate the conduct of others. Just as a discourse 'rules in' certain ways of talking about a topic, defining acceptable and an intelligible way

to talk, write or conduct oneself, so also, by definition, it 'rules out', limits and restricts other ways of talking, of conducting ourselves in relation to the topic or constructing knowledge about it. (Hall 1997: 44)

Being 'ruled' by discursive patterns defining what can and cannot be said by whom and how, the negotiation of the past regulates participation, citizenship and exclusion. It mirrors and influences power relations. The simple question is: Which elements of the unlimited multitude of past events will be regarded as meaningful in the present and the future and thus will be preserved and handed down to coming generations? This indicates that the 'preserving' of the past is always a 'construction' of narratives and images and thus connected to choice and interpretation.

Discourses about the past serve to build and stabilize identities, both for individuals and for collectives. Each social group has its collective narrative, which supplies ideas about a common identity and common values. National narratives about common roots and heritages are the most striking example of the use of the past in the construction of 'imagined communities' (Anderson 1983) in modern times. This 'unifying' function of the past is essential in the creation and maintenance of social order. It can serve to prevent or at least silence social and political conflicts. But this powerful notion of the past is, on the other hand, the evident reason for the contentedness of the past. The authorized version of the past and its anchorage in public memory culture can be understood in Foucault's term as a power constellation (Foucault 1974) which regulates what can be said and, more importantly, what is intelligible (or can be thought) about the past.

Having looked at ideas about the connection between systems of representations of, or discourses about, the past within a society, I want to next turn to the concept of hegemonic struggle as developed by Ernesto Laclau and Chantal Mouffe (2000). Laclau and Mouffe view power as a dynamic force which regulates the construction and change of possibilities of thinking, articulating and transferring discourse into social practice. Power in this sense is the power to create mental, social, economic and politically institutionalized order. A discourse and the subject positions it generates are power related since they regulate articulation. This has a double notion: someone is enabled and authorized to articulate (subject position) and something can be articulated (intelligibility). There is, in other words, a possibility in interfering in the power/knowledge game which regulates social order. On the other hand, this mechanism implies that individuals and groups can be denied the possibility of appearing as speaking and acting subjects.

Taking these premises into consideration, we can define public and private memories as elements of a hegemonic constellation, which regulates articulation, agency and power relations. Negotiating the meaning of the past has the crucial function of legitimizing a subject's former and present actions, but, furthermore, it has the function of constituting the subject as an agent – in contrast to being a passive object of the course of historical events. What does this mean with regard to gendered power relations in post-war Norway?

In the case of Norway, as with almost all other Western European countries, post-war efforts were directed at building up the country, both materially and morally and with regard to a stable political order. But despite this focus on the future, the past was by no means lacking importance. Having been an active member of the resistance movement, having been a political prisoner in a German concentration camp and having been in exile gave some people a kind of political credibility and authority. If one looks at the Norwegian political elite after 1945 one finds there many men who had been engaged in the resistance movement. Having been a 'patriotic housewife' during the five years of the Occupation, however, did not grant a woman the same political authority; rather, it led to the same traditional division of labour which had been there all the time. In other words, the gendered way the Occupation was seen and commemorated after 1945 was an integral part of the conservative restoration of a social and gender order. Interestingly enough, having been on 'the wrong side' during the Occupation – having collaborated with the Germans – led to exclusion from social and political life for both women and men. But whereas men who had been members of the Nazi party or SS volunteers faced legal sanctions, women who had had love affairs with German soldiers were punished with ostracism by their neighbours or by vigilante gangs who strolled around shaving the heads of what they called 'German whores' (Olsen 1999; Ericsen and Simonsen 2002). The stigmatization and silencing of these women has been so long lasting that even the initiative of their children some forty years later to claim rehabilitation and compensation did not lead to rehabilitation for their mothers.

It is, thus, interesting with regard to a gendered order of memories to ask the following questions: Are men and women alike offered the opportunity to speak and present themselves as historical agents? In which way do narratives of the past reproduce and stabilize gendered power relations? Cultural systems of representation are not mere mirrors of social order but are also part of the negotiation and change of power relations. The following paragraphs will demonstrate that gender is one central category in this process in which authority is generated and regulated. Men and women relate themselves and are related to different historical themes and topics, which are regarded as more (male) or less (female) relevant. Further, men and women are assigned asymmetric positions as speakers and actors, which has consequences for their self esteem as social agents.

Gendered Representations of the Past

As I have already mentioned, the basic narrative of the five years of the Occupation was built upon the idea of a resistance movement gradually supported by every 'real' Norwegian. This inclusive narrative was accompanied by a culture of commemoration which reduced the idea of 'all the people' (which obviously includes both men and women) to the representation of some outstanding male figures – the male heroes of the organized resistance movement. Women were thus reduced to 'patriotic housewives', effectively excluded from those authorized to talk 'in the name' of the past and to build the future. In what follows I will analyse some examples of representations of the Occupation and the resistance movement from popular memory: an image taken from an exhibit of the museum dedicated to commemorating the resistance, the Norges Hjemmefrontmuseum; an autobiographical report from one of the 'boys in the woods'; and one of the best known Norwegian feature films about the Occupation.

The Gendered Order of Wartime in a Picture Frame

There are not many women shown in the permanent exhibition of the Norges Hjemmefrontmuseum.[3] This is a logical consequence of the way the Occupation and the resistance movement were conceptualized by the exhibition's producers. Opened in 1970, it is based on resistance movement veterans' narratives about the five years of the Occupation. When it comes to forms of civil resistance some women are to be found in the exhibit; for example, the teacher's strike in 1942 and symbols of resistance such as wearing a paper clip on one's clothes. But the 'real' – that is, military – resistance is portrayed as nearly exclusively male business. However, there is one picture which brings to life the saying of one of the most prominent Norwegian resistance heroes, Gunnar Sønstreby, that without women, nothing of all that would have worked.[4] Is it here that, finally, women's courage and actions seem to be acknowledged? The large picture that is shown in the last part of the exhibition shows two people, a sitting woman and a standing man in a traditional living-room interior of the 1940s. The man wears an overall, the typical 'uniform' of members of Milorg, the resistance movement, which, although supported with weapons and partly trained by the British army, was not equipped with full military uniforms. The woman is wearing a cardigan, traditional Norwegian knitwear, and is looking down at something she is sewing. If you look closely you can see that she is sewing a brassard in the Norwegian national colours. The narrative of the picture is clear: Soon, he will put the brassard on his uniform and then he will move out, into the woods, to be with his (male) comrades, ready to fight the Germans. She, however, will not move out; she will stay at home and keep house, not only her private home but in a symbolic sense 'the house of the nation'. She is a patriotic housewife and will not betray him while he is away, because she will not betray their country. The picture tells the tale of the patriotic, 'sober' housewife. Her presence is necessary to keep the house and the country clean while the boys are prepared to do the dirty work – fight a war against the enemy.

In fact, this war was not fought inside Norway. The military resistance movement did not fight a partisan war against the German occupiers but was built up and trained for the country's expected liberation by allied troops. The allied invasion started from France and Norway was liberated by German capitulation on 8 May 1945. That day, some 400,000 German soldiers left in the country simply surrendered. There had been some acts of sabotage during the later years of the war, some of them being very spectacular and successful, such as the attack on a heavy-water plant, an event which made its way into several movies.[5] But the majority of the estimated 10,000 members of the Milorg had not been involved in direct confrontations with the enemy. Nevertheless a wave of 'hero stories' came out immediately after the war, in which members of the resistance movement reported narratives about their patriotic mission spiced with notions of masculinity and male comradeship. A book containing a narrative of this kind is Arne Kyhring's novel *Gutta på skauen* ('The boys in the woods'), which was published in summer 1945.

A Story of Masculine Initiation and Comradeship: The Boys in the Woods

Accounts published by other, more prominent, resistance heroes – like Max Manus (1945) and Gunnar Sønstreby (1960) – which Stein Uglevik Larsen (1999) has called the nation's 'collective property', are surely better known and have in a way been more influential than the book of this relatively unknown man. But when looking at Kyhring's report one is reminded of a point made by Claus Bryld and Anette Warring: 'The master narrative builds the framework for all [these stories], be it implicitly or explicitly. When you read one of those saboteur-accounts, you know all of them' (Bryld and Warring 1998: 354).

Kyhring's narrative is basically structured in three parts, the three-step structure of a mythical tale:

a) initiation – the entrance into the extraordinary state of being;
b) probation – the formation of an ideal community
c) transition – returning to normality as a changed person.

The plot of the book is easily told. The main character decides to join the resistance movement; he leaves his home town and accompanies a group of Milorg men hiding in the woods. Large parts of the book are filled with descriptions of military exercises, which strengthen and harden the main character's body but also turn a group of young men into a collective of patriots. After a while the group has to move and seek new hiding places; sometimes they have to collect some weapons dropped by British military planes, which is the most dangerous of the 'boys' activities. But there is no fight for liberation, the military skills they learn do not come into use, and the war ends with the German capitulation.

There would be much to say about the details of this male and patriotic story of initiation but I will concentrate on the only two parts of the story where women appear. The first meeting with women is a very distanced one, when the group is on its way to collect some weapons. Crossing a little town the hero of the story sees couples out on the streets, which provokes no sentimentality but alienation in him: 'Strange view, to see people running around in their coats and hats. Some Germans were passing with their tarts' (Kyhring 1945: 72). Obviously the narrator is concerned with the patriotic and sexual attitude of the Norwegian girls. They might have fun with German soldiers while he does his patriotic duty; he might be about to lose control over the way in which their sexuality is being deployed.

The next episode in which women appear involves the unexpected appearance of the female owner of a cabin in the woods which the group has 'requisitioned'. The owner who is escorted by a young girl reacts with panic and hysteria, something which according to Kyhring 'forces' the men to make both of them stay in the cabin until the group leaves. The unspoken logic here is that the men had to confine the women, otherwise they would have blabbed out about the hiding resistance fighters. In seeking to assure his readers how gentlemanly the 'boys' behaved towards the women, Kyhring creates an even more infantile image of them.

Summing up, Kyhring creates the image of the ideal national community as one consisting of patriotic comrades, a male-biased view in which women are of no importance at all. If they appear, they are not represented as acting subjects but rather as a threat: they either represent the danger of active (sexual) betrayal or that of unintended betrayal because of their hysterical behaviour and stupidity.

Even though Kyhring states in his introduction that he doesn't want to write about 'big heroes and extraordinary events during the time of occupation' (ibid.: 5), he makes it very clear that his intention is to inscribe himself into a narrative including all 'brave Norwegian men': 'All the boys I met were of the same calibre: Men, for whom their future dedication and comradeship were the most important. All regarded their work to be mere duty' (ibid.: 7). Portraying himself as one of the brave patriots who were willing to sacrifice their lives for their country puts Kyhring on the same level as Max Manus and Gunnar Sønstreby. His narrative, thus, is the story of a masculine rite of passage in which he becomes a real man-and-patriot, and in which a group of young men living in hiding become a masculine community representing the real nation. This pointing at the past is also a pointing at the present and future. It is a claim that 'we', the patriots who realized the ideal of a national community even under harsh conditions, now have the authority to define social and political order in the future. How could a post-war order based on these idea(l)s lead to gender equality?

The Lonesome Hero and the National Family: Ni liv

My third example from popular memory does not deal with male comradeship in the woods; instead, it is based on the story of a lonesome national hero who struggles not against foreign occupiers but with the powers of nature – an issue which touches the core of Norwegian identity discourse. This story is the focus of the film *Ni liv* ('Nine lives'), released in 1957 and based on the real story of the resistance fighter Jan Balsrud, a member of the famous Linge Company who was wounded in a German attack in March 1943 but managed to flee from the west coast of Norway to the Swedish border, crossing a rock mass on his way. Balsrud was already a legend when the film was released and it contributed to making his story a national myth – a tale that not only dealt with a concrete historical event, that occurred at a concrete time in concrete places, but also – and in a different way to Kyhring's novel – with the ideal national community. Beside showing Balsrud's struggle with natural and human powers, the film shows him being supported in his struggle by 'the people' of Norway, or more precisely by 'the good Norwegians'. And this representation of 'the people' again has a gendered structure that culminates in the image of the traditional nuclear family: father Martin, mother Agnes and their new-born child.

These 'good people' take care of Balsrud when he comes to their house, snow-blind, suffering from frostbite and completely exhausted. They hide him while there is a German raid going on in their town and they take part in attempts to get him over the Swedish border. Their courage and their determination to help this man, even if his presence puts them in danger, fits with the national master narrative of collective patriotic attitude and support for the resistance movement, something which includes the whole population, men and women alike. But not all contributions to this patriotic struggle were represented in the same way, there is a division of labour and a system of gender roles. Not only is the outstanding hero male, it is also up to his male supporters to do the 'hard work' of bringing him to the Swedish border. Agnes, on the other hand, is portrayed as physically weak but morally strong. She, the young mother, has to keep hope when her husband no longer believes that Balsrud can survive. But when she follows Martin on a ski trip to the place where Balsrud is hidden she becomes exhausted and Martin has to carry her. The scene when both enter their house where an anxious grandfather is taking care of the baby and Agnes sinks down by the child's cradle puts her, literally, in the place 'where she belongs'. The message implied here is that she should have known about the limits of a patriotic housewife.

Ni liv was an enormous success. Within a few weeks hundreds of thousands of Norwegians saw it. The newspapers discussed the authenticity of the shootings which led to an intermingling of historical reality and fiction within an all-embracing myth. Consequently, the director of the movie, Arne Skouen, and the actor playing Balsrud, Jack Fjeldstad, became national heroes themselves. There were even public events arranged where Skouen and Fjeldstad appeared together with veterans of the Linge Company, where together they merged into a virtual 'community of war heroes'. The success of the film has been long lasting: It is considered a classic of Norwegian cinema, has been shown again and again in Norwegian TV, and over the years it has been repeatedly nominated as the best film of all time.[6] Obviously, this tale about male heroes, loyal citizens and patriotic housewives touched the need for a national historical narrative offering role models and emotional glue to Norwegian society after 1945.

This and the other two examples discussed above show to what extent visual, written and cinematic cultural representations of the war mirrored and fed into a general tendency in post-war Norway, namely to re-establish the traditional order of the sexes in which men were responsible for public affairs and women for privacy. Everything which might have undermined this division of labour and responsibilities during the war – for example, the politicized meaning of women's duties in the support for members of the resistance or refugees – was neglected or reinterpreted by the traditional gender pattern. It was nearly thirty years before a younger generation of feminist historians and political activists set about discovering female role models or, in other words, a female line of tradition in their struggle for equal rights. In the last part of this chapter I want to look at one of the protagonists of the gendered rewriting of Occupation history. The varied nature of her activities show that the integration of women's resistance stories into the national master narrative of the Second World War was a cultural and political project.

Elisabeth Sveri: Feminist Interventions in the Politics of History

Elisabeth Sveri is the first Norwegian woman with a top military career reaching the position of a lieutenant colonel. From 1959 to 1987 she was superintendent for female members of the Norwegian armed forces.[7] In this position, she was responsible for equal opportunities for women and men within the army. In 1975 she became a member of a parliamentary commission which formulated recommendations which led to major advances in this field. This engagement included a historical dimension. Sveri wanted to show that there is a tradition of women's active participation in warfare in Norway reaching back to the foundation of the organization Lottas in 1928, which actively participated in combat during the German invasion of Norway in 1940 and became part of the exile forces built up in Britain after the Norwegian surrender.[8] Sveri fought for the recognition of women as ordinary, even fighting, members of the army. Including them in the history of Norway's military self-defence was one aspect of this struggle. In the 1990s, when the fiftieth anniversary of the liberation came closer, she successfully campaigned for many of these women to be decorated for their contribution to the resistance, both inside Norway and in exile. But she did not leave it with the Lottas and the military resistance. By and by she became interested in the varying ways in which women participated in resistance activities. Sveri initiated cooperative work between different institutions and started projects within different fields of public memory culture to call attention to women's contributions to the resistance movement in the Second World War. In the following paragraphs, I want to elaborate on the ways in which Sveri's activities contributed to a change in cultural representations of the resistance and the gendered division of labour in wartime – something which would not have been possible without a coalition of feminist activists and without the whole of society having opened itself up to questions of gender equality from the 1970s onward.

The Politics of Decorating Resistance Heroes

Some of the resistance heroes of the Second World War are as much decorated as the highest-ranked members of the Norwegian forces. Anniversaries of the liberation held each decade after the war have always been occasions for awarding medals to some veterans, but this had traditionally been men's business. These jubilee celebrations called attention to the veterans' heroic efforts and strengthened (or maintained) their authority. This was the case when the fortieth anniversary was celebrated in 1985, even if feminist historians and activists had already begun to dig up stories of female protagonists in the resistance movement. Sveri allied herself with the Kvinners Frivillige Beretskap (KFB), a group of female voluntary workers which is an umbrella for different women's organizations. Together, they started a campaign aiming to ensure the invitation of at least two female members or supporters of the resistance movement to the – hitherto all male – celebrations in each of the former districts in which the resistance was organized. In addition, on the occasion of the fiftieth anniversary in 1995 they claimed that these women should be decorated with a 'participant's medal' (*deltagermedalje*), the most basic of all official recognitions after 1945 (Lenz 2004). Sveri and her 'combatants' lobbied the former leaders of each resistance district, and their campaign seems to have been successful: in 1995 women attended the liberation celebrations for the first time after the war *as members* of the military resistance organization, Milorg.[9]

The success of this campaign lies, of course, not only in the number of medals given to female members of the resistance. It lies, moreover, in the changed public representation of the resistance, which is connected to women's attendance at the celebrations. This success has probably been possible because of the support of women's organizations, which in the late 1980s and early 1990s represented a serious political force within Norwegian society.

Creating Public Images: Changing Representations of the Resistance

Closely connected to the campaign for the decoration of female members of the resistance was another intervention into public memory culture, namely an exhibition about women's contributions to the resistance and their assignment to the exile forces during the Second World War. In 1995 this exhibition was shown for some months in Trondheim, and from February to August 2001 an extended version was shown at the Norwegian Armed Forces Museum in Oslo under the title 'Women in the Norwegian Army'. The Armed Forces Museum is one of the major arenas for the public representation of the Norwegian army's history, a history which has always been written by men about men. This exhibition was meant to give women a place – even if only a temporary one – in the official memory of the armed forces. It is obvious that Sveri's campaign had two aims: to force the army to include women in its institutional memory in order to open the doors for contemporary women's careers in the army; and to change the public image of the army as a merely male business and make it a place attractive to women. Again, Sveri sought public attention for women's role in the resistance when she prompted the organizers to include a public tribute to those women who had been part of the resistance movement in their speeches at the opening of the exhibition.

To maintain the effect of the exhibitions and public recognition of women's wartime contributions, Sveri published a reader with a selection of women's reports about their activities in the resistance (Sveri 1998). This publication was based on material she had collected over several years. Since 1996, Sveri has published advertisements in local newspapers encouraging women to send her all kinds of written reports, diaries or letters connected to resistance activities. By doing so she appealed to women as agents of the resistance movement who for decades had carried stories that were worth being told. The effect was that she received hundreds of answers, including pictures, newspaper clippings and other sources. The most effective achievement of Sveri's campaigning has been a booklet on women's activities in the resistance movement which was published in a series of the Norges Hjemmefrontmuseum, which is still the most powerful and productive institution when it comes to the creation of a public and, one would say, official, memory about the resistance movement (see Sveri 2002).

There is one other generation-crossing activity in which Elisabeth Sveri has been involved. It uses the core idea of all kinds of commemorative and memory work, that 'history teaches'; in other words that it helps people, especially the younger generations, understand political phenomena, to judge and to actively take part in social and political life. But a culture which only tells stories about men who go out fighting and housewives who embody moral virtue delivers hardly any role model for active female citizens, not to mention women who want to take part in the military defence of their country. These are probably some of the considerations which led to the development of courses for young women which Elisabeth Sveri organized together with the organization of female voluntary workers (*Kvinners Frivillige Beretskap*) from 1998 onwards. In an information brochure about the courses one learns that they want to show 'what women fought for and what they achieved'.[10] The connection between women's active participation in the armed forces during the war and their active participation in civil society and in the struggle for gender equality in general can very clearly be seen here.

In stark contrast to the message of films like *Ni liv* or the heroic veteran literature, these courses offer great potential for identification with strong, active and independent women. Even if the impact of Sveri's activities on Norwegian society have not been seen as important or significant as, for example, *Ni liv*, the discursive order of the master narrative about the German Occupation and the resistance is turned upside down in all of them. Their representational logic involves a shift from attempts at re-establishing a traditional division of labour between the sexes to an arena where struggles for gender equality are fought.

Conclusion

The aim of this chapter was to show in what ways Norwegian public memory culture relating to the Second World War was structured in terms of gender and, thus, was connected to gender 'regimes' after 1945. In the first phase, it could be argued, popular memories contained narratives of active men fighting for the nation and patriotic housewives who kept home and maintained moral standards. This corresponded to the traditional social order where men performed paid labour and women were responsible for housework and childcare. The idea that political representation and leadership was 'naturally' a man's business was also mirrored and maintained by the connection between the patriotic efforts of the resistance veterans and the political authority they enjoyed after 1945.

It was some decades until a younger generation of women started to question this division of labour and the imbalance of power between the sexes. Second-wave-feminism, which became a strong political force in Norway from the 1970s onward, resulted in the need for new female role models and for narratives on which claims for social, political and economic participation could be based. Alongside stories of male heroes, a culture of stories and cultural representations emerged that offered new images of courageous and active women who had participated in the struggle for national independence – some using means which had been traditionally regarded as 'female' (smuggling food, hiding and helping refugees to flee), some using weapons.

But despite adding female heroines to them, narratives about the 'the boys in the woods' and women's involvement in the resistance remained linked to the myth of the 'resisting nation'. Further deconstruction was – and is – to come. History is not told in simple terms of patriots and traitors any longer. There are shades of grey between black and white. The fact that most Norwegians acquiesced in the face of German occupation; the fact that many simply got on with their everyday lives as before; that fact that it was not necessarily members of the resistance movement but individual men and women who saved persecuted Jews in 1942; and the fact that acts of resistance were often single, uncoordinated, but nonetheless important and courageous, acts of disobedience have started to be investigated and recognized in recent years (e.g., Levin 2007). This means that there is still a need for gender-sensitive historical research and that attention still needs to be paid to the gendered ways history and 'the lessons of the past' are told.

Notes

1. These numbers are taken from: 'NS, Nasjonal Samling'. 2003. Retrieved 15 August 2008 from: http://www.norgeslexi.com/krigslex/n/n4.html#nasjonal-samling.
2. Source: 'Tyskerarbeid'. 2003. Retrieved 15 August 2008 from: http://www.norgeslexi.com/krigslex/t/t3.html#tyskerarbeid.
3. See the museum's homepage: http://www.mil.no/felles/nhm/start/eng/. See also the exhibition's description: http://www.mil.no/felles/nhm/start/eng/exhibition/. Last retrieved 15 August 2008.
4. Sønstreby's remark is taken from the TV documentary *Report from No.24* (2002), about the famous Norwegian resistance fighter Gunnar Fridtjof Thurmann Sønsteby, alias 'No.24', alias 'Kjakan'. See: http://www.mil.no/felles/nhm/start/Publikasjoner/Videokassetter/article.jhtml?articleID=14006. Retrieved 15 August 2008.
5. The Norwegian film *Kampen mo Tungvannet* (1948), directed by Jean Drèvill and Titus Vibe-Müller, was followed by the U.K. production *The Heroes of Telemark* (1965), directed by Anthony Mann and starring Kirk Douglas, and the documentary *The Real Heroes of Telemark* (2003), directed by Martin Pailthorpe.
6. This occurred, for example, in a 1991 Norwegian TV poll and at the 2005 Bergen film festival.
7. See the biographical note published on the webpage of the Norwegian armed forces when Sveri was decorated with the St. Olaf's medal in 2008: http://www.mil.no/felles/nvkb/start/article.jhtml?articleID=155358. Retrieved 15 August 2008.
8. The Lottas – previously the Kvinners Frivillige Verneplikt ('Women's voluntary military service'), today the Norges Lotteforbund – was created as voluntary organization for women willing to support the efforts of the Norwegian armed forces. The organization was built after the model of the Finnish Lotta Svärd.
9. Unfortunately it is impossible to find out how many women were decorated in that year because the Norwegian ministry of defence has so far not published statistics about it.
10. KFB information handout. Oslo: Kvinners Frivillige Beretskap, 1998, p.2.

10

Sissi: Popular Representations of an Empress

Sylvia Schraut

Sissi Mania I

'Sissi lives!' a book recently published declared (Webson 1998).[1] A recent Google search of the term 'Elisabeth von Österreich' yielded 56,300 hits; a search of the term 'Sissi' in combination with Romy Schneider, the actress who played Sissi in the successful film of the same name, yielded 151,000 hits; while 303,000 hits were obtained from a search with the single term 'Sissi'.[2] The German *Books in print* (*Verzeichnis lieferbarer Bücher*) recently listed fifty-five historical biographies, coffee-table books and novels on the subject of Elisabeth von Österreich. Keep-sakes and devotional objects are in as well. The ZVAB (a central catalogue of antiquarian and second-hand books) offers, for example, original photos for up to €450. In 1998, on the occasion of the centennial of Elisabeth's death, a pay-as-you-go phone card with Elisabeth's portrait on it was issued in Austria. The model railway company Märklin produced a freight car named 'Elisabeth – Empress of Austria – Queen of Hungary'.[3] In May 2006 a Playmobil figure of 'Elisabeth', manufactured 'for a good cause', was made available on the market. Supposedly, all the proceeds from sales of this limited edition are donated to the Society of Friends of the German Heart Centre, Berlin.[4] Even the vaguest traces left by Elisabeth's life are used to organize tourist events. In Passau, for example, a guided two-hour tour titled 'Following Empress Sissi's Traces' is offered, costing no less than €56.50. The tour description reads as follows: 'Empress Sissi stayed three times in Passau: when she travelled to Vienna to get married, for a family convention and incognito. Follow her traces and visit the Empress Sissi room at the Hotel Wilder Mann'.[5] The Viennese Hotel Kaiserin Elisabeth tries to attract guests with a poem by Elisabeth. It reads:

I write those little songs;
A heart full of grief and sorrow pushes my spirit down.
How once I was so young and rich of cheers and hope;
Never thought of anyone stronger than me, watching at an open world;
I loved, I lived, I travelled throughout the world but never achieved
    what I've longed for, I was fraud and got cheated.

There is even a Sissi 'syndrome', a condition 'when the soul loses its balance' (Voll 1998), and there are of course minutes of spiritualist sessions with Sissi (Webson 1998). Obviously, the Austrian Empress Elisabeth is very popular today, and yet she was not very popular with her contemporaries. During her lifetime she offended the supporters of the monarchy rather than contributed to the enhancement of the reputation of the endangered Austrian emperorship.

In this chapter I want to show how the unpopular and aloof empress of the second half of the nineteenth century became today's media star. I will give a short overview of Elisabeth's life and follow the process of legend-building around the empress in historiography. I also examine the stage and film adaptations of her life and have a closer look at the image of Elisabeth in films about her made in the 1950s. Finally, I will analyse the current image of Elisabeth in the popular media and offer an explanation of the changes in the popular image of Sissi that have occurred over the course of the last one hundred years and more.

The Historical Elisabeth

According to the current internet edition of the *Brockhaus*, the most widely used German encyclopaedia, 'Elisabeth Eugenie Amalie, Empress of Austria and Queen of Hungary, [was] born in Munich, 24 December1837, [and] died in Geneva on 10 September 1898'. The text continues:

> The second daughter (called Sisi) of Duke Maximilian Joseph of Bavaria married Emperor Franz Joseph I of Austria on 24 April 1854. From this marriage, which was also based on dynastic interests, sprang Crown-Prince Rudolf (1858–1889), [and] the Arch-Duchesses Sophie (1855–1857), Gisela (1856–1932) and Marie Valerie (1868–1924). Elisabeth, who – after the birth of her children – was regarded as one of the most beautiful women of her time, remained an outsider at the imperial court because of her aversion to the court's restrictions (final break at about 1860). Her sympathy for the Hungarian part of the Empire where she often stayed in the 1850s and 1860s (Gödöllö) was used by Count G. Andràssy, the Hungarian prime minister, for politics. Thus, her only explicit and emphatic political intervention led to the sanctioning of the Austrian–Hungarian settlement (June 1867) and to the union of Austria and

Hungary in a dual monarchy (coronation to Queen of Hungary in June 1867). By travelling abroad, Elisabeth increasingly withdrew from court ... and, especially after 1885, became enthusiastic about Greece. The empress, who had become isolated and, especially after the death of Crown-Prince Rudolf, suffered from depression and inner conflicts, was assassinated by the Italian anarchist Luigi Lucheni. By this unnatural death and fed by rumours, legends and sustained media-interest, very quickly a process of mystification and glorification of an ambiguous personality set in.[6]

As we know, encyclopaedias mirror the agreed upon, popular knowledge about a historical person. The entry in the *Brockhaus* in fact summarizes the knowledge presented in standard biographies of the Austrian empress. But this short overview of Elisabeth's life does not only contain the hard historical facts. It also conveys elements of the popular 'Sissi legend', which has not yet been examined critically by historiography. It is known, for example, that Elisabeth had sympathies for Hungary and that she supported the political interests of this country. However, whether Elisabeth was actively involved in the settlement between Austria and Hungary and the establishment of the dual monarchy, or whether her contemporaries simply assumed that she was involved, still awaits historical examination. This also applies to the assertion, that Sissi was regarded as a European beauty during her lifetime. It seems that this claim is an example of historical legend-building rather than based on a critical examination of the sources. Even a matter-of-fact encyclopaedia, it seems, mixes historical facts with legends.

Legend-Building

Even during her lifetime, the Austrian court and Elisabeth herself consciously contributed to the legend-building around her person. According to the sources, Elisabeth put great effort into enhancing her image as a beautiful and forever-young monarch. In the second half of her life, the empress did her best to prevent the circulation of photographs that revealed her ageing (see Figures 10.1 and 10.2).

The first photograph, which was used as the basis for several lithographs, shows the seventeen-year-old teenager. It cannot be said that this photo is evidence of her much renowned beauty and aura. Meanwhile, several photos from the 1860s verify that Elisabeth mastered the art of producing an ideal image of herself and that she was content with her appearance. The publication of official photos of Elisabeth ceased at the end of the 1860s, when Elisabeth was thirty-five-years old. From then on, the imperial court and the media satisfied the existing public demand with several photo-montages and drawings. They staged the monarch as part of the imperial family during social gatherings as a tender, beautiful and forever-young woman, a policy that was maintained

Figure 10.1: Portrait of Sissi in 1854 at the age of 17 (photograph by Franz Hanfstaengl).

after Elisabeth's death. A painting commissioned by Emperor Franz Joseph as a gift for Ida Ferency, Elisabeth's friend and lady-in-waiting, shows the empress as an icon of youthful beauty in a black gown against a golden backdrop. The small picture disseminated on the occasion of her death, aged sixty, was a photo of Elisabeth aged about thirty touched up to make her look older. This picture was reproduced on numerous postcards and shaped the picture-based memory of the empress (Mraz and Fischer-Westhauser 1998: 36).

Figure 10.2: Portrait of Sissi in 1867 at the age of 39 (photograph by Emil Rabending).

As I have already mentioned, both the court and Elisabeth herself were involved in creating a legend around the empress. The suicide of Elisabeth's son Rudolf in 1889 and Elisabeth's assassination in 1898 contributed to a high degree to developing an image of an imperial life marked by tragedy. Tragic subjects intend to arouse sympathy in the observer. Thus, the aloof monarch all of a sudden turned into a person many sympathized with. Newspaper obituaries are characteristic of the elaborate legend-building which started immediately after Elisabeth's assassination:

> Destined to everlasting happiness by birth, she blossomed in cheerful Bavaria. She came down to our joyful country on the blue waters of the Danube like a fairy of beauty and youth. However, she was not spared

human pain, fate measured out a part for her, even more than for a common mortal. Bodily pain and the soul's woe were her steady companions. Now, her martyrdom has come to an end ... She long walked the earth like a pilgrim from the land of shadows, before her heart was hit by the murderer's weapon. Reclusive and restless she lived ... With her, a shining angel sank into the realm of the shadows. A noble, fate-stricken life ended at the shores of Lake Leman. Although standing in solitary splendour high above mankind, she never left the modest and noblest circle her sex is bound to. It was only by her charitable and good deeds that she came into contact with the world. Her unique, genuine and tender femininity kept her away from the bustle of politics; her noble, refined and introverted nature did not take pleasure in superficial things, meaningless splendour and pageantry ... After all, we have learned about her secret benefaction, although she shunned nothing more than publicity when she gave ... Her crown gave off rays of mildness and love, with her charming gracefulness and her noble soul she won all hearts. Those who saw her, keep her in mind as an angel of mildness and pain with her soft, careworn face, and her infinitely kind eyes.[7]

In these obituaries we can already recognize some of the ways in which the life of an empress who hardly fulfilled the duties of her role was turned into one of suffering, making her a true royal and superhuman idol. A woman who performed an intensive body and youth cult, and who was – in today's terms – doubtless anorexic, becomes a 'fairy of beauty and youth' and is transferred from reality to the realm of fairy tales. Life-long poor health, restless travelling and taking cures are interpreted as the result of a mother's suffering from, rather than a failure to come to terms with, the suicide of her son. It is a conscious strategy that the real or assumed causes of her suffering are obscured: by implicitly evoking the knowledge of the reader, it becomes possible to characterize Elisabeth as a woman who had to endure more suffering than a 'common mortal'. In this way, Elisabeth appears as a *mater dolorosa*. Spontaneous, unsystematic charitable deeds are reinterpreted as deeds of compassion. They value them more as Elisabeth shuns publicity. Because of her refusal to fulfil the ceremonial duties of court, Elisabeth finally appears as the representative of middle-class concepts of femininity and modesty. This way, contemporary criticism of the empress is re-evaluated and embedded in an image of a martyr and who indulges in deeds of compassion, which are connoted with middle-class feminine values.[8]

Only a few years after Elisabeth's assassination, historiography about the *mater dolorosa* on the imperial throne began. In 1901 two biographies were published. One of them, written by A.D. Burgh (1901), an English author, depicts an empress who fully complied with her role: a child of nature when she was young, a loving wife and mother, beautiful, religious, charitable, committed to the Hungarian cause, an enthusiastic reader, a builder and sports enthusiast, her mind broadened by travelling and a friend of King Ludwig II. Due to the death of her son Rudolf in 1889 she turns into a mater dolorosa distanced from court and, as can be seen by her mourning, longed for her own death in the last years of her life. According to Burgh, the tragedy lies in Elisabeth's death, not in her life:

> What stroke of fate, that the beautiful empress who renounced the bustle of the world and, for long years, wandered from place to place doing good deeds, who, far from the court and politics and grief-stricken, was seeking a rest for her wounded soul, was murdered in cold blood by a brute who did not know her and who persecuted her with the same hatred he harboured against all who lived in better conditions than he himself. (ibid.: xiv)

The second biography of Elisabeth published in 1901 was written by the Norwegian Clara Tschudi, an author of many biographies of the nobility (Tschudi 1901).[9] In contrast to Burgh, for Clara Tschudi, Elisabeth's life rather than her death was marked by tragedy. Tschudi introduces the description of Elisabeth's life with two citations, for which she gives no sources. Remarkably striking, they describe Elisabeth's problems with her role as empress. Arch-Duchess Ludovica supposedly said to her daughter Elisabeth: 'You are gifted by nature and you have a noble character. You are, however, not able to lower yourself to the vision of those who surround you. You are unable to adapt to what the conditions require. You belong to another time than ours'. Elisabeth's reply, it is claimed, was, 'All I wish from people is to leave me alone' (ibid.: 7). Tschudi turns the tragedy about the meaningless destruction of an exemplary noble life into a drama about a woman wrestling with a conflict between social requirement and individual inclination.

It seems that interest in Elisabeth waned in the 1910s. After the First World War and the downfall of the dual monarchy, the unpleasant conditions of the time apparently helped nourish an interest in the subject again, but now it was coupled with nostalgia for the monarchy. In the 1920s the first magazine articles about Elisabeth were published. They tell of the very young and beautiful empress who was bound by romantic love to Emperor Franz Joseph, who was loved by the people and who met a tragic end (Unterreiner 2001: 18–19).

In 1934 Egon Caesar Conte Corti published a biography, which contains a certain nostalgia for the monarchy, titled 'Elisabeth: the strange woman' (Corti 1934). The picture of Empress Elisabeth in – even current – historiography is based on this book, which is cited again and again. Corti tried to meet scientific standards of historiography. 'On the basis of genuine and credible sources which have not yet been published', Corti wrote in the preface, 'I will try to draw the picture of a woman of whom the countess of Fürstenberg, one of Elisabeth's ladies-in-waiting once said: "Neither chizel nor brush can render how she really was and what made her so attractive; she was unique. She will survive in legend, not in history"' (ibid.: v). The author stressed his intention to 'put the empress of legend into the blazing light of history' and to 'stick to the truth' (ibid.). Corti meticulously evaluated all sources that were available to him as well as the then published literature about Elisabeth, thus writing the first sound biography of her. Judging by the many editions of this work, the study was enthusiastically welcomed. By the end of 1935, one year after publication, the book had been reprinted fifteen times, and within two years 45,000 copies had been sold. The Austrian publisher Puszet printed a new edition with 3,000 or more copies almost every year, and new editions were later published by Styria, who took over Puszet in 1953. By 1996 about 260,000 copies of the hardback had been sold, and licensed paperback editions appeared in 1977. The licensed edition that sold best is probably the one published by Heyne, reprinted fourteen times between 1977 and 1995 (Corti 1977). Corti's biography was also translated into many languages. Thus for more than half a century Corti apparently shaped the scientific and the popular image of Elisabeth.

Despite the fact that Corti's work was based on credible sources, he nevertheless took part in the weaving of the Sissi legend. The structure and emphasis of his biography seems to have served as a blueprint for many biographies and literary renderings of the subject which were published later. There is the childhood of a nature-loving tomboy in Bavaria from 1837 to 1853, which is followed by the phase of the Austrian emperor's passionate courting. Then come the first years of married life (1854–1856) which are characterized by 'longing for home and golden fetters' and the power struggle with the emperor's mother and aunt. A phase of changing states of health, unsteady motherly ambitions, of family conflicts and of rebellion is described as a period of increasing self-assertion which comes to a climax in Elisabeth's speaking up for the Hungarian cause. After that the main themes are restlessness, travelling, riding and hunting, detachment from court life in Vienna, increasing depression and anorexia, whose symptoms are described by Corti though he does not name the disorder. Finally, the shadow of death falls on the last years of Elisabeth's life – Ludwig II dies in 1886, crown-prince Rudolph in 1889 – and her execution by the anarchist Luigi Lucheni merely 'helps' Elisabeth end her life. 'Surely Elisabeth would have excused Lucheni', Corti writes. 'With her own, sometimes joyful, sometimes sorrowful irony, with the charming and beguiling smile around her lips, she perhaps would have said: "Well done, Lucheni, that's just how I wished it"'(Corti 1934: 529).

Corti has the merit of having historically founded and differentiated the picture of Elisabeth and of having gone beyond the then existing clichés. The author meticulously evaluated Elisabeth's correspondence and poems, accounts of people who were close to her, and reconstructed many facets of the opinions, interests and activities of the empress.[10] But, at the same time, his biography shows a lack of critical distance from the sources. Corti regards Elisabeth's poems as evidence of her emotions and principles; he completely equates the lyrical 'I' with the author's self and often equates Elisabeth's view with historical reality.

The criticism of seventeen-year-old Elisabeth by her mother-in-law, for example, leads Corti to the conclusion that this mother-in-law was in fact too rigorous. He leaves out Elisabeth's contemporaries' perception of her. As there is no critical analysis of the sources which might shed light on Elisabeth's commitment to the Hungarian cause, or which allow one to categorize this in the framework of the politics of the time, her enthusiasm for Hungary appears to be just a personal preference.

In comparison to Clara Tschudi's biography Corti draws a more differentiated picture of Elisabeth but with the shortcoming of being less clear cut. Corti evidently admired Elisabeth and, in his view, she did the Austrian monarchy credit. He attempts to paint a balanced picture of her conflicts and the situations in her private life. If there is tragedy in his account, then it is only in so far as Corti thinks that life may 'not end very happily' despite the 'good will of the acting persons' (ibid.: v). In his story Elisabeth does not have a hard time because of the working of fate, as in Greek tragedy, but because of the troubles of daily life – tragedy from a day-to-day point of view. 'We easily jump to conclusions, though it is important to try to understand. With this work I intended to learn to know the Empress Elisabeth and to get a clear view of the conditions in which she lived … What counted was to provide people with a better understanding and a better judgement on the matter-of-fact basis of truth', Corti explains (ibid.: vi). Apparently hundreds of thousands of readers accepted Corti's vindication of the empress and the Austro–Hungarian monarchy.

Corti's work lacked competitors until 1981, when Brigitte Hamann, the well-known author of popular histories, published her biography of Elisabeth (Hamann 1981).[11] Hamann's biography conquered the market with the same breathtaking speed as Corti's. Between 1981 and 1996 the Viennese publisher Amalthea published fifteen hardcover editions, and successful licensed paperback editions followed from 1983 onwards. The most successful edition was probably that by Piper, who issued ten editions between 1989 and 1996. In 1997 Hamann brought out a revised version which also appears to be a bestseller; meanwhile, eight paperback editions of this version have been published. On top of this, a gift edition was brought out by Piper in 2005. Like Corti's book, Hamann's biography has found its way onto hundreds of thousands of bookshelves. It must be assumed that sympathy-arousing tragedy spiced with glamour still sells best, although Brigitte Hamann's portrait of Elisabeth differs from Corti's: she modernized it by adding sex and crime. Whereas Corti remained silent about the love affairs of Emperor Franz Joseph, Hamann lifts this taboo. As she uses many citations from Elisabeth's letters and poems her book is more vivid than Corti's. In addition, Hamann's picture of Elisabeth is influenced by the films about Sissi that came out in the 1950s, to which I will come to later. Finally, Hamann echoes the line of interpretation suggested by Clara Tschudi in 1901, although she never mentions Tschudi. Using the available sources and employing modern language, she stages again the drama of the hapless struggle between individual freedom and social constraints. Elisabeth, the author tells us:

> did not accept the roles assigned to her by tradition and her surroundings: not the role of the loving and devoted wife, not the role of family mother, not the role of the foremost representative of a giant empire. She insisted on her right to be an individual and succeeded. It is the tragedy of her life that this did not result in her being happy. (Hamann 1996: 11)

But Hamann goes further than characterizing the empress as a representative of the middle-class tragically torn between self-realization and social expectations. Hamann's Elisabeth has a critical attitude towards nobility and she flouts social barriers. Thus despite her high nobility, and always having taken the privileges of her class for granted, Elisabeth nevertheless criticized courtly life and ceremonies and all of a sudden becomes the poor relative whose husband came from a higher social stratum. This motive is also apparent in the 1950s films about Sissi. Like ordinary people Elisabeth has to fight against the disdain of established elites. In this way she becomes the unhappy, tragic personification of middle- or lower-class people who try to realize themselves in an inhospitable world.

In the Sissi renaissance which accompanied the centennial of the empress's death many biographies and historical novels followed the path prepared by Hamann. But popular perception of Sissi has not only been shaped by literature but also by film.

Sissi on Stage and Screen

Films about Sissi came out quite soon after the film industry was born.[12] Between 1921 and 1955 six German and French films were made with the empress as the main character, and many others featured her as minor character. Their success varied, and none was a box-office success. It was not until the 1950s, when Ernst Marischka adapted the life of Sissi for a feature film, that this form of her biography reached the broad public. Marischka had been a scriptwriter in the 1930s and in the 1940s he had directed three films. He was versed in 'very light entertainment and the lavish representation of prominent historical persons who have remained good-hearted despite the splendour they live in' (Bessen 1989: 320). Marischka's script for *Sissi* was a free adaptation of the play 'Sissi's bride journey' (*Sissis Brautfahrt*), by Ernst Descey and Gustav Holm (1931) and the operetta *Sissy* (1932) which Marischka co-wrote with his brother Hubert.[13] Ernst Marischka was not only the scriptwriter but also directed *Sissi*, a German–Austrian production which was released in Germany and Austria in 1955. Romy Schneider starred as Elisabeth, and rapidly captured the hearts of the German audience. Almost seven million cinema goers laughed and suffered with the noble Cinderella who managed to rise to the Austrian imperial throne. Carrying on with this success, Marischka shot 'Sissi, the young Empress' (*Sissi, die junge Kaiserin*) in 1956 and 'Sissi: fateful years of an empress' (*Sissi: Schicksalsjahre einer Kaiserin*) in 1957. He was prevented from making further films, however, because the actress Romy Schneider got tired of being addressed by people on the street as 'Sissi'.

Ernst Marischka's trilogy was not the last film adaptation of the empress's life. In 1962 *Sissi: Forever my Love*, a version that combined the three German films, conquered the Anglo–American market. Since then there have been several unsuccessful film adaptations, such as those of the 1970s which dealt rather critically with the Sissi image, and more recently there has even been a French-Canadian animated TV series, *Princess Sissi* (1997). 'The smart and beautiful Sissi does everything to be with her beloved charming Prince Franz, but many people try to stop the couple from living happily', was the production's theme.[14] The cartoon character 'Princess Sissy' even has her own web-site, which, for example, offers browsers the opportunity to dress the princess. In other interactive scenes the players can experience adventures with Sissi, horses and dogs.[15] In 2002, Sissi mania provoked the German TV comedian and director of well-know comedies Michael Herbig (known as Bully) to produce a 23-minute TV programme, *Bully Special: Sissi*, with Bully starring as Sissi. A few years later, Herbig also released a feature-length animated satire about Sissi, *Lissi und der wilde Kaiser* (2007). All in all, Empress Elisabeth and historical works about her have apparently triggered a number of film adaptations. None of them, however, was as successful as Marischka's films from the 1950s.

Marischka's *Sissi*: Turning a Princess's Tale into a Middle-class Story

How does Marischka portray the Austrian empress? What made the picture he draws of Elisabeth so attractive to the audiences of the 1950s? And why are the *Sissi* films so well known today in German-speaking countries?

We have to begin with a short summary of the films. In 1853 the Austrian Archduchess Sophie looks for a suitable wife for her son, the Emperor Franz Joseph. She selects her niece Helene, offspring of a branch of the Bavarian royal house. The emperor's mother arranges a meeting in Bad Ischl between her son, her sister and her niece to prepare the engagement. But Emperor Franz Joseph falls in love with Sissi, the younger sister of the designated bride. Sissi is a charming nymph who captivates Franz Joseph by her naturalness and her love of nature. Sissi does not intend to stand in her sister's way, but Franz Joseph gets what he wants. After the engagement the prospective bride takes leave of her home and travels to Vienna. The film ends with the wedding festivities in 1854. The two films that followed – *Sissi, die junge Kaiserin* (1956) and *Sissi: Schicksalsjahre einer Kaiserin* (1957) – focus on the first years of Elisabeth and

Franz Joseph's marriage and end with the coronation of Elisabeth as Queen of Hungary in 1867. The films deal rather sketchily with the historical background and such matter-of-fact things as dates. As central themes they pick out misunderstandings between the imperial couple, Elisabeth's commitment to the cause of Hungary, marital crises, Elisabeth's illnesses, and conflicts between the empress and her mother-in-law. There is, of course, a happy ending.

Critics attacked the films for their schmaltzy style and lack of critical perspective which allegedly reduced world history to triviality (see *Der Spiegel* [11 January 1956] cited in Bessen 1989: 328). Cinema goers, however, did not agree and developed an almost unrestrained enthusiasm for the *Sissi* trilogy.

Film studies explain the success of the Sissi films against the background of the political, social and cultural conditions and attitudes of 1950s Germany and Austria. The trilogy is regarded as a courtly version of the popular *Heimatfilme* (sentimental films set against the background of unspoilt nature) of the 1950s, which the German audience watched to escape from the historical guilt prompted by the Second World War (Bandmann and Hembus 1980: 132). 'In the historical *Heimatfilm Sissi* the scenery is as important as the royal imperial décor. In nature, we learn, there is humanity, whereas in castles cool etiquette dominates ... In *Sissi*, the world exists as beautiful landscapes and castles. There is no urban life or memory of such life in this film' (Bessen 1989: 327). Film studies also stress that the family image conveyed by the films is typical for the 1950s. The story is about the seemingly ideal world of a noble family that has rather agrarian or middle-class traits rather than those of a family of high nobility. There are tiny hints that this family's life is also less than ideal: the parents have different aims and do not really appreciate each other. 'Judging by West German films, people had a great longing for intact families in which the parents were a loving couple', Gerhard Bliersbach writes (Bliersbach 1989: 157). He adds:

> the Bavarian Duchess and Duke are a West German couple: Duchess Ludovika, in her early forties, is a dissatisfied woman who grieves over the hopes she has lost in post-war Germany and who expects that her children will fulfil them for her ... Duke Maximilian, in his early fifties, is a father whose position is undermined and who is fighting to pick up the pieces of his shattered life. Ernst Marischka, who tries to present a family idyll, is imprecisely precise: the noble family from Possenhofen fits well with the post-war era. (ibid.: 157–58)

The films can also be interpreted as narratives about the gender relations of this time. On the surface, strong mothers have their say; besides them, fathers fade into insignificance. But in the end real manliness gains the upper hand, be it personified in the son, Emperor Franz Josef, or the tomboy Sissi, who admires her father. '*Sissi* is a film in which – almost in silence – men reassert their rights' (Bessen 1989: 326).

In my view it is not sufficient to explain the attractiveness and success of the *Sissi* films with the image they convey about nature, the family and gender relations. What is more important with regard to the effect of the films is how the plots handle the tragic moment inherent in Sissi's biography. It is remarkable that all the *Sissi* films have a happy ending. In contrast to the historical biographies the films show only snapshots of the life of the Austrian empress. Although they depict episodes of conflict and invite the audience to sympathize with both the empress's happiness and unhappiness, the conflicts all end well. Tragedy is turned into conflicts that can be solved. Moreover, the version of Sissi presented by the Marischka films is not that of a woman of high nobility who struggles for liberation from social conventions and courtly ceremonies. She is a minor member of the landed gentry torn from historical context, almost a petty bourgeois without history. Social conventions and historical context fade in favour of individual characteristics, especially in favour of a gender-specific role model. There is a clear message: all historical conflicts can be solved by recollecting simple, true virtues; with regard to women these virtues are motherliness and the ability to love.

We can see this in a scene from *Sissi: Schicksalsjahre einer Kaiserin* (1957). In 1856 the imperial couple travel to Italy in an attempt to favourably influence anti-Austrian opinions in the context of the growing Italian nationalist movement. Corti's biography, which served as historical reference of the Marischka-films, writes the following about the unsuccessful visit to Venice: 'The welcome seemed to be a satisfying and fine one, had it not been necessary for the imperial couple to walk through the crowd to the church San Marco after having landed on the Piazetta. There was icy silence among the people standing there closely together. There was no "Eviva", only "Hurrays" from native civil servants and officers' (Corti 1934: 68). In the film portrait of the same scene, the emperor and the empress land on the piazza San Marco while the crowd stands in icy silence. The film emphasizes the rejection by the Italians, which is not lost on the imperial couple. But suddenly Elisabeth sees her little daughter, whom she has missed for so long, standing among the crowd. She forgets etiquette and the political situation, hurries towards her and takes her into her arms. A cry of '*Viva la mamma!* comes from the crowd. The spell is broken; the mood changes: Italian critics of Austrian domination turn into ardent supporters of the empress who, in fact, has the same feelings as, and is just like, every young mother. It is evident that the German audience of the 1950s was open to the message that historical and political problems – in this case showing responsibility for the past – can be solved in the private realm, within the family, and in a gender role consistent with motherliness.

Although German society changed during the 1960s and 1970s, the *Sissi* films were not forgotten. Over more than three generations the fairytale of the sweet, noble Cinderella of the Austrian imperial throne embodied by Romy Schneider has been kept alive in the hearts of girls and teenagers. The sustained presence of the Sissi films on German TV has certainly contributed to this. Since

1967 there has been no Christmas TV schedule without the *Sissi* films, and satellite and cable TV make it possible to watch *Sissi* several times a year.[16]

Marischka's *Sissi* films are amongst the most-shown German films on TV. Although the films are met with derision by film critics and have been deemed in film guides as 'pretentious rubbish for simpletons',[17] 'royal kitsch for the soul' and *Kaiserschmarrn,*[18] the films still have an audience. Internet forums, however, indicate that current responses to the films are controversial. The comments range from '*Sissi* films are the best on the market' to 'Gee! What cheap rubbish' and 'the *Sissi* films offer a distorted picture of history. But never mind, those who enjoy heart, soul and sugar-sweet kitsch in noble décor and costumes, are served excellently by these films'.[19] By early 2007, 972 people had rated *Sissi* (1955) on the internet movie database (Imdb), giving it an average of 6.7 on a scale of 10.[20] But apart from the rating, internet forums show that the *Sissi* films also have young viewers. It is indicative that attempts to demystify the Sissi myth have failed. *Sissi and the Emperor's Kiss*, for example, produced in 1991, was a box-office flop. The various DVD editions available on the English and German-speaking market also show that there is still an audience for Marischka's *Sissi* films.[21]

Sissi Mania II and the Changing Picture of Sissi

It may be due to the lasting influence of the films, maybe also to the boom often triggered by anniversaries, but since the centennial of Elisabeth's death in 1998 publications have poured down on readers. In general they are nothing more than varied versions of the biographies of Corti and Hamann. 'Is there anything more exciting than experiencing interesting historical characters in their daily life "at close range"? To watch them like people of flesh and blood in their most intimate moments, so to say "through the keyhole?" For example, Elisabeth, Empress of Austria. Dealing with this very "modern" women is a major adventure, even 100 years after she died', the cover of a recent publication claims (Reisinger 1998). Again and again the empress's alleged desire for emancipation and her Cinderella-like story are evoked. It has also become popular to construct similarities between the hapless lives of Elisabeth and the Princess of Wales. 'She was the yardstick for the royal rebels who followed her, especially for the late Diana, Princess of Wales' (Sinclair 2000: 7).[22] The many attempts to use the Austrian empress as a projection screen for people's fantasies were met by the trustees of Elisabeth's memory by an effort to correct the portrait of Sissi on the one hand and with effective marketing measures on the other. In 2004, in the imperial apartments of the Hofburg in Vienna, a Sissi museum was opened which attempts to contrast the so-called 'myth' – not just 'legend' – with 'historical reality'.[23] Although there have also been attempts at serious historiographical research into the Austrian empress, the wave of Sissi mania since the end of the 1990s has not really resulted in new insights (Vogel 1992; Amtmann 1998).

Sissi mania reached a new climax with the premiere of the hitherto most successful German musical *Elisabeth* in Vienna in 1992. The musical, with a libretto by Michael Kunze and music by Sylvester Levay, centres on the tension between Elisabeth's desire for freedom and her longing for death. Elisabeth sings: 'I do not want to be obedient, tamed and well-behaved; I do not want to be modest, popular and betrayed; I am not your property, because I only belong to myself' (Kunze and Levay 1993: 15–20). 'By stylizing personified death her life-long companion, the musical also gives an esoteric-morbid response to conditions at the turn of the millennium which are marked by gender conflict and an increasing inability to keep up close relations' (Exner 2004: 140). The musical has had more success than any other musical in German and has been performed in several countries;[24] to date it has been watched by more than 8 million visitors worldwide. In Japan it has even been adapted for dance. Titled *Elisabeth: Ai To Shi No Rondo* ('Elisabeth: a dance between life and death'), it has been part of the repertoire of the Japanese Takarazuka Revue since 1996. In this adaptation death is the main character; he appears in almost every scene and has his own song. In this production the Sissi legend seems to have been brought to a consistent end. In what way will future adaptations bring Elisabeth back to historical life?

Explanations

'There has hardly been a destiny, a life of suffering, a life-long unfulfilled longing for happiness which has in the same way prompted the stage-managing of romantic and tragic, trivial and profound stories as the life of Elisabeth' (Becker 2001: 413–14). We can summarize a number of different versions of Elisabeth's life that have circulated in different media:

- the romantic middle-class fairytale of the Sissi films of the 1950s;
- the Elisabeth of modern historical biographies who condenses futile desires for emancipation and self-realization;
- and, taking up again elements of Greek tragedy, the Elisabeth who flirts with death in the musical and dance productions.

As these versions are contradictory, a mono-causal explanation of the 'reception and impact history' (*Wirkungsgeschichte*) of Elisabeth is inadequate. It seems reasonable to assume that the attractiveness of fairytales about a queen comes from the longing of the public for royal splendour and an ideal world, a world, in which good triumphs. It also seems reasonable to interpret the fascination with power and the mourning for lost freedom for which Elisabeth also stands as a mirror of the tragedy of 'the conditions of modern middle-class societies' (ibid.: 414). But when there is no higher aim than a body-cult and egocentrism then all the attempts to fight for individual freedom and self-realization one can arguably detect in Elisabeth's life become meaningless and the longing for freedom – one of the key terms of bourgeois society – is in danger of becoming banal and trivial. This danger can be seen in the latest dance and musical interpretations. They stage Elisabeth's longing for death and thus give her once again a tragic aura, something which is apparently – still or again and again – fascinating.

It might be that death is the only tragic motive the audience can agree upon in a pluralistic world in which anything goes with regard to values. But I would like to conclude by suggesting that the core of the fascination with Elisabeth – in addition to the attractiveness of power and royal splendour – lies in the fact that an ambiguous character who cannot be easily understood can be used as a projection screen onto which can be cast anything for which there is demand in the popular occupation with historical matters.

Notes

1. Sisi is the traditional spelling of Elisabeth's nick-name, but especially since Marischka's 1950s biopic entitled *Sissi* this spelling is the most popular and therefore preferred here.
2. Google search, 30 January 2007.
3. Märklin model number HO 4890.029.
4. The singer and musical performer Ross Antony is the official ambassador of the donation campaign; Antony played Crown-Prince Rudolf in the Stuttgart production of the musical *Elisabeth* (of which, more below). See: http://www.musicalfriends-stuttgart.net/html/23_5__play-sissi.html. Retrieved 30 August 2008.
5. See: http://www.passau.de/public_main_modul.php?bm=&unit=4676b519ef205&ses=&document_id=371. Retrieved 30 January 2007.
6. Brockhaus Enzyklopädie. 2007. 'Elisabeth von Österreich', *Brockhaus Enzyklopädie Online*. Retrieved 30 January 2007 from: http://www.brockhaus-enzyklopaedie.de.
7. *Österreichische Forst- und Jagd-Zeitung*, 16 September 1898.
8. There are also numerous monuments that were erected soon after Elisabeth's death: see Kassal-Mikula (1987: 82ff).
9. Reclams Universal Bibliothek published several biographies by Clara Tschudi, such as biographies of King Ludwig II of Bavaria, Queen Maria Sophia of Naples, the French Empress Eugenie, Marie Antoinette, and Napoleon's mother and son. Tschudi's biography of Elisabeth was well known, and Reclam published at least two editions for a broad German-speaking readership.
10. Corti also used a number of reports by eyewitnesses (e.g., Heyden-Rynsch 1983). Meanwile, further excerpts of Elisabeth's unpublished works have appeared; see Hamann (1984).
11. Before Hamann's biography was published there were some other attempts at biographies: see, e.g., the literary version by Barbara Cartland (1959) or the historical biography by Joan Haslip (1965) which was published in many editions. Haslip's biography, however, added only minor aspects from an English perspective – references to Elisabeth's visit to England – to the well-known facts.
12. See the film listing in Kraus-Kautzky (1987).
13. The play deals with the period between 16 and 18 August 1853 and concerns the falling

in love of Franz Joseph and Elisabeth. There were other stage adaptations too: see. e.g., the play by Georg Rendl, *Elisabeth, Kaiserin von Österreich* (1935).

14. See plot summary on the internet movie database (imdb), http://www.imdb.com/title/tt0283213/. Retrieved 30 August 2008.

15. See: http://www.teletoon.com/Games/Sissi/eng/index2.htm. Retrieved 30 January 2007.

16. The TV channels ARD, SAT.1, ORF 2 and SF 2 have all shown the Sissi trilogy once a year recently.

17. See *Lexikon des internationalen Films*. Munich: Systhema. 1999, p. 5129.

18. Adolf Heinzlmeier; Berndt Schulz: *Lexikon der deutschen Film- und TV-Stars*. Schwarzkopf & Schwarzkopf, 2000, p.321. *Kaiserschmarrn* is the name of a dish popular in the region of the Austro–Hungarian Empire; *Schmarrn* also means 'nonsense, rubbish' – i.e., *Kaiserschmarrn*, 'royal rubbish'.

19. Contributions #10054, #21683 und #21684 see: http://www.new-video.de/f-forum-sissi. Retrieved 30 January 2007.

20. See http://www.imdb.com/title/tt0048624/. Retrieved 30 August 2008.

21. These were released on DVD in 1998. New DVD editions by different companies followed in 2001 and 2003, and in 2005 a limited, three-disc 'royal' edition was released.

22. See, e.g., Boscontri (1998), Daimler (1998) and Mayer and Vogl (1998).

23. The term *Mythos Sisi* is used by Unterreiner (2001).

24. *Elisabeth* ran in Vienna in the 1990s and again between 2003 and 2005. There were further productions in Japan (Osaka, 1996), Hungary (Szeged, Budapest, 1992–), Sweden (Karlstad, 1999), the Netherlands (Scheveningen, 1999/2000), Germany (Essen 2001–2003; Stuttgart, 2005–2006), Finland (Turku, 2005) and Switzerland (Thun, 2006).

11

Scientists as Heroes? Einstein, Curie and the Popular Historiography of Science

Beate Ceranski

In 2005, Germans encountered Albert Einstein virtually everywhere. The jubilee of his *annus mirabilis*, 1905, when he published three epochal discoveries, among them the special theory of relativity, brought Einstein to the title pages of all major journals and magazines. A government campaign using the physicist's quotations and portrait encouraged Germans to become actively involved in cultural, scientific and public life. People queued for hours at the entrance of an Einstein exhibition at the famous Kronprinzenpalais, Berlin, which was one of several important exhibitions about the scientist. Official activities like the Festakt of the German physics society (Deutsche Physikalische Gesellschaft) and the scientific activities of this World Year of Physics were joined by broad media coverage of this most famous of all physicists. The omnipresence of Einstein in Germany in 2005 demonstrated that science and scientists can succeed splendidly in figuring as subjects of popular historiography. The latter, on the other hand, has been connected intimately and almost exclusively with biographical literature. Most interestingly, the unfaltering success of the biographical genre within popular historiography has led recently to a renaissance of biography in the academic historiography of science. Among recent publications (e.g., Söderqvist 2007), a leading international journal published a special issue on biography that clearly acknowledged its indebtedness to the enduring popularity of the biographical genre (Jo Nye 2006).

In this chapter I will explore the characteristics and historical development of the popular historiography of science by looking at the cases of Albert Einstein (1879–1955) and Marie Curie (1867–1934). Both are the subjects of a considerable body of pertinent literature which allows us to situate popular historiography within historiographic as well as more general cultural contexts. Furthermore, a look at the cases of Curie and Einstein raises the question of gender. An analysis of the biographical literature on Einstein and Curie respectively is the subject of the main part of this paper. Both Einstein and Curie, however, became famous in their lifetimes so that historiography, popular and academic alike, was not a wholly posthumous endeavour. Both scientists actively developed their own relationship with the media, contributed to their own image and thereby also laid the foundations for what would become their popular biography. I will argue that, at least as far as the twentieth century is concerned, the analysis of the popular historiography of science inevitably leads back to the public image developed by scientists (or their close friends) themselves. I will conclude my paper with some reflections on the relationship between the popular and academic historiography of science.

The Changing Faces of Popularity: The Popular Historiography of Albert Einstein

When Einstein died in 1955 he had been world famous for more than three decades, though he had published his first truly revolutionary work fifty years beforehand while working as a clerk at the patent office in Bern. The special theory of relativity and the other research he published in 1905 was widely accepted by 1910, and after short stays as a professor in Zurich and Prague Einstein received a generous offer from the Berlin Academy of Sciences in 1913. At this time he was working on his theory of general relativity which took him until 1915 to complete. Only a few people knew about it and Einstein repeatedly tried in vain to have astronomers search for the small astronomical effects predicted by his theory. Soon after arriving in Berlin, Einstein's wife Mileva and two sons returned to Zurich although the couple divorced only in 1919. A few weeks after the divorce Einstein married his cousin Elsa with whom he had had an affair since 1912. His fame came out of the blue (or rather the black) in the same year as a British solar eclipse expedition confirmed the very feeble displacement of light in the sun's gravity field. When the Royal Society, in November 1919, officially announced that the effect predicted by Einstein's general theory of relativity had indeed been observed, he became famous all over the world virtually over night. The mysteries of the 'relativity of space and time' aroused the attention of the press. The fact that this sophisticated theory, requiring advanced mathematical techniques, was comprehensible to very few scientists only added to its attraction. From 1920 onwards Einstein began lecturing all over the world and from 1921 he actively supported the Zionist cause. Einstein, who had been a lonely pacifist during the First World War, also committed himself to the causes of pacifism and international cooperation – with the single exception of his signature on the famous letter that started the American atomic bomb project. As his fame rose, however, opposition was not far behind. In 1920 Einstein had to deal with an ugly 'anti-relativistic movement' which garnered considerable attention in the press and caused some uproar at the conference of German physicians and scientists in September

1920. Though this movement was supported by only a tiny minority of physicists it added to Einstein's uneasiness with the political and ideological situation in the German physics community and society. In 1933 he accepted a professorship at the Institute for Advanced Study at Princeton and left Germany forever. For the rest of his life he searched in vain for a general theory uniting both gravitational and electromagnetic effects. When he died in 1955 his last important scientific work was exactly thirty years old. But his repeated announcements (and withdrawals) of the general theory, as well as his political activities, had kept his name and his fame alive.

It is, therefore, hardly surprising that a steady stream of historiographic literature began to emerge during his lifetime. Beginning with the biography by the Austrian physicist Philipp Frank (1949), there were at least half a dozen books about Einstein published before his death in 1955 and a similar number in the following decade (Highfield and Carter 1993). The authors of the first generation of books were related to Einstein in one way or another and drew on personal knowledge and that of their contemporaries.[1] They included former colleagues, assistants or (remote) relatives as well as journalists who had got to know Einstein. These authors usually do not indicate their sources, employ the first person singular and speak from their position as an eyewitness. One can differentiate two strands in this literature. One renounces all scientific details and rather presupposes than explains the importance of Einstein's achievements. A lively example is to be found in the book by Antonina Vallentin (1955).[2] A professional writer and translator, Vallentin got to know Einstein's second wife Elsa and wrote her book as an easy-to-read conversation concentrating upon the human sides of her subject. The other type of popular literature on Einstein – written by colleagues, assistants or successors – provides both a narrative of Einstein's life and an introduction to his thinking. The book by Einstein's personal assistant Banesh Hoffmann, written in collaboration with Einstein's long-time secretary Helen Dukas, is an excellent example in this genre (Hoffmann and Dukas 1972).

From the very first books on Einstein to the most recent publications, we thus observe a structure typical of, and peculiar to, the popular historiography of science when compared to other fields of historiography: Popularization can (but need not) include more than one layer. Besides the portrait of lives and times, the web of contexts and circumstances, it may include the popularization of scientific results. Where, for example, the intricacies of polite etiquette in the German courts may be taught in passing and with some amusement to the reader, the exposition of scientific results quickly reaches a complexity that requires considerable length and detail of explanation, and of effort on the reader's side. Needless to say, this popularization of science can only be carried out successfully by those with expert knowledge of the relevant field. Moreover, it also requires the readers' willingness to read more slowly and to reflect more deeply in order to understand (as far as they can within a limited time) not only the people and developments concerned but also the science itself. As far as I can see, the number of such popular historiographies of science published is declining rather than rising, probably because these books are far more difficult to read and, therefore, to sell.[3]

This development, however, is counterbalanced by another which deeply affects the historiography of science. With a growing realization of the need for scientific literacy, as well as a need for more science students, the explanation of scientific achievements has received major attention within both museums and temporary exposition projects such as the Expo fairs. Moreover, ever-expanding technical means have provided a much more attractive way of exhibiting scientific research; for example, relativity theory can be more easily explained using computer simulations and film than in printed texts alone. Coming back to Einstein, all major expositions in 2005 devoted considerable attention to Einstein's physics and, in some cases, to Einstein's legacy today. In doing so – as, for example, the Deutsche Museum in Munich explicitly did – they followed a trend that has influenced science and technology museums in recent years.[4]

Independent of their devotion to physics, all early Einstein biographies depict the image of a 'perfectly simple' man whose character has not been compromised by glory or vanity (ibid.: 11). His revolutionary scientific ideas stand in stark contrast to his apparently childlike innocence in worldly matters, such as socks and haircuts, food and money, thus eliciting in the reader both admiration and sympathy. There is no flaw in this creator (of a new attitude towards time and space) and rebel (against old scientific concepts as well as nationalism and McCarthyism). All the biographies use positive adjectives throughout and describe Einstein in terms of a genius. In those books dealing with his scientific work his personal life is mentioned only in passing; in the others (e.g., Vallentin 1955) Einstein is also described in terms of his home and family circle: his wife Elsa and daughters Ilse and Margot.

Beginning in the 1970s, this idyllic picture was destroyed, though not by investigative journalists from the tabloid press but by serious scholars of the then new discipline of the history of science. Einstein had bequeathed his papers and copyrights to the Hebrew University in Jerusalem but had entrusted his friend and economic counsellor Otto Nathan, and his secretary Helen Dukas, with the immediate trusteeship and entitlement to all copyright royalties as long as they lived. Dukas and Nathan, for their part, were probably more conscious of Einstein's honour and public image than Einstein himself had ever been (Highfield and Carter 1993). This situation led to serious conflicts with Einstein's son, Hans Albert. He and his wife had come into possession of Einstein's letters to his first wife, Mileva Maric, from which could be drawn quite a different picture of Einstein's character. They wanted to publish excerpts of these letters as well as some of the correspondence between Hans Albert and his father but the manuscript had to be withdrawn. Dukas and Nathan also sued the editors of Einstein's collected papers, the preparation of which had begun in the 1970s (ibid.: 349). Though Dukas and Nathan could not in the end prevent the publication of Einstein's letters and papers, their relentless activities ensured a long delay. The first volume of Einstein's *Collected Papers*, arranged in chronological order and therefore concerning his early years, appeared only after the death of Nathan in 1987 (see Einstein 1987).[5]

In Einstein historiography, this publication of sources on the young Einstein marks the watershed in both popular and academic discussion. Ironically, the delay brought about by Nathan and Dukas was probably the precise cause of the vigorous effect of the publication. Inspired by the second women's movement of the 1970s, the historiography of science – both academic and popular – had, by the 1980s, turned its attention to the question of gender and science with the explicit aim of laying open the patriarchal and unjust political and historical treatment of women and women's achievements in the sciences (Fox Keller 1983; Alic 1985). When the first volume of Einstein's papers appeared in 1987, Einstein's letters to Mileva Maric, his first wife, found an exceedingly interested audience. The 'love letters', as they soon became known (see Einstein and Maric 1992), not only revealed new facets of the private Einstein, they also raised questions about whether and how much Mileva had contributed to Albert's theory of special relativity. Feminist magazines dubbed Mileva 'the mother of relativity theory' (Rauch 1990) and major quality newspapers such as the renowned weekly *ZEIT* discussed the subject in their pages. Even if the overwhelming majority of authors was not persuaded of Maric's importance to Einstein's work no serious author could ignore her any longer. From the 1990s on, every Einstein book, be it academic or popular, had to deal with Mileva and find its own position. With the availability of Albert's letters to her – both the early intimate ones and, as the publication of the Einstein papers went on, the later hostile, even brutal, ones – the image of Einstein underwent severe reconstruction. Einstein came to be seen no longer as a scientific genius whose personal life did not matter but as a scientific genius with severe deficits in other – emotional and social – respects. Alongside the discussion of Mileva, the couple's children came into focus and evoked pressing questions concerning Albert's responsibilities as father.

The Einstein hype in 2005 further radicalized the image of Albert Einstein's personal life. Now his adulterous behaviour towards his second wife Elsa was added to that towards his first wife Mileva. The question which (and how many) women had been Einstein's lovers became one of the recurring themes in recent popular historiography.[6] I see this preoccupation as an intense appropriation of Einstein's personal life which is intimately related to the tabloid press behaviour towards prominent contemporaries. It resonates perfectly with other spectacular extra-scientific aspects of his person, such as his CIA file and the fate of his brain.[7] The Einstein of today, in short, is still the 'inventor of time and space'[8] but he is also a contradictory and not always lovable person whose apparent perfection has been compromised by the unrelenting activities of biographers, journalists and historians. The beautiful simplicity of the 'creator and rebel' of the early biographies has long gone.

Remarkably, Einstein is also the subject of a new literary form of popular historiography. With the expansion of the Einstein 'industry' in 2005 we can observe what one might call at first sight a topographic turn, one perfectly in tune with developments in academic historiography. Books on Einstein in Berlin (Hoffmann 2006) and Bern (Hentschel and Grasshoff 2005) concentrate on a certain period of Einstein's life connected to a particular city. Combining historical and tourist background information with short chapters on sites related to the life of the physicist, they invite us to walk literally in Einstein's footsteps. Providing city maps and, in the elaborate example of Bern, signposts and signs on streets and buildings, such books are perfect for the scientific tourist. What might at first seem a consequence of the sheer growth and differentiation of the Einstein industry thus reveals itself as a genre superbly adapted to our contemporary leisure society. Moreover, this genre does not require hundreds of pages of concentrated reading but small units of easy-to-digest, colourful information.

Einstein has also been adapted for younger readers. Besides the classical biography we also find other formats, such as a historical mystery for children with a lot of historical background information provided in the last part of the book (Rodik 2006). This book is part of a successful series of historical mysteries for children. Characteristically, this story around a theft of Einstein's manuscript was the first one when the series was expanded towards the history of science – together with a story around Leonardo da Vinci. Einstein and Leonardo were those scientists whom the publisher obviously regarded as the most attractive for this new series.[9]

Concluding this sketch of 'the popular Einstein' it is finally worthwhile having a look at Einstein in other media. This adds another important facet to our subject. Einstein figures explicitly or implicitly in a variety of genres, from romantic comedies to strategy computer games.[10] The most remarkable fact is the identification of Einstein as a scientist in films or works of art, as well as the abundant use of his portrait in advertising campaigns.[11] The use of his portrait on popular encyclopedias and science books also testifies to his iconic status as a scientist. Drawing out the lines of popular historiography one can easily identify the elements that made Albert Einstein such an attractive icon: his dealing with the most fundamental entities of time and space, his outspoken political (mostly pacifist) attitude, and, last but not least, his unconventional appearance.

Popularity through Tragedy? The Popular Historiography of Marie Curie

While there are numerous books about Albert Einstein, none of which came to dominate his public image, the biographical landscape concerning Marie Curie is dominated by a single and singularly successful book. In 1937, Eve Curie – Marie Curie's 33-year-old youngest daughter – published *Madame Curie* which became both an immediate and enduring success (see Curie 1938). It has been translated into more than thirty languages, among them English, Spanish, German and Norwegian as well as Arabic and Hebrew, with many of these published soon after the book's first appearance, and the book still appears in new editions today. It has been the basis of film productions, abbreviated for Reader's Digest and adapted for children, inspiring hundreds and thousands of children and adults alike.

Eve Curie, who had been Marie's constant companion in the last months of her life, managed to publish this book, her first publication, within four years of Marie Curie's death (Curie 1938). Quoting amply from family documents, among them letters from Marie to her family in Poland which were subsequently destroyed in the Second World War, she depicts Marie Curie as a brave, tragic heroine. Indeed, Marie Curie's life lent itself easily to an exciting and romantic story. From the many difficulties she had to overcome in her native Poland before studying in Paris to the romantic love story between her and fellow physicist Pierre Curie, and from their successful work on radio-activity – a word coined by Marie Curie in 1898 – to the Nobel Prize for physics in 1903, her story is that of a dream come true. When the tragic death of her husband Pierre shattered this life, Marie struggled to obtain a laboratory and continue their work. The most difficult period in her life began in 1910 when she applied for membership of the Académie des Sciences in Paris. Conservative and Catholic forces initiated a hostile campaign against a woman's membership and Curie became the object of several ugly newspaper articles. The situation was further aggravated when, in 1911, a love affair between Curie and the married physicist Paul Langevin was made public. At this point Curie was to be awarded the Nobel Prize a second time – for chemistry in 1911 – but the Swedish academy asked her to renounce the prize because of the Langevin affair (Blanc 1999). Curie did accept the prize but the relentless public campaign against her led to a severe breakdown from which she recovered only slowly. By her fearless and untiring medical work in the First World War – Curie invented and used mobile X-ray machines to help wounded soldiers – the French public became reconciled with her and the 1920s became a period of worldwide fame for Marie Curie. When she died in 1934 she had seen her daughter and successor Irène Joliot-Curie make another major discovery which would bring her own Nobel Prize the year following Marie's death. No wonder then that the first of several films of Curie's life, full of struggles and achievements, love and bereavement, appeared in 1943.[12]

In Eve Curie's representation of her mother's eventful life, the overarching theme is the deep loneliness which characterized both Marie Curie's youth and her mature years. The Curie we come to see through Eve's eyes suffered loneliness in the years she served as a governess in order to enable her elder sister Bronia to study medicine in Paris; she sought loneliness when studying at the Sorbonne, becoming 'a pitiful and incurably lonely woman' (Curie 1938: 247) for the rest of her life when her husband Pierre Curie died from an accident in 1906, aged 46, when Eve Curie was only eighteen-months old. She stayed singularly solitary even 'in the storm of acclamations' (ibid.: 348). This utter loneliness was only lifted (or rather suspended) during her tragically short ten-year marriage to Pierre Curie, which is represented as a beautiful and coherent union of conjugal love and a mutual love of science. Consequently, more than in any other period of her life, Marie the wife is depicted as a person juggling her various responsibilities. Readers are presented with a Marie who coped – not without effort, but successfully – with her various roles and achieved a beautiful unity between family life and scientific work.[13] If anybody was harmed by this it was never her husband or her children or her scientific work but Marie herself, who overburdened herself. And if she suffered it was not for lack of strength in the impassioned struggles with nature in their poor laboratory, but because of those 'other struggles', both she and Pierre were obliged to fight (ibid.). Eve Curie's biography focuses on the point of view of Marie Curie herself, who throughout the book is usually called by her first name only. Its poetic language, together with frequent quotations from letters and the diary Marie kept after Pierre's death, draws readers very closely to the book's subject and invites identification with the struggles and victories, joys and sorrows of the person it depicts. Marie is not only the protagonist, she is a heroine. The Marie Curie that emerges from this book – flawless and saintly to the point of frustration – drew hundreds and thousands of people into its story, whether they were interested in science or not.

In this respect it is interesting to observe that students in a class I taught recently reacted equivocally towards the book. Most of them felt deeply repelled by the supposed perfection of Marie Curie and argued that such a person was both highly improbable as well as unpleasant. The saga of a lonely and sacrificial devotion to science seems no longer to spellbind young people. In criticizing the overwhelmingly perfect protagonist my students unconsciously expressed the basic historiographic tenet that people of each period need and write their own (popular) historiography. Thus, the heyday of Eve's hagiographic portrait of Marie Curie may come to an end. However, in contrast to Einstein, it is not yet clear what the future image of Marie Curie will be like.

Quite remarkably, Eve Curie did not write the biography from the point of view of a daughter but from a neutral third-person perspective. This seemingly objective and impersonal stance is broken in only a few instances where Eve figures as an eyewitness (ibid.: 366, 382). Recently, this has been interpreted as a sign of emotional distance between mother and daughter (Goldsmith 2005: 146). However, in my opinion Eve Curie may very well have chosen this detachment in order not to undermine the book by using an all too obvious family perspective. Eve Curie – and probably her sister Irène too – was desperately determined to bring to light the 'true' story of her mother, who in her life had been both the darling and the villain of the press. More than fifty years after writing the book, Eve Curie said that it was important to her and her sister that they prevent anyone else from writing about her mother who might not 'get it right' (Quinn 1995: 14; Goldsmith 2005: 145). In view of the fact that critical voices commented bitingly upon Marie's simple funeral ceremony, Eve and Irène's concerns appear not at all far fetched. Throughout the book we get to know Marie Curie as a person who has deep personal feelings but who is (with the exception of her relationship to Pierre Curie) incapable of showing them. Eve Curie may have written her biography to show this hidden side of her mother's apparently cold personality, which was commented upon even by friendly colleagues like Einstein who, in a letter to his cousin Elsa, described her as 'the soul of a herring, which means that she is poor when it comes to the art of joy and pain' (Einstein 1993: 554). At this point in time Einstein was courting Elsa, so he may have described Marie in such a way to avoid jealousy on the part of his cousin. Einstein's judgement has been widely cited, especially in the popular Einstein historiography (e.g., Hermann 1994: 198) and thus contributed to the Curie image. However, it is even more probable that Eve Curie wrote her book in order to avoid any reference to the Langevin affair in the public memory of her mother. What had broken Marie Curie's health and happiness forever would not be allowed to taint her image ever after. This opinion is strongly supported by the fact that the Curie papers were closed after the publication of Eve's book. Thus, for several decades no other biographer was able to draw a different or even supplementary portrait. The tragic and superhuman Madame Curie prevailed.

If it had been Eve Curie's intention to cover up the Langevin affair, she was reasonably successful. It took more than thirty years before the affair became part of the Curie story. The English-speaking audience had to wait until the 1970s, when Robert Reid's biography appeared (Reid 1974), but it was only in 1981 that the French journalist Françoise Giroud published a detailed account of the Langevin affair (Giroud 1981). These books added a great deal to knowledge about Marie Curie, yet they did not seem to alter her image permanently. Revealing a love affair in the 1970s had quite a different effect to doing so in the 1930s. All major biographies written after 1975 include a chapter on the Langevin affair, stressing, among other things, its role in forming Marie's reclusive behaviour. It is precisely in their dealing with the Langevin affair that we can follow the deep dependency of popular historiography upon larger social and cultural contexts. In the most recent literature the story has taken another fascinating turn. Not only is Curie's image no longer endangered by speaking about her affair with a married man, but it is precisely the Langevin affair that renders Curie more sympathetic to the audience. She is all the more 'at once human and heroic' (Quinn 1995: 16; Strathern 1999: 76) because – not although – she succumbed to an unwise love affair. In spite of the twists and turns the historiography of Marie Curie has taken since Eve Curie's book, she is still cast in the model of a heroine, a person inviting emotional commitment and identification.

Since the biography was written immediately after her mother's death, Eve's sister Irène Joliot-Curie had no opportunity to take part in it, even if she had wished to author or co-author it. The mid 1930s was a particularly exciting and busy time in the Curie laboratory, of which she had become director. In 1934, shortly before Marie's death, Irène and her husband discovered the phenomenon of artificial radioactivity and together – or rather in competition – with laboratories in Rome and Berlin they were frantically busy in the new field. Consequently, Marie Curie's scientific achievements were treated accurately but superficially in her first and most influential biography, 'a sentimental romance by the wrong daughter' as a professional historian of science has put it (Badash 1975: 566). Eve Curie's biography concentrated heavily on radium, thereby neglecting both Marie's groundbreaking early conceptual and procedural contributions to the new science of radioactivity as well as the importance of her laboratory as a place of reference over the next few decades.[14] The concentration upon radium is more easily understood if one remembers that at the time of Eve Curie's book radium cures were highly fashionable and radium held the place of the most promising and most mysterious of all elements. It is therefore no great wonder that virtually all scientific achievements were overshadowed by the story of its discovery. Many years later, Irène wrote a detailed study of her parents' laboratory notebooks (Joliot-Curie 1955) which showed the intricacy and sophistication of their work. This, however, never became part of *Marie Curie*.[15]

In contrast to Einstein, Marie Curie was subject of a popular biography which was not written by a scientist and did not popularize her science. Instead, it focused on her dramatic life story and the strength of her personality despite difficult circumstances. Even more than in the treatment of her personal life, this seminal biography set the trend for later books. It was not until Susan Quinn's monumental biography (Quinn 1995) that one could read a comprehensive description of Marie's (early) work on radioactivity, including her arguments with other scientists regarding polonium. Finally, her work after the First World War is not prominent even in the latest popular books, which focus on laboratory building and laboratory administration but fail to discuss the subjects of research. Curie's journeys to America in the 1920s clearly play the most important role in the treatment of her life after the war. Interestingly, it is precisely within academic historiography that an adequate description and judgement of her work was long prevented by clichés that appear to have sprung from the tabloid press:

> Marie Curie's laboratory in Paris continued to be haunted by her husband's ghost ... Mme. Curie was a woman overwhelmed with grief, a burden ... which she had to bear for nearly thirty years, sweeping in corners and tidying up the details of radioactivity ... Marie Curie had become a slave to the past, expending great efforts on the isolation of polonium and towards perpetuating the memory of her husband's work. (Malley 1976: 146–47; cf. Badash 1975)

Only very recently have new approaches in the historiography of science permitted one to see Marie Curie's work as a very specific and highly purposeful strategy which made her laboratory a centre of radioactivity research far beyond purely 'academic' questions, if such ever existed (Boudia and Roqué 1997;

Ceranski 2005). The amassing of radium and polonium was not just Curie's personal whim but constituted a resource. The Nobel Prize-winning discovery of artificial radioacitivity, for example, was possible only because of the unique polonium preparations in Curie's laboratory, which constituted the best alpha-ray source available in the world. Thus, more than thirty years after Curie's personal life was brought to full light, academic historiography has finally opened up a new avenue for the consideration of her work as well (see Boudia 2001).

The Roots of Popularity: Einstein, Curie, the Public and the Media

When the first books on Einstein and Curie appeared, their personae were already well fixed in the public's consciousness. Both were international renowned celebrities and both had repeatedly toured the U.S. in the 1920s. In the case of Marie Curie, fame went back further, to 1903 when she and her husband received the Nobel Prize. In late 1903 the image of the self-sacrificing scientist was born:

> The image propagated was not only linked to the person of Marie Curie, however, for in the future the several themes of which it was composed – the pursuit of pure science for its own sake, the wondrous and totally unexpected results that might flow from such endeavours, and the struggle of the individual to overcome formidable obstacles – were to recur.... Here, a poignant image of the experimental scientist at work was forged by the descriptions of Marie Curie grinding down tons of pitchblende in order to extract a minute quantity of radium. (Crawford 1984: 194)

This image was readily confirmed by Marie Curie herself. In her 1923 biography of her husband, Pierre Curie, which she supplemented with a short autobiographical note, she stresses their miserable working conditions and the hard labour she had to invest in her research over and over again. Moreover, she also explicitly stated that she and Pierre had renounced a patent on the production process for radium in order not to prevent scientific progress (Curie 1923: 92). Thus the virtue of disinterestedness added to that of hard work and poverty. It was this image which was taken to the U.S. and made both fund raising and her trip in 1921 singularly successful. American women were strongly moved by this pure soul and her tragic life. They contributed enough money to endow first Curie herself and later the Polish radium institute with the huge amount of one gram of radium salt for each. But fame and money came at a price. In the U.S. Curie was pursued by the press, which she did not like at all. Soon she was so exhausted by the programme of engagements prepared for her that she had to give a considerable number of her appointments to her daughters accompanying her. And if she had hoped in turn to open-up scientific careers for women in the U.S. by her visit, these hopes proved ambivalent at best. Although the number of American women studying in the sciences grew considerably after Curie's visit, this did not lead to women gaining top career positions in the sciences (Rossiter 1993: 129; Quinn 1995: 396). For her fame, her laboratory and her country of birth, however, Curie's intense interaction with the American public, mediated through American journals, proved most satisfactory. Not the least result was her being asked to write a biography of Pierre Curie for the American public (Curie 1923). This proved to be a singular opportunity to tell people about his and their lives without exposing herself to the criticism of self-publicity. The miserable conditions and hard work mentioned above, which Marie Curie depicted here, were later repeated and expanded by Eve Curie in her own biography of her mother. In this way they determined the image of the Curies for more than half a century in what has to be regarded as a quite successful self-fashioning.

It is a fascinating parallel that Albert Einstein and his second wife Elsa travelled to the U.S. in the same months of late spring 1921 as the Curie women. Just as the American journalist Mary Meloney had coaxed Curie to visit North America, Einstein succumbed to the wishes of someone else. He accompanied Chaim Weizmann on a fundraising journey devoted to the Zionist project for a Hebrew university in Jerusalem. The rich press material, now available in a beautiful collection (Illy 2006), constantly refers to Einstein as the creator of a theory which only half a dozen men in the U.S. could understand. Curie, in the same mood of exaggeration, had been introduced as the woman who had found a cure against cancer. Unlike Curie, Einstein gave many lectures in which he undertook to explain (a tiny bit of) his theory of relativity. But Einstein, even more so than Curie, also experienced the pitfalls of celebrity: when a Dutch journalist cited some of Einstein's less than flattering impressions of America, Einstein had to work hard for several days to soften the American public. Fame was a mighty helper as well as a dangerous companion, and Einstein learned much about both during this first big international visit.

Women and Men, Genius and Obsession: On the Justice of Popularity

There are a fascinating multitude of parallels in Einstein's and Curie's relation-ship with the public. Both had an ambiguous relationship to the public and media of their time. On the one hand both shunned public exposure – Curie by cold reticence, Einstein by a clownish attitude and by stressing repeatedly the importance of his thoughts as compared to his private life and his personality. On the other hand in the 1920s both sought the public – in both cases outside their home countries. Whereas Einstein used his reputation for Zionist, socialist and pacifist causes, Curie traded her public appearance for the material means of scientific and medical radium research. During her second visit to the U.S., the humanitarian agenda was strengthened by the final destination of the radium she obtained: it was given to the Polish radium institute to further research in Curie's country of birth. Because of their prominence both Curie and Einstein were strongly exposed to ugly campaigns during their lifetimes. After their death, those to whom they had been dear accordingly put their efforts into ensuring their image was untainted by impropriety or scandal: Dukas and Hoffmann prevented the publication of any of Einstein's early family letters which would have showed him in a light far from advantageous; and Eve Curie devoted three years of her life to the writing of her mother's biography lest somebody else might do it and expose the Langevin affair. In both cases restricted access to the sources played a key political role and the wealth of papers and letters open to researchers today give us a singular glimpse into these scientists' most intimate moments and relationships.

There are, however, differences as well. Whereas Einstein was exposed to hostile campaigns because of his scientific work and being Jewish, Curie at first suffered because she had dared to apply to the Académie des Sciences. In her case anti-semitic, xenophobic and, above all, misogynistic arguments were used against her.[16] Whereas Einstein's work was condemned as false and sterile – and defended by many friends and colleagues, both privately and publicly – Curie's work was threatened by attempts to ascribe it solely to Pierre Curie. The debate about who, in her partnership with her husband, was really responsible for the discoveries that the Curies made, an issue which Marie had to confront from 1910 onwards, only concerned Einstein posthumously in debates about the role of Mileva Maric in his scientific work. Popular historiography, fuelled by a growing awareness of the more subtle forms of the oppression of women, then created a new perspective which might appear to offer a kind of posthumous justice with regard to gender discriminations both in Marie Curie's and in Mileva (and Albert) Einstein's cases, although the virulence of both debates is not of the same scale.[17]

There is one other obvious difference with regard to gender issues. Curie's love affair with Pierre Langevin almost led to her losing her second Nobel Prize which means that her personal life threatened the acknowledgement of her scientific work. Einstein, on the other hand, never had to protect his work against condemnations of his private life (nor, incidentally, did Langevin). The Curie–Langevin case, as well as the Curie–Einstein comparison, follows the all too well-known pattern in history, according to which women were punished much harder than men for sexual relationships outside marriage. In this respect, as we have seen, the situation has profoundly changed. Today Curie's once unwise love affair is a subject of empathy in popular historiography. On the other hand side, Einstein's affairs, if not condemned, have been investigated to the last female visitor. In both cases the impact of these questions is limited: in popular as well as academic historiography private behaviour is no longer a battlefield for claiming or refuting scientific worth.

This is not to say, however, that concepts and clichés of gender difference are no longer at work. Looking at book titles we find specific and very different semantic fields related to the two scientists. Popular historiographic books, among them recent ones, dealing with Curie depict the Curies as 'the most controversial family in science' (Brian 2005) and Marie Curie as an 'obsessive genius' (Goldsmith 2005) driven by a 'grand obsession' (Pflaum 1989). By representing Curie's unrelenting quest for radium and radium research as an obsession – something which verges on illness and mental instability – she is subtly discredited as an exceptional yet not quite rational human being. Even if academic historiography has repeatedly and with growing emphasis insisted upon the importance of categories such as passion and obsession when capturing the lives of scientists (Jo Nye 2006: 324, 328), the distribution of this attribution is suspiciously asymmetrical: nobody ever called Einstein's futile thirty-five-year search for a unified theory of relativity an obsession in a book title; rather, Einstein is the 'chief engineer of the universe' (Renn 2005), and besides the still-frequent attribution of genius (Hoffmann 2006; Illy 2006) we find others of the same colour (Hermann 1994). I am inclined to regard these subtly gendered titles as indicative of the fact that Einstein and, even more so, Curie remain trapped in gendered clichés that have long dominated people's perception. And one thing is for sure: as long as the best-known male scientist to date is called a genius and the best-known woman scientist is called an obsessive there is still much to be done within popular historiography – and beyond.

Looking at the relationship between the popular and academic historiography of science, probably the most remarkable characteristic of the present situation is the self-conscious reflections of historians of science on their profession and their handicraft. This is related to two contrasting developments. On the one hand the academic historiography of science has become ever more informed by cultural studies. This growing sophistication has resulted in a vast ramification of approaches as well as the widespread use of jargon. The resulting loss of audiences inevitably leads to the question: For whom and why should the academic historiography of science be written? On the other hand, the history of science has fared remarkably well in the popular book market. When Dava Sobel's study of the eighteenth century clocksmith John Harrison (Sobel 1995) was awarded the British Book of the Year award in 1997, a serious dilemma for academic historians of science arose: Should they enjoy, despise or fear such a popular and successful book, written by a professional author on their own subject? What to do with the emphasis on heroic individuals? What to do with historian's thick descriptions, prosopographic studies and complex contexts? Answers have been manifold and may also have been influenced by gender issues (see Govoni 2005: 9–10). And whatever one might say, the history of science as a subject has certainly been changed by the 'Sobel effect' (ibid.). The explicit rehabilitation of biography as a legitimate genre for academic historiography is to be regarded as one major consequence of this process. Another conclusion that can be safely drawn from recent Einstein mania is the tremendous importance of the appropriation of the scientist's persona as a route to public attention. One of the publicly best-known German historians of science of the younger generation is working on the history of neurophysiology. The way in which he made it into the public's consciousness involved the history of Einstein's brain (Hagner 2004; see also K. Michel 2004).

Notes

1. For example, Philipp Frank was Einstein's successor at the University of Prague and had often discussed physics with Einstein during his Zurich years; Rudolf Kayser (who published under the pseudonym Anton Reiser) was married to Einstein's stepdaughter Ilse.
2. The book was first published in English in 1954.
3. This point refers mainly to the more popular literature. With regard to academic historiography, ongoing research in the development of Einstein's ideas has resulted in several excellent but highly technical publications accessible only to readers with considerable expertise in mathematics and physics.
4. A major example is Baden-Württemberg's central museum for the history of technology, industry and labour, the Landesmuseum für Technik und Arbeit in Mannheim), a conceptually and didactically ambitious and reformist museum project of the 1980s. A few years ago it created the first of what are now several sections with hands-on experiments only loosely related to the museum's historiographic agenda. Political pressure, the Pisa debate on better school training, especially in the natural sciences, and the constant need for high numbers of visitors all add to this broad reorientation.
5. Nathan died aged 87; Dukas died in 1982 aged 85.
6. See the magazine Focus 52 (2004).
7. *Focus* framed 'his true story' as 'the genius, the secret service, the diary, the women' (*Focus* 54, 2004).
8. *Der Spiegel* March 2005.
9. The series has continued, dealing with Darwin, Newton and Curie amongst others. In this section I refer to the German book market for young readers only.
10. See, e.g., Fred Schepsi's comedy *I.Q.* (1994) and the successful computer game *Red Alert* in the 'Command and Conquer' series (London: Virgin Interactive, 1996).
11. Figures like Dr. Know in Steven Spielberg's *Artificial Intelligence* (2001) are modelled on Einstein. The brand 'Albert Einstein' is sold by an American advertising agency and the Hebrew University of Jerusalem is entitled to all fees arising from these merchandising activities.
12. This was *Madame Curie*, directed by Mervyn LeRoy (1943). On the image of Curie in films, see Bensaude-Vincent (1994) and Elena (1997).
13. See, e.g., Curie (1938: 145), where the author, by using parallel sentences, establishes a coherent identity for the Marie Curie working in the laboratory and the Marie Curie preparing the meal; or where Marie is sitting in the laboratory and watching radium in an 'attitude which had been hers an hour earlier at the bedside of her sleeping child' (ibid.: 177).
14. For example, under Marie's directorship the Paris laboratory tackled the highly controversial experiments of the English chemist William Ramsay in 1908/9, which were

finally proved erroneous. One might interpret this and other instances as 'busywork' (Badash 1975: 567), but one might also read them as testimony to Curie's unique authority in the field.

15. Irène Joliot-Curie's study was instead published as an appendix to a revised edition of Marie Curie's short biography of Pierre Curie: see Joliot-Curie (1955).

16. Not only a sign of the times, the anti-semitic remarks are noteworthy because Curie was not even Jewish.

17. Those voices who point to the ironical fact that Einstein, after his separation from Mileva, had, with one exception, virtually finished his creative phase, remain few.

12

Das Wunder von Bern: The 1954 Football World Cup, the German Nation and Popular Histories

Franz-Josef Brüggemeier

The title of this chapter implies that what follows will be an article about football.[1] Or, to be more precise, about Germany winning the World Cup in Switzerland in 1954. However, the chapter will deal only briefly with football and the extraordinary sporting event that took place in the summer of that year. Instead, it will deal with how Germans reacted to their team winning the World Cup, and what their reactions tell us about German society and the German nation in the early 1950s, just ten years after the war.[2]

The reaction of the German public was quite extraordinary and surprised everybody when the team returned home. The final was played on a Sunday and the team left Switzerland the next day, using a special train provided by the Bundesbahn, the German state railway. Victory in the final had come completely unexpectedly and there had been no time to make any preparations – apart from painting *Fussball Weltmeister 1954* on the train. Everything else happened spontaneously. Nobody had any idea what to do or what was going to happen when the team returned, and everybody was taken aback when hundreds of thousands, if not millions, of Germans gave the players a tumultuous welcome. Wherever the train passed, the stations were bursting with people who could not move, and often neither could the train. People were standing everywhere, not just at the stations but also on the tracks. They wanted to welcome the players, to give them presents or just to shake their hands. And when the train reached Munich on the Tuesday afternoon, more than 500,000 people – almost as many as the population of Munich itself – lined the streets and assembled on the Marienplatz, in front of the Rathaus (see Figure 12.1) (Frei 1994).

Even today, pictures of these events are rather impressive, and the World Cup triumph – known as the *Wunder von Bern*, or 'miracle of Bern', after the city in which the final was played – left a lasting impression. In 2004, Germany

Figure 12.1: Waiting for the team, Munich 6.7.1954. Source: Alfred Georg Frei: Finale Grande. Die Rückkehr des Fußballweltmeisters 1954.

celebrated the fiftieth anniversary of this victory, and the event obtained widespread coverage in the newspapers and on TV and radio. Special ceremonies and festivities took place and a very successful film was released, *Das Wunder von Bern* (2004). Almost everybody agreed that fifty years ago something special had taken place, something that was much more than a mere football game. As a leader in the *Süddeutsche Zeitung* put it:

> 4 July 1954 was an unforgettable day in Germany's postwar history ... Jubilations turned into patriotic manifestations, and already in the stadium tens of thousands sang the national anthem, of course the opening words of the first stanza (Germany, Germany above all) since they did not know the officially stipulated third verse. ... [This day] was the real birthday of the Federal Republic, more important than the currency reform, the passing of the constitution or the fall of the Berlin wall.[3]

For others these events did not so much mean the birth of a new nation-state as the rebirth of an aggressive German nationalism. For them the winning team 'repaired the injuries suffered during and after the war' (Gebauer 1999: 107). The players achieved what the German military had not, and they displayed the same qualities: self-sacrifice, team spirit and modesty.[4] The young republic, 'celebrated itself. Didn't Bern somehow make up for Stalingrad?' (Kistner and Schulze 2001: 63).[5]

With these comments in mind I began my research expecting to find an abundance of sources in newspapers and archives. After all, these events took place less than ten years after the end of the Second World War and I assumed that, while many contemporaries were celebrating a newly found national pride, others might be afraid that they were witnessing the re-emergence of a dangerous nationalism. These different reactions may have occurred, but if they did they left very few traces. In fact I found almost nothing in the archives, neither at the local, regional nor national level. No major politician publicly talked about the events, they do not show up in the cabinet papers, and Adenauer, the then chancellor, does not even mention them in his memoirs. The newspapers, it is true, covered the World Cup and the matches played in some detail, but I found very few articles that went beyond the sporting event itself and dealing with the questions that interested me. So if the *Süddeutsche Zeitung* leader writer is right, and the new Germany was born in the summer of 1954, contemporaries obviously did not notice it or talk about it.

Nor for that matter did later historians. Not even one of the many books recently published on postwar Germany mentions the World Cup and the public celebrations it created (see, e.g., Görtemaker 1999; Kielmannsegg 2000; Winkler 2000). Studies specifically dealing with German nationalism and German identity after 1945 – of which there are quite a few – do not attribute the 'miracle of Bern' any significance (e.g., Gabbe 1976; Mögenburg 1993; Winkler 1993: 12–33; Moeller 1997; Assmann and Frevert 1999; Wolfrum 1999). This in itself is an interesting observation. Even if some of the claims were exaggerated, there can be no doubt that something special took place in 1954 and that we should try to explain what was going on.

This is what this chapter will try to do, taking up two themes. First it will ask the question of why the World Cup triumph of 1954 did not cause a new outburst of nationalism and why it did not create a new national identity. If it resulted in neither of these things, there remains, of course, the question of how the enormous enthusiasm that occurred can be explained. About this enthusiasm there can be no doubt, and the second part of the chapter will offer an explanation for this phenomenon.

On the theme of nationalism and national identity, there are, of course, many areas one would have to look into but I will mention just two: Firstly, the distinction between low and high culture, which has been and in many ways still is particularly marked in Germany (Schildt 1999). This is especially true when it comes to football (and sport in general). My second area of interest is the widespread uncertainty which, I will argue, existed in the early 1950s about all aspects concerning the nation, nationalism, national symbols and so on, including an uncertainty about how to behave towards foreigners – be it in Germany or abroad.

Let us look first then at the distinction between low and high culture, and in this context the attitude towards sport, especially football. In the 1950s football in Germany – as in Britain – was by far the most popular sport and one of the most important elements of popular culture. It figured prominently on radio as well as in newspapers and football supporters were to be found among all classes of society. It would be wrong, therefore, to see it as a mere working-class or even a proletarian sport. However, it is true to say that this was the class where football enjoyed the widest support and it was generally seen as a pastime and indulgence of the lower classes. As a consequence, in all the highbrow journals I analysed for the period between the end of the war and the months after the World Cup, I could find only three articles dealing with football.[6] They read like reports from a foreign country.

The first piece appeared as late as 1952 in the *Frankfurter Hefte*, and the author is at pains to inform his readers about the 'sports for the masses: football' (*Massensport Fussball*), of which he assumed they knew very little. As a consequence, he describes in some detail what it is all about, how it is played and what the rules are. In addition he emphasizes that football educates the workers, who still see themselves as excluded from the world of culture and education. On the football field, in contrast, they feel at home and practise the solidarity they need in their fight for recognition in society. But not all aspects of football are as positive. The author also describes spectators who completely lose control, scream and yell, 'creating fear and horror of the unleashed behemoth of the masses'. These spectators have lost all orientation in life and need help from those members of society who – like the author and his readers – carry a moral responsibility. They cannot afford to neglect such an important area of modern mass society as sport and especially football (Baukloh 1952: 862–64).

This plea was not taken up. I did not find any other article dealing with sport, let alone football, even though the sporting bodies tried hard. In 1954 the Deutsche Sport Bund (DSB), the main German sporting organization, invited Ortega y Gasset to give the keynote speech at its annual convention in order to achieve the 'breakthrough of the intellectual elite to sport'. In Germany in the early 1950s Ortega y Gasset was probably the most widely read serious author. His book *The Revolt of the Masses* (Ortega y Gasset 1932) was a bestseller, since it was seen to support a widely held explanation for the rise of Nazism, according to which Hitler had come to power because he had seduced the masses.[7] Whatever the merits of this argument, numerous recent studies have shown that among the political parties no other conviction was as widely shared as the need to fight the 'mass attitude', or *Massengeist* (Ehrenstein 1955: 96; Schildt 1999). On the Right and Left, from Gehlen to Habermas, mass culture and mass consumption were attacked and vilified (Gehlen 1952: 579–94; Habermas 1954: 701–24). They were seen as the result of alienation, expressions of 'false consciousness', manifestations of lower instincts and so on. Football fell into this category; indeed, it provided a particularly negative manifestation of mass culture.

As a consequence, it was not only highbrow journals that wrote little about football. Middle-brow newspapers, too, by and large restricted their coverage to the sport pages. Even the World Cup made no difference: football only rarely made it to the front pages. Readers of the *Süddeutsche*, to give just one example, had to wait until the semi-finals before finding a column – of six lines! – informing them about the result. The following Friday they found nothing, and even on Saturday, the day before the final, football was not seen worthy of a headline – although the newspaper did comment upon the enthusiasm that had broken out.

Of course, these findings are not easy to interpret, since newspaper front pages have their own rules. But in other pages, too, football rarely featured, except for the days just before and after the final when one can find the occasional report describing the country's growing interest. Meanwhile in the feuilleton – a very German institution – not one single article about the sport can be found. This was all in stark contrast to the fiftieth anniversary of the Bern victory in 2004, and the avalanche of comments, reports and documentaries on football in all sorts of magazines, newspapers and journals that marked Germany's hosting of the World Cup in 2006.

To sum up: In 1954, the media and those people in society who shaped debates about the nation and national identity were just not interested in the German team winning the World Cup. Indeed, if you had asked them to include football among their considerations, or to suggest that it was as important a part of Germany's cultural heritage as Goethe, Schiller, Beethoven and others, they would have been shocked.

Moving on now to attitudes towards the nation and national symbols, these are best characterized as marked by a widespread feeling of uncertainty. A good example is the photograph of the two teams before the kick off. If one looks closely, there is something missing: the German flag. It should be on the left, and after the match the West German government asked its embassy in Bern to inquire why it was missing. According to its report the flag had been properly raised, but strong winds and heavy rain had caused it to become entangled in the ropes. Zealous spectators had tried to untangle it, but doing so had torn the ropes so that the flag fell off and was carried away by the wind. By then, it was too late to replace it.[8]

This explanation may be true, but that is not the interesting part of the story. More interesting is that only two of the newspapers I consulted reported the missing flag. One of them did not directly deal with it let alone complain about it; rather, it referred to a Hungarian newspaper which had wondered why the flag was missing and why the Germans had not complained about it.[9] The other newspaper only briefly mentioned the incident and was at pains to emphasize that no sabotage had taken place.[10] The German government did not complain about the missing flag, nor did the German football association. Furthermore, none of the books published immediately after the World Cup and in the following years even mentioned this episode – until 2003. In that year, Rudi Michel, who was a junior reporter in Bern and later became a famous and widely respected TV commentator, published a book about the World Cup where for the first time he mentioned the missing flag. In an interview he said that in 1954 he had, of course, seen what had happened and that he was somewhat angry about it. But he did not dare to mention it in public. In fact, he waited fifty years to tell the story (R. Michel 2004: 77).

Rudi Michel may have been more sensitive than others, but it is striking that the national anthem and the national flag only played a very limited role in the celebrations. After the final, when the cup was presented to the German team, the national anthem was played as protocol demanded. German spectators in the stadium sang along – but, to the horror of many, they sang the first verse. Ever since, there has been a debate about why they did not sing the official, non-provocative third one. Some see this as an outburst of an emerging and long-suppressed nationalism, but this is a minority view. Even Eduard Schnitzler, a journalist from East Germany who was notorious for constantly attacking West Germany as a citadel of capitalism and militarism, described the behaviour of the spectators as 'more or less thoughtless' and almost all other commentators agreed.[11] In fact, they and the politicians went out of their way to prevent an outburst of nationalism.

To give but one example: On the Monday after the final, the conservative Christian Democratic Union (CDU) warned against describing the victory in Bern as a 'German football miracle'. The great sporting success should not be in national phrases. It was not Germany that had won in Bern but the eleven players of the German team. One should not see the events in Switzerland as an indication that nine years after their capitulation Germans would again know how to prevail.[12] These warnings were not necessary. On the contrary, the newspapers agreed with the CDU and also played down the significance of the event in Bern, describing it as being just about football. Reading their articles one gets the impression that they felt uneasy and expressed an uncertainty towards nationalism and national symbols which was a marked feature of the Federal Republic from its very beginning.

When the Federal Republic of Germany was founded in 1949, the question arose whether or not it should have a national flag, a national anthem and a national holiday. Other states have all three – though not necessarily a national holiday (which, for instance, Great Britain does not have). In Germany, considering its recent history, it proved very difficult to agree upon these symbols. The flag did not cause a major problem. The colours black, red and gold symbolize the democratic traditions of the nineteenth century and were chosen to wide acclaim. In contrast, a date for a national holiday could not be found, since all possible dates were tarnished by often disastrous events. For example, 9 November, the date when the Weimar Republic was proclaimed in 1918, also stands for the pogrom against the Jews in 1938, the failed Hitler Putsch in 1923 and the killing of Robert Blum in 1848, signalling the defeat of the revolution in Germany and Austro–Hungary. Other dates were as complicated, so that the attempt to find a national holiday was given up, at least until the uprising in East Germany (GDR) in June 1953. This revolt offered an ideal opportunity, since in this case Germans stood up for liberty, democracy and freedom and were willing to die for it. Within a month, the German parliament declared 17 June a national holiday, which first celebrated a year later when the German team played its first match in the World Cup in Switzerland (Gabbe 1976; Kiefer 1993; Wolfrum 1999; Bialas 2002).

International sporting events require a national anthem, which was also difficult. The most popular choice contains the infamous first verse – 'Germany, Germany above all' (*Deutschland, Deutschland über alles*) – and it encountered widespread opposition, including from Theodor Heuss, the then head of state. He commissioned a new anthem, which found even less support, so that in the end he reached a compromise with Adenauer, in which they agreed that the first verse should be banned. Instead, the third verse was chosen, which calls for unity and freedom for the German fatherland. Here, however, an additional problem arose. In 1952, when the first German team was allowed to take part in the Olympic Games, Adenauer and Heuss had not yet reached their compromise. Furthermore, the German team included participants from the GDR which had its own national anthem but which was not yet a member of the International Olympic Committee and therefore could not send its own team. As a consequence, a decision was made to play the 'Ode to Joy' from Beethoven's Ninth Symphony as the German team's anthem. But when the first German athlete was to be presented his gold medal at the games in Norway, the band refused to play the tune, assuming they had been given the wrong score. The ceremony was broken off and phone calls were made to the German government to find out whether they were serious about choosing Beethoven's music as their national anthem. When the choice was confirmed, the ceremony was repeated the next day (Blasius 2001: 102).

There exist many other examples of this uncertainty towards national symbols and nationalism. How, for instance, were Germans to behave when they visited Holland, Denmark, France or other countries they had attacked and occupied just a few years earlier? Around Easter 1954, few months before the World Cup, visa restrictions with several of these countries had been eased. A special permit was no longer required to cross the border and go, for example, to the Dutch coast for a holiday. Easter was a traditional holiday period and the German newspapers wondered what was going to happen in the Netherlands and how German tourists would behave. Reading the articles published after Easter, you can sense the relief. For one thing, the vast majority of Germans obviously behaved rather well. But, more importantly, they were more or less well received. In fact, they came in such great numbers that the hotels and guest houses could not offer enough beds. On the radio, therefore, Dutch people were asked to put them up privately, and many did (Brüggemeier 2004: 139–40).

Given this uncertainty towards nationalism and national symbols and given the huge gulf between high and popular culture, it should be no surprise that, in 1954, contemporaries did not see the victory in Bern as the date on which the Federal Republic was born. Nor can we talk about the rise of a new nationalism. But the enormous enthusiasm has still to be explained. Why – as a newspaper letter put it – 'did old ladies, who hardly knew what a football looks like, burst into tears of joy when they saw the players of the national squad?'.[13] This is a difficult question, one which the second part of this chapter will deal with. It cannot, of course, give definite answers, but it can offer a few suggestions worth considering.

In a nutshell, the most convincing explanation is to consider the enthusiasm to be the result of a media event. This allowed new experiences and created a new form of community. This virtual community was characterized by emotions of the utmost intensity, ones which could be shared by anybody who cared to join, but which – at the same time – disappeared very quickly once the event was over. This community was thus marked by intensity as well as volatility.

To begin with the media event: The final was broadcast live, which in itself was not new, especially for sporting events, where live broadcast had a long tradition. But this time, the final was broadcast not only on the radio but also on television. More importantly, so many stations transmitted it that one could listen to it anywhere in Germany. According to the reports, almost everybody who could get near a radio or television did so. In 1954 there were only about 40,000 TV sets in entire West Germany, but so many wanted to watch the match that televisions on that afternoon ceased being private property. Whoever owned one had to accept that friends, relatives, neighbours, colleagues and so on came to visit. Others hired buses to travel to towns which had better reception; and still others queued for hours at cinemas and other places where televisions were set up. But the vast majority had to put up with radio, where they could listen to just about the best and most exciting transmission ever to be broadcast in Germany. For this there are two reasons: one was the commentator, who lived up to the occasion. The other was the final itself and the way the German team reached it which created an almost unbearably tense atmosphere (ibid.: 209–22).

To recap: The West Germans came to the World Cup as rank outsiders. In effect, bookmakers in London had stopped taking bets on the team since nobody gave it a chance. But they had also stopped taking bets on the Hungarian team, though for the opposite reason.[14] In the early 1950s the Hungarians were widely acknowledged to be by far the best team in Europe, if not worldwide. They were the first non-British side to beat England at Wembley with six goals to three. Worse was to come in the return match, when the Hungarians beat England by seven goals to one. A new era had started in football and nobody had any doubt that the Hungarians would win the World Cup – including the London bookmakers, who therefore stopped taking on them..

In Switzerland, the German team played in the same group as Hungary, and the German fans were looking forward to the first match, only to be bitterly disappointed. The Hungarians won by eight goals to three, having led seven at one point until they stopped taking the game seriously so that the final result looked slightly less disastrous. In the final the two teams met again. In the meantime, the German team had improved a little, but the Hungarians were still overwhelming favourites. Some Germans may have harboured hopes, against their better judgement, while the commentator assumed that his main task was to comfort the audience at home if their team got another thrashing. He therefore hoped that this time it would take longer for the first goals to be conceded, but he was wrong. Whilst in the first match it took the Hungarians seventeen minutes to score two goals, now it took only eight minutes. All hope had been in vain and an even worse result seemed to be on the cards. But all of a sudden, the West German team scored a goal and in the eighteenth minute they equalized.

The commentator and his audience could not believe what was happening. The first signs of hope reappeared and they grew stronger as the Germans held out. The tension grew by the minute. Several times both teams were close to scoring a goal, but neither did. To quote a Freiburg newspaper: 'Two hours were filled with unbearable tension. Breathless silence alternated with deafening noise, which threatened to detonate the room, when the decisive goals were scored. People jumped off their chairs, threw up their arms, and their beer glasses started dancing on the table ... The tension could not have been greater in Bern, which was 300 kilometres away'.[15]

The same atmosphere was to be found all over Germany and it affected people of all ages and from all strata of society, irrespective of religion, political beliefs, regional provenance, education, gender or profession. The feelings were so intense and the desire to be part of this community so strong that – as Dolf Sternberg, a liberal intellectual, observed – everybody, including academics, the educated elites and others wanted to belong, even though they knew nothing about the game and normally went to great lengths to cultivate individual feelings and thoughts. But now they could not help but let 'themselves go and they were glad that they were not unmoved by the event' (Sternberger 1954: 461).

This community, as argued before, was characterized by a combination of intensity and volatility, and it created a situation where normal rules and ways of behaviour were suspended. Men who did not know one another hugged each other, crying in public, overcome by emotions and behaving like little children beneath the Christmas tree. They were not ashamed to show their feelings and to behave in ways which even today seem unbelievable, when, for instance, Fritz Walter and Toni Turek, two of the German players, 'hugged and kissed each other for minutes, like a loving couple', as one of the newspapers reported.[16]

These feelings and emotions were intense but they were also volatile and disappeared once the event was over. They were reignited when the players returned and when huge crowds awaited them – including grandmas and grandpas (see Figure 12.2). In these moments, the atmosphere of the final was recreated, and for an hour or two similar emotions prevailed – affecting not just children and the young, as was the case in 2006 when the World Cup was played

Figure 12.2: Welcoming the players, Kaiserslautern, 7.7.1954. Source: Gerhard Bahr (ed): *Fußball-Weltmeisterschaft* 1954.

in Germany. In 1954 almost everybody joined in, including elderly and frail ladies who queued for hours to welcome the players home and share in the emotion. But when everybody went home, these emotions disappeared as did the virtual community – with the consequence that these events did not have a lasting impact: the intensity of the feelings and their volatility were two sides of the same coin.

One other factor has to be mentioned: despite the intensity of feelings nothing much was at stake. This may sound surprising since the two teams competed for the World Cup. But apart from the desire to win the title there were no other objectives, no shared values or common beliefs which held the virtual community together. On the contrary, this community could only exert such an attraction and appeal to almost everybody because it did not demand anything from its members apart from their willingness to participate in the event.

In the German context, the term 'community' normally has a different meaning. There is a tradition of juxtaposing 'community' (*Gemeinschaft*) and 'society' (*Gesellschaft*), and to ascribe to community all the values and convictions which are seen as lacking in modern society. But it is precisely this lack of values and common commitments which brought about the virtual community on 4 July 1954. Contemporaries made the same observation, but assessed it very differently. The value-system of the masses – as a letter writer to the *Frankfurter Allgemeine Zeitung* complained – had sunk to almost zero. For him, the enthusiasm that accompanied the victory was coupled with a complete lack of meaning and it symbolized an 'exponentiated nothing'.[17] He was right: the community was largely empty, devoid of profound meanings. But in contrast to his judgment, this emptiness was not something to deplore. On the contrary, it was a liberating factor, allowing everybody to join and – as important – to leave again.

This is putting the argument very crudely. It could, of course, be pointed out that not everybody was allowed to join since this community was very much a German affair. To a degree, this is true, and it seems very unlikely that so soon after the war people from other nations wanted to celebrate a German victory. But this is exactly what happened in Bern. Spectators from Switzerland and other countries were so carried away by the sheer intensity of what was going on that they started to support the German team, the underdog which had come back from an almost hopeless situation. For a moment the virtual community included not only Germans but other spectators from other nations too, some of whom even sang the German anthem. Still, it can be safely assumed that their allegiance to this spontaneous community was, though momentarily intense, also extremely volatile and disappeared once they left the stadium.

Another example of the openness of these virtual communities, and the possibility of joining and leaving them almost at will, concerns the 2004 European Championship matches, which garnered the highest TV ratings in Germany. This may not seem surprising, but in fact these ratings are rather astonishing since the German team was eliminated in the first round of the competition. By way of a substitute many Germans chose to support the Greek team. One reason for this choice may have been that the Greeks had a German coach. But more important was the fact that the Greek team was almost more of an underdog than the German team in 1954. It was fun to support them and it became quite exciting when they eliminated one favourite after the other. In the final, as in 1954, the tension became enormous and for a short moment Greeks, Germans and people from many other nations formed a community which was intense but also very volatile and quickly disappeared.

This, however, is not always the case. Virtual communities created by special events can have a lasting influence – as was the case in Germany after the 1954 World Cup. For many, the events of 4 July remained an important part of people's lives and, maybe even, of their identity. But that was very much a private matter, while in public the event was quickly forgotten – as was the film made about the World Cup which came out a few weeks later and proved to be a great success in Germany. However, after it had toured the cinemas all the copies were thrown away, since the producers did not expect a lasting interest (Brüggemeier 2004: 320). When interest grew again many years later there were only a few minutes of the film left, and when the fiftieth anniversary approached a hectic search for remaining footage began – without much success.

When I looked at German newspapers published over the decade after the 1954 victory I found no articles marking the anniversary of the 'miracle of Bern'.

In most years nothing at all was mentioned, with the exception of 1958, when the next World Cup was played in Sweden and Germany had to defend the title. In this situation, articles appeared looking back at 1954, but they were fairly short and concentrated on the sporting aspects.

So all the assertions and assumptions made in 2004, on the fiftieth anniversary of the victory in Bern, do not have an empirical basis. For a few hours on 4 July Germans went wild with excitement, but they did not really see this event as the day on which the new Germany was born nor did their jubilations turn into patriotic, let alone nationalistic, manifestations. For this there are many reasons, as I have tried to show.

Football was largely seen as a sport of the working classes or – worse – the despised masses, and for the majority of the middle, especially the educated, classes, it was out of the question to accept a football event as a national symbol. This holds especially true for academics, intellectuals, politicians, journalists or authors whose contributions are an essential part of the shaping of collective memory. Public memory, as we know, does not come into existence on its own. Rather it has to be constructed, especially if it is to survive. The agents in charge of constructing cultural memory at that time, however, did not pay attention to the events described here. On the contrary, they would have been appalled if they had been asked to include them in their canon of national symbols. Many years later this attitude changed, but to date there has not been enough research carried out to say when and why and who was responsible for it. To my knowledge, the first attempts to give the events of 1954 a greater meaning appeared in the 1980s, and increased in the 1990s. But it was only when the fiftieth anniversary approached that we find the hyperbolic and exaggerated statements quoted above.

Having said that, the current generation can, of course, declare 4 July 1954 to be an important date in Germany's postwar history. It can even declare it a national holiday, since each generation has the right to rediscover historical events and to give them new meanings. It can even try to disguise the fact that it is effectively inventing a tradition (see Hobsbawm and Ranger 1992). As is well known, Germany still does not have a proper national holiday. Officially it is 3 October, when the GDR ceased to exist. But the Berlin Wall was broken down on 19 November, and that is the highly emotional day when unification actually happened. However, for the reasons mentioned above, 19 November cannot be a national holiday.

As an alternative, 3 October was chosen when the new and enlarged Germany came into existence, but the way this happened had about the same charm and popular appeal as the signing of a new EU treaty in Brussels, and the date does not arouse great public enthusiasm. Personally, I have no objection if today's Germans decide to choose 4 July 1954 instead. In doing so, they would celebrate the success of an underdog, which beat the best team in the world; they would celebrate a day full of enthusiasm and joy; and they would celebrate a virtual community which was emotional and volatile at the same time and which did not proclaim any greater meaning to their actions. In the context of Germany's history and its often fatal 'sense of mission' (*Sendungsbewußtsein*) that would be a message many Germans and especially our neighbours can easily live with. But I am afraid this is not realistic. And to be honest I am glad about that. The day of the 'miracle of Bern' should be looked back upon as a great sporting success, a day about which we can reminisce, let our imaginations blossom and tell ever more outrageous stories. That is what great sporting events are all about. Nothing more and nothing less.

Notes

1. I would like to thank David Gamston, Anne Sutherland and Joan Brüggemeier for their comments and their help with the translation.
2. The argument advanced here is more fully developed in Brüggemeier (2004).
3. *Süddeutsche Zeitung*, 3 July 2004. In 1922, the 'Song of Germany' (Deutschlandlied) was chosen for the national anthem. During the Nazi era only the first stanza was used, and after the Second World War only the third stanza was accepted. The issue of which verses were sung, and the significance of this, is discussed below.
4. Schindelbeck, cited in Schweer (1994: 10).
5. The reference here is to German defeat in the Battle of Stalingrad, 1942/3.
6. The journals were: *Frankfurter Hefte, Merkur, Christ und Welt, Neues Abendland, Wort und Wahrheit, Magnum* and *Gewerkschaftliche Monatshefte*.
7. The book was first published in Germany in 1931, but became widely read only after the war. By 1953 more than 100,000 copies had been printed.
8. Report from 10 July 1954: Politisches Archiv des Auswärtigen Amtes, B 10, AZ 471-00, Bd. 1913, Bl. 212.
9. *Westdeutsche Allgemeine Zeitung*, 7 July 1954.
10. *Schwäbische Zeitung*, 9 July 1954.
11. Eduard von Schnitzler, 'Missbrauchte Sportbegeisterung', Sendemanuskript vom 07.07.1954, Deutsches Rundfunkarchiv, Dokument des Monats April 2000. Retrieved 14 August 2008 from: http://www.dra.de/dok_0400a.htm.
12. Remarks cited in *Basler Nachrichten*, 7 April 1954.
13. *Süddeutsche Zeitung*, 10–11 July 1954.
14. *Die Welt*, 3 July 1954.
15. *Badische Zeitung*, 6 July 1954.
16. *Münchener Merkur*, 6 July 1954.
17. *Frankfurter Allgemeine Zeitung*, 12 July 1954.

References

Adorno, T.W. 1977. 'Spengler nach dem Untergang', in idem, *Werke*, vol. 10. Frankfurt am Main: Suhrkamp, pp. 48–71.

Agde, G. (ed.) 2000. *Kahlschlag. Das 11. Plenum des ZK der SED 1965. Studien und Dokumente*, 2nd edn. Berlin: Aufbau.

Albisetti, J.C. and P. Ludgreen. 1991. 'Höhere Knabenschulen', in C. Berg (ed.) *Handbuch der deutschen Bildungsgeschichte*, vol. 4. Munich: Beck, pp. 228–303.

Alic, M. 1985. *Hypatia's Heritage: A History of Women in Science from Antiquity to the Late Nineteenth Century*. London: Women's Press.

Altermatt, U. 2005. 'Das komplexe Verhältnis von Religion und Nation. Eine Typologie für den Katholizismus', *Schweizerische Zeitschrift für Religions- und Kulturgeschichte* 99: 417–32.

Altwegg, J. 2003. 'Geschichte zweier Deutscher. Blick in französische Zeitschriften: Haffners Triumph und Noltes Niedergang', *Frankfurter Allgemeine Zeitung* 15 February, B34.

Aly, G. 1995. *'Endlösung'. Völkerverschiebung und der Mord an den europäischen Juden*. Frankfurt am Main: Fischer.

Amtmann, K. 1998. *Elisabeth von Österreich. Die politischen Geschäfte der Kaiserin*. Regensburg: Pustet.

Anderson, B. 1983. *Imagined Communities*. London: Verso.

Angehrn, E. 1991. *Geschichtsphilosophie*. Stuttgart: Kohlhammer.

Annegarn, J. 1895–96. *Annegarns Weltgeschichte in 8 Bänden*, 8 vols, 7th edn. Münster: Theissing.

Ariès, P. 1988. *Zeit und Geschichte*. Frankfurt am Main: Athenäum.

——— 1994. *Geschichte der Kindheit*, 11th edn. Munich: Deutscher Taschenbuch-Verlag.

Arnold, G. 1967[1729]. *Unparteiische Kirchen- und Ketzerhistorie. Vom Anfang des Neuen Testaments bis auf das Jahr Christi 1688*, 2 vols. Hildesheim: Olms.

Assmann, A. 1999. *Erinnerungsräume. Formen und Wandlungen des kulturellen Gedächtnisses*. Munich: Beck.

———— 2005. 'Jahrestage. Denkmäler in der Zeit', in P. Münch (ed.) *Jubiläum, Jubiläum. Zur Geschichte öffentlicher und privater Erinnerung.* Essen: Klartext, pp. 305–14.

———— 2006. *Der lange Schatten der Vergangenheit. Erinnerungskultur und Geschichtspolitik.* Munich: Beck.

Assmann, A. (ed.) 1993. *Mnemosyne. Formen und Funktionen der kulturellen Erinnerung.* Frankfurt am Main: Fischer.

Assmann, A. and U. Frevert. 1999. *Geschichtsvergessenheit – Geschichtsversessenheit. Vom Umgang mit deutschen Erfahrungen.* Stuttgart: Deutsche Verlagsanstalt.

Assmann, J. 1995a. 'Collective Memory and Cultural Identity', *New German Critique* 65: 125–33.

———— 1995b. 'Erinnern um dazuzugehören', in K. Platt and M. Dabag (eds), *Generation und Gedächtnis. Erinnerungen und Kollektive Identitäten.* Opladen: Leske and Budrich, pp. 51–75.

———— 1997. *Das kulturelle Gedächtnis. Schrift, Erinnerung und politische Identität in frühen Hochkulturen.* Munich: Beck.

———— 1999. *Das kulturelle Gedächtnis. Schrift, Erinnerung und politische Identität in frühen Hochkulturen,* 2nd edn. Munich: Beck.

———— 2005. *Das kulturelle Gedächtnis. Schrift, Erinnerung und politische Identität in frühen Hochkulturen,* 5th edn. Munich: Beck.

Assmann, J. (ed.) 1988. *Kultur und Gedächtnis.* Frankfurt am Main: Suhrkamp.

Augstein, R. et al. (eds). 1987. *'Historikerstreit'. Die Dokumentation der Kontroverse um die Einzigartigkeit der nationalsozialistischen Judenvernichtung.* Munich: Piper.

Badash, L. 1975. 'Decay of a Radioactive Halo', *Isis* 66: 566–68.

Bamm, P. 1955. *Frühe Stätten der Christenheit.* Munich: Kösel.

Bandmann, C. and J. Hembus. 1980. *Klassiker des deutschen Tonfilms 1930–1960.* Munich: Goldmann.

Bauer, D. 2006. *Geschichtskultur als Instrument zur staatlichen Identitätsstiftung. Feste, Feiern und Denkmalpflege in Bayern im 19. Jahrhundert und in der DDR.* Neuried: Ars Una.

Bauer, J.M. 1955. *So weit die Füße tragen.* Munich: Ehrenwirth.

Baukloh, F. 1952. 'Massensport Fußball', *Frankfurter Hefte* 7: 859–64.

Beck, U. and W. Bonß (eds). 2001. *Modernisierung der Moderne.* Frankfurt am Main: Suhrkamp.

Beck, U. and A. Giddens. 1996. *Reflexive Modernisierung: Eine Kontroverse.* Frankfurt am Main: Suhrkamp.

Beck, U. and C. Lau (eds). 2004. *Entgrenzung und Entscheidung: Was ist neu an der Theorie der reflexiven Modernisierung?* Frankfurt am Main: Suhrkamp.

Becker, C. 1932. 'Everyman his own Historian', *American Historical Review* 37: 221–36.

Becker, E.W. 2005. 'Biographie als Lebensform. Theodor Heuss als Biograph im Nationalsozialismus', in W. Hardtwig (ed.) *Geschichte für Leser: Populäre*

Geschichtsschreibung in Deutschland im 20. Jahrhundert. Stuttgart: Steiner, pp. 57–92.

Becker, F. 2001. *Bilder von Krieg und Nation. Die Einigungskriege in der bürgerlichen Öffentlichkeit Deutschlands 1864–1913.* Munich: Oldenbourg.

Becker, K.F. 1891–93. *K. F. Beckers Weltgeschichte, neu bearbeitet und bis auf die Gegenwart fortgeführt von Wilhelm Müller,* 12 vols, 3rd edn. Stuttgart: Union Deutsche Verlagsgesellschaft.

Becker, S. 2001. 'Die Macht des Herzens und die Einsamkeit der Macht. Sisi als kulturphilosophische Projektion', in idem et al. (eds), *Volkskundliche Tableaus. Festschrift für Martin Scharfe.* Münster: Waxmann, pp. 413–30.

Belgum, K. 1998. *Popularizing the Nation: Audience, Representation, and the Production of Identity in* Die Gartenlaube, *1853–1900.* Lincoln: University of Nebraska Press.

Bensaude-Vincent, B. 1994. 'Une robe de coton noir', *Cahiers de Science et Vie* 24: 76–85.

Benson, R.L. and J. Fried (eds). 1997. *Ernst Kantorowicz.* Stuttgart: Steiner.

Benz, W. 1986. 'Zeitgeschichte und Fernsehen', *Studienkreis Rundfunk und Geschichte* 12: 41–54.

Berg, C. and U. Herrmann. 1991. 'Industriegesellschaft und Kulturkrise. Ambivalenzen der Epoche des Zweiten Deutschen Kaiserreichs 1870–1918', in C. Berg (ed.) *Handbuch der deutschen Bildungsgeschichte,* vol. 4: *1870–1918. Von der Reichsgründung bis zum Ende des Ersten Weltkrieges.* Munich: Beck, pp. 1–56.

Bergenthum, H. 2002. 'Weltgeschichten im wilhelminischen Deutschland. Innovative Ansätze in der populären Geschichtsschreibung', *Comparativ* 12: 16–56.

————— 2004. *Weltgeschichten im Zeitalter der Weltpolitik. Zur populären Geschichtsschreibung im wilhelminischen Deutschland.* Munich: Meidenbauer.

Bergmann, W. 1997. 'Die TV-Serie Holocaust als Medienereignis', in idem, *Antisemitismus in öffentlichen Konflikten. Kollektives Lernen in der politischen Kultur der Bundesrepublik 1949–1989.* Frankfurt am Main: Campus, pp. 351–81.

Berking, H. 1984. *Masse und Geist. Studien zur Soziologie in der Weimarer Republik.* Berlin: Wissenschaftlicher Autoren-Verlag.

Bernecker, W.L. and S. Brinkmann (eds). 2006. *Kampf der Erinnerungen. Der Spanische Bürgerkrieg in Politik und Gesellschaft 1936–2006.* Nettersheim: Verlag Graswurzelrevolution.

Bessen, U. 1989. *Trümmer und Träume. Nachkriegszeit und fünfziger Jahre auf Zelluloid.* Bochum: Studienverlag Brockmeyer.

Beutelschmidt, T. and R. Steinlein (eds). 2004. *Realitätskonstruktion, Faschismus und Antifaschismus in den Literaturverfilmungen des DDR-Fernsehens.* Leipzig: Leipziger Universitätsverlag.

Bialas, W. (ed.) 2002. *Die nationale Identität der Deutschen. Philosophische Imaginationen und historische Mentalitäten.* Frankfurt am Main: Lang.

Biedermann, K. 1969[1854]. *Deutschland im 18. Jahrhundert.* Reprint edn. Aalen: Scientia.

Billig, M. 1995. *Banal Nationalism.* London: Sage.

Black, J. 2005. *Using History.* London: Arnold.

Blaha, T. 2003. *Willi Graf und die Weiße Rose. Eine Rezeptionsgeschichte.* Munich: Saur.

Blanc, K. 1999. *Marie Curie et le Nobel.* Uppsala: Avdelningen för Vetenskaps-historia.

Blanke, H.W. 1991. *Historiographiegeschichte als Historik.* Stuttgart: Frommann-Holzboog.

Blanke, H.W. and D. Fleischer (eds). 1990. *Theoretiker der deutschen Aufklärungshistorie,* vol. 1: *Die theoretische Begründung der Geschichte als Fachwissenschaft.* Stuttgart: Frommann-Holzboog.

Blasius, T. 2001. *Olympische Bewegung, Kalter Krieg und Deutschlandpolitik 1949–1972.* Frankfurt am Main: Lang.

Bleicher, J. 2002. 'Zwischen Horror und Komödie. Das Leben ist schön von Roberto Benigni und Zug des Lebens von Radu Mihaileanu', in W. Wende (ed.) *Geschichte im Film. Mediale Inszenierungen des Holocaust und kulturelles Gedächtnis.* Stuttgart: Metzler, pp. 181–99.

Bliersbach, G. 1989. *So grün war die Heide.* Weinheim: Beltz.

Bloch, M. 1985. *Apologie der Geschichte oder der Beruf des Historikers.* Munich: Deutscher Taschenbuch-Verlag.

Blumenthal, L.J.L. von. 1797. *Lebensbeschreibung Hans Joachims von Ziethen, Königlich-Preußischen Generals der Kavallerie, Ritters des Schwarzen Adlerordens, Chef des Regiments der Königlichen Leibhusaren, und Erbherrn auf Wustrau.* Berlin: Rieger.

——— 1803. *The Life of General de Zieten,* 2 vols, trans. B. Beresford. Berlin: Blumenthal.

Böge, V. (ed.) 2004. *Geschichtswerkstätten gestern – heute – morgen. Bewegung! Stillstand. Aufbruch?* Munich: Dölling and Galitz.

Bösch F. 1999. '"Das Dritte Reich" ferngesehen. Geschichtsvermittlung in der historischen Dokumentation', *Geschichte in Wissenschaft und Unterricht* 50: 204–20.

——— 2007. 'Film, NS-Vergangenheit und Geschichtswissenschaft, Von *Holocaust* zu *Der Untergang', Vierteljahrshefte für Zeitgeschichte* 55: 1–32.

Boscontri, L. 1998. *Sissi, Glanz und Last der Krone.* Cologne: Eco.

Boudia, S. 2001. *Marie Curie et son laboratoire. Sciences et industrie de la radioactivité en France.* Paris: Editions des Achives Contemporaines.

Boudia, S. and X. Roqué (eds). 1997. *Science, Medicine, and Industry: The Curie and Joliot-Curie Laboratories.* Amsterdam: Harwood.

Brandt, S. 2003. 'Wenig Anschauung? Die Ausstrahlung des Film „Holocaust" im westdeutschen Fernsehen (1978/79)', in C. Cornelißen et al. (eds), *Erinnerungskulturen. Deutschland, Italien und Japan seit 1945.* Frankfurt am Main: Fischer, pp. 257–68.

Braudel, F. 1969. *Ecrits sur l'histoire*. Paris: Flammarion.

Brendecke, A. 2005. 'Reden über Geschichte. Zur Rhetorik des Rückblicks in Jubiläumsreden der Frühen Neuzeit', in P. Münch (ed.) *Jubiläum, Jubiläum. Zur Geschichte öffentlicher und privater Erinnerung*. Essen: Klartext, pp. 61–83.

Brian, D. 2005. *The Curies: A Biography of the Most Controversial Family in Science*. Hoboken, NJ: Wiley.

Brock, C. 2006. *The Feminisation of Fame 1750–1850*. Basingstoke: Palgrave Macmillan.

Broszat, M. 1979. 'Holocaust und die Geschichtswissenschaft', *Vierteljahreshefte für Zeitgeschichte* 27: 285–98.

Brown, D. 2004. *Sakrileg*. Bergisch Gladbach: Lübbe.

Browning, C. 1992. *Ordinary Men: Reserve Police Battalion 101 and the Final Solution in Poland*. New York: HarperCollins.

Bruch, R. von. 1980. *Wissenschaft, Politik und öffentliche Meinung. Gelehrtenpolitik im Wilhelminischen Deutschland (1890–1914)*. Husum: Matthiesen.

Brüggemeier, F.-J. 2004. *Zurück auf dem Platz. Deutschland und die Fußball-Weltmeisterschaft 1954*. Munich: Deutsche Verlagsanstalt.

Bryld, C. and A. Warring. 1998. *Besættelsestiden som kollektiv erindring. Historie- og traditionsforvaltning af krig og besættelse 1945–1997*. Roskilde: Universitetsforlag.

Burgh, A. de. 1901. *Elisabeth. Kaiserin von Österreich und Königin von Ungarn, Blätter der Erinnerung*. Vienna: Moritz Perles.

Buschmann, N. and D. Langewiesche (eds). 2003. *Der Krieg in den Gründungsmythen europäischer Nationen und der USA*. Frankfurt am Main: Campus.

Carlson, M. 2000. 'Performing the Past: Living History and Cultural Memory', *Paragrana* 9: 237–48.

Cartland, B. 1959. *The Private Life of Elisabeth, Empress of Austria*. London: Ferderick Muller.

Ceranski, B. 2005. 'Die Arbeit mit dem Radium. Radioaktivitätsforschung 1896–1914', Ph.D. dissertation. Stuttgart: Universität Stuttgart.

Champion, J. 2008a. 'Entertainment or Instruction?' Retrieved 7 August 2008 from: http://www.doingpublichistory.org/pag_1200582779032.html.

———— 2008b. 'What are Historians For?' Retrieved 7 August 2008 from: http://www.doingpublichistory.org/pag_1200582779032.html.

Charle, C. 1997. *Vordenker der Moderne: Die Intellektuellen im 19. Jahrhundert*. Frankfurt am Main: Fischer.

Chladenius, J.M. 1985[1752]. *Allgemeine Geschichtswissenschaft*. Vienna: Böhlau.

Christian, D. 2005. *Maps of Time: An Introduction to Big History*. Berkeley: University of California Press.

Classen, C. 1999. *Bilder der Vergangenheit. Die Zeit des Nationalsozialismus im Fernsehen der Bundesrepublik 1955–1965*. Cologne: Böhlau.

———— 2005. 'Ungeliebte Unterhaltung. Zum Unterhaltungs-Diskurs im geteilten Deutschland 1945–1970', in J. Ruchatz (ed.) *Mediendiskurse deutsch/deutsch.* Weimar: Verlag und Datenbank für Geisteswissenschaften, pp. 209–33.

Conrad, S. 2006. *Globalisierung und Nation im Deutschen Kaiserreich.* Munich: Beck.

Conrad, S. and J. Osterhammel. 2004. 'Einleitung', in idem (eds), *Das Kaiserreich transnational. Deutschland in der Welt 1871–1914.* Göttingen: Vandenhoek and Ruprecht, pp. 7–27.

Cook, A. 2004. 'The Use and Abuse of Historical Reenactment: Thoughts on Recent Trends in Public History', *Criticism* 46: 487–96.

Cooter, R. and S. Pumfrey. 1994. 'Seprarate Spheres and Public Places: Reflections on the History of Science, Popularization and Science in Popular Culture', *History of Science* 32: 234–67.

Corbin, A. 1990. *Meereslust. Das Abendland und die Entdeckung der Küste.* Berlin: Wagenbach.

Cornelißen, C. 2003. 'Was heißt Erinnerungskultur? Begriff – Methoden – Perspektiven', *Geschichte in Wissenschaft und Unterricht* 54: 548–63.

Cornelißen, C. et al. (eds). 2003. *Erinnerungskulturen. Deutschland, Italien und Japan seit 1945.* Frankfurt am Main: Fischer.

Corti, E.C. 1934. *Elisabeth "die seltsame Frau".* Salzburg: Pustet.

———— 1977. *Elisabeth von Österreich: Tragik einer Unpolitischen.* Munich: Heyne.

Crawford, E. 1984. *The Beginnings of the Nobel Institution: The Science Prizes, 1901–1915.* Cambridge: Cambridge University Press.

Crivellari, F. et al. 2004. 'Einleitung', in idem (eds), *Die Medien der Geschichte. Historizität und Medialität in interdisziplinärer Perspektive.* Konstanz: UVK, pp. 9–48.

Curie, E. 1938. *Madame Curie*, trans. V. Sheehan. Garden City, NY: Doubleday.

Curie, M. 1923. *Pierre Curie.* Paris: Editions Payot.

Daimler, R. 1998. *Diana and Sisi. Zwei Frauen – ein Schicksal.* Munich: Deuticke.

Daniel, U. 2005. 'Bücher vom Kriegsschauplatz. Kriegsberichterstattung als Genre des 19. Jahrhunderts', in W. Hardtwig (ed.) *Geschichte für Leser: Populäre Geschichtsschreibung in Deutschland im 20. Jahrhundert.* Stuttgart: Steiner, pp. 93–122.

Danyel, J. (ed.) 1995. *Die geteilte Vergangenheit. Zum Umgang mit Nationalsozialismus und Widerstand in beiden deutschen Staaten.* Berlin: Akademie Verlag.

Daum, A.W. 1998. *Wissenschaftspopularisierung im 19. Jahrhundert. Bürgerliche Kultur, naturwissenschaftliche Bildung und die deutsche Öffentlichkeit 1848–1914.* Munich: Oldenbourg.

Daston, L. 2001. *Wunder, Beweise und Tatsachen. Zur Geschichte der Realität.* Frankfurt am Main: Fischer.

Davies, K. 2005. *Catharine Macaulay and Mercy Otis Warren: The Revolutionary Atlantic and the Politics of Gender.* Oxford: Oxford University Press.

Davis, N.Z. 1980. 'Gender and Genre: Women As Historical Writers, 1400–1820', in P.H. Labalme (ed.) *Beyond their Sex: Learned Women of the European Past*. New York: New York University Press, pp. 153–82.

Degele, N. and C. Dries. 2005. *Modernisierungstheorie*. Munich: Fink.

Demandt, A. 2003. *Kleine Weltgeschichte*. Munich: Beck.

Demandt, A. and J. Farrenkopf (eds). 1994. *Der Fall Spengler. Eine kritische Bilanz*. Cologne: Böhlau.

Demantowsky, M. 2005. 'Geschichtskultur und Erinnerungskultur – zwei Konzepte des einen Gegenstandes. Historischer Hintergrund und exemplarischer Vergleich', *Geschichte, Politik und ihre Didaktik* 33: 11–20.

Diem, P. 1979. *'Holocaust'. Anatomie eines Medienereignisses*. Vienna: Österreichischer Rundfunk.

Diner, D. 2000. *Das Jahrhundert verstehen. Eine universalhistorische Deutung*. Frankfurt am Main: Fischer.

Diner, D. (ed.) 1987. *Ist der Nationalsozialismus Geschichte? Zur Historisierung und Historikerstreit*. Frankfurt am Main: Fischer.

Drehsen, V. and W. Sparn. 1996. 'Die Moderne. Kulturkrise und Konstruktionsgeist', in idem (eds), *Vom Weltbildwandel zur Weltanschauungsanalyse. Krisenwahrnehmung und Krisenbewältigung um 1900*. Berlin: Akademie Verlag, pp. 11–29.

Dunk, H. v.d. 1994. 'Dargestellte und erlebte Zeit. Gedanken zum Zeitbewußtsein und zur Periodisierungsfrage', in G. Hübinger and J. Osterhammel (eds), *Universalgeschichte und Nationalgeschichten. Ernst Schulin zum 65. Geburtstag*. Freiburg: Rombach, pp. 11–29.

Dussel, K. 2002. *Hörfunk in Deutschland. Politik, Programm, Publikum (1923–1960)*. Potsdam: Verlag für Berlin-Brandenburg.

Ebbrecht, T. 2007. 'Docudramatizing History on TV: German and British Docudrama and Historical Event Television in the Memorial Year 2005', *European Journal of Cultural Studies* 10: 35–53.

Eco, U. 1982. *Der Name der Rose*. Munich: Hanser.

Ehrenstein, W. 1955. 'Die Mitarbeit der Schule im Kampf gegen den Massengeist', *Aus Politik und Zeitgeschichte* 5: 96.

Einstein, A. 1987. *Collected Papers*, vol. 1: *The Early Years, 1979–1902*. Princeton, NJ: Princeton University Press.

———— 1993. *Collected Papers*, vol. 5: *The Swiss Years: Correspondence*. Princeton, NJ: Princeton University Press.

Einstein, A. and M. Maric. 1992. *The Love Letters*, trans. S. Smith. Princeton, NJ: Princeton University Press.

Elena, A. 1997. 'Skirts in the Lab: Madame Curie and the Image of the Woman Scientist in the Feature Film', *Public Understanding of Science* 6: 269–78.

Eley, G. and A. Grossmann. 1997. 'Watching Schindler's List and Holocaust Fiction, Reception, Criticism: Not the Last Word', *New German Criticism* 71: 41–62.

Epple, A. 2003. *Empfindsame Geschichtsschreibung. Eine Geschlechtergeschichte der Historiographie zwischen Aufklärung und Historismus.* Cologne: Böhlau.

———— 2007. 'Von Werwölfen und Schutzengeln. Historiographiegeschichte als Analyse des historischen Apriori', in J. Eckel and T. Etzemüller (eds), *Neue Zugänge zur Geschichte der Geschichtswissenschaft.* Göttingen: Wallstein, pp. 171–200.

Epple, A. and F. Haber. 2005. *Vom Nutzen und Nachteil des Internets für die historische Erkenntnis.* Zurich: Chronos.

Epple, A. and A. Schaser (eds). 2009. *Multiple Histories? Changing Perspectives on Modern Historiography.* Frankfurt am Main: Campus.

Ericsen, K. and E. Simonsen (eds). 2002. *Children of World War II: The Hidden Enemy Legacy.* Oxford: Berg.

Eriksen, A. 1995. *Det var noe annet under krigen. 2. Verdenskrig i norsk kollektivtradisjon.* Oslo: Pax Forlag.

Erll, A. 2005. *Kollektives Gedächtnis und Erinnerungskultur.* Stuttgart: Metzler.

Estermann, A. 1995. *Inhaltsanalytische Bibliographien deutscher Kulturzeitschriften des 19. Jahrhunderts (IBDK),* vol. 3: *Die Gartenlaube (1853–1880).* Munich: Saur.

Estermann, M. and S. Füssel. 2003. 'Belletristische Verlage', in G. Jäger (ed.) *Geschichte des deutschen Buchhandels im 19. und 20. Jahrhundert,* vol. 1: *Das Kaiserreich 1870–1918.* Frankfurt am Main: Buchhändler-Vereinigung, pp. 164–299.

Evans, J. 2000. 'What is Public History?' Retrieved 7 August 2008 from: http://www.publichistory.org/what_is/definition.html.

Evans, R.J. 1991. *Im Schatten Hitlers? Historikerstreit und Vergangenheitsbewältigung in der Bundesrepublik.* Frankfurt am Main: Suhrkamp.

Exner, L. 2004. *Elisabeth von Österreich.* Reinbek: Rowohlt.

Febvre, L. 1988. *Das Gewissen des Historikers.* Berlin: Wagenbach.

Felken, D. 1988. *Oswald Spengler. Konservatives Denken zwischen Kaiserreich und Diktatur.* Munich: Beck.

Fest, J. 1973. *Hitler.* Berlin: Propyläen.

———— 1994. *Das tragische Vermächtnis. Der 20. Juli 1944.* Heidelberg: Müller.

———— 1999. *Speer. Eine Biographie.* Berlin: Fest.

Fest, J. and B. Eichinger. 2004. *'Der Untergang'. Das Filmbuch.* Reinbek: Rowohlt.

Fischer, J.-U. 2001. '"Man soll nicht vergessen" – Stalingrad-Deutungen im Hörfunkprogramm der SBZ/DDR in den späten vierziger und fünfziger Jahren', in U. Heukenkamp (ed.) *Schuld und Sühne? Kriegserlebnis und Kriegsdeutung in deutschen Medien der Nachkriegszeit (1945–1961),* vol. 1. Amsterdam: Rodopi, pp. 127–38.

Fischer, T. and R. Wirtz (eds). 2008. *Alles authentisch? Popularisierung der Geschichte im Fernsehen.* Konstanz: UVK.

Fleck, L. 2002[1935]. *Entstehung und Entwicklung einer wissenschaftlichen Tatsache. Einführung in die Lehre vom Denkstil und Denkkollektiv.* Frankfurt am Main: Suhrkamp.

Follett, K. 1990. *Die Säulen der Erde*. Bergisch Gladbach: Lübbe.

Foucault, M. 1974. *Die Ordnung der Dinge. Eine Archäologie der Humanwissenschaften*. Frankfurt am Main: Suhrkamp.

———— 1978. *Dispositive der Macht. Über Sexualität, Wissen und Wahrheit*. Berlin: Merve.

Fox-Genovese, E. and E. Lasch-Quinn (eds). 1999. *Reconstructing History: The Emergence of a New Historical Society*. New York: Routledge.

Fox Keller, E. 1983. *Reflections on Gender and Science*. New Haven, CT: Yale University Press.

Frank, P. 1949. *Einstein. Sein Leben und seine Zeit*. Munich: List.

Franzke, H.-G. 2007. 'Gesetzgeber als Geschichtslehrer? Zur Entscheidung des französischen Verfassungsrates über das HeimkehrG 2005', *Europäische Grundrechte-Zeitschrift* 34: 21–24.

Frei, A.G. 1994. *Finale Grande. Die Rückkehr der Fußballweltmeister 1954*. Berlin: Transit.

Frei, N. 1996. *Vergangenheitspolitik. Die Anfänge der Bundesrepublik und die NS-Vergangenheit*. Munich: Beck.

Friedlaender, S. 2006. *Nazi Germany and the Jews*, 2 vols. New York: HarperCollins.

Friedrich, J. 2002. *Der Brand. Deutschland im Bombenkrieg*. Berlin: Propyläen.

Fritz. J. 2003. 'Geschichtsverständnis via Computerspiel', in J. Fritz. and W. Fehr (eds), *Computerspiele. Virtuelle Spiel- und Lernwelten*. Bonn: Bundeszentrale für Politische Bildung, pp. 168–90.

Frölich, M. and H. Loewy (eds). 2003. *Lachen über Hitler – Auschwitz-Gelächter? Filmkomödie, Satire und Holocaust*. Munich: Text and Kritik.

Fuchs, E. 2001. 'Reshaping the World: Historiography from a Universal Perspective', in L.E. Jones (ed.) *Crossing Boundaries: The Exclusion and Inclusion of Minorities in Germany and America*. Oxford: Berghahn, pp. 243–63.

Fuhrmann, H. 1996a. *'Sind eben alles Menschen gewesen'. Gelehrtenleben im 19. und 20. Jahrhundert*. Munich: Beck.

———— 1996b. 'Ernst H. Kantorowicz: Der gedeutete Geschichtsdeuter', in idem, *Überall ist Mittelalter. Von der Gegenwart einer vergangenen Zeit*. Munich: Beck, pp. 252–70.

Fulda, D. 1996. *Wissenschaft aus Kunst. Die Entstehung der modernen deutschen Geschichtsschreibung 1760–1860*. Berlin: de Gruyter.

Füßl, W. and S. Ittner (eds). 1998. *Biographie und Technikgeschichte*. Opladen: Leske and Budrich.

Füßmann, K. 1994. 'Historische Formungen, Dimensionen der Geschichts-darstellung', in K. Füßmann and H.T. Grütter (eds), *Historische Faszination. Geschichtskultur heute*. Cologne: Böhlau, pp. 27–44.

Gabbe, J. 1976. *Parteien und Nation. Zur Rolle des Nationalbewusstseins für die politische Grundorientierung der Parteien in der Anfangsphase der Bundesrepublik*. Meisenheim: Hain.

Gassert, P. 1997. *Amerika im Dritten Reich. Ideologie, Propaganda und Volks-meinung 1933–1945*. Stuttgart: Steiner.

Gawlick, G. and L. Kreimendahl. 1987. *Hume in der deutschen Aufklärung. Umrisse einer Rezeptionsgeschichte*. Stuttgart: Frommann-Holzboog.

Gebauer, G. 1999. 'Les trois dates de l'équipe d'allemagne de football', in H. Héla and P. Mignon (eds), *Football. Jeu et société*. Paris: INSEP, pp. 101–11.

Gehlen, A. 1952. 'Mensch trotz Masse. Der Einzelne in der Umwälzung der Gesellschaft', *Wort und Wahrheit* 8: 579–94.

Gehrke, H.J. 2001. 'Myth, History, and Collective Identity: Uses of the Past in Ancient Greece and Beyond', in N. Luraghi (ed.) *The Historian's Craft in the Age of Herodotus*. Oxford: Oxford University Press, pp. 286–313.

Geiss, I. 1993. 'Welt und Weltgeschichte 1991. Ein universalhistorischer Besinnungsaufsatz', in G. Diesener et al. (eds), *Karl Lamprecht weiterdenken. Universal- und Kulturgeschichte heute*. Leipzig: Leipziger Universitätsverlag, pp. 421–43.

Gerlach, C. 2003. 'Nationsbildung im Krieg. Wirtschaftliche Faktoren bei der Vernichtung der Armenier und beim Mord an den ungarischen Juden', in H.-L. Kieser and D.J. Schaller (eds), *Der Völkermord an den Armeniern und die Shoah*. Zurich: Chronos, pp. 347–422.

Geserick, R. 2004. 'Vom Erziehungsinstrument zum Konsumgut? Zur Entwicklung des DDR-Rundfunks in der Honecker-Zeit', in K. Arnold and C. Classen (eds), *Zwischen Pop und Propaganda. Radio in der DDR*. Berlin: Links, pp. 151–62.

Gilzmer, M. 2007. *Denkmäler als Medien der Erinnerungskultur in Frankreich seit 1945*. Munich: Meidenbauer.

Giroud, F. 1981. *Une femme honorable*. Paris: Fayard.

Glassberg, D. 2001. *Sense of History: The Place of the Past in American Life*. Amherst: University of Massachusetts Press.

Goldsmith, B. 2005. *Obsessive Genius: The Inner World of Marie Curie*. London: Weidenfeld and Nicolson.

Görtemaker, M. 1999. *Geschichte der Bundesrepublik. Von der Gründung bis zur Gegenwart*. Munich: Beck.

Govoni, P. 2005. 'Historians of Science and the "Sobel Effect"', *Journal of Science Communication* 4: 1–17.

Graus, F. 1987. 'Epochenbewußtsein im Spätmittelalter und Probleme der Periodisierung', in R. Herzog and R. Koselleck (eds), *Epochenschwelle und Epochenbewußtsein*. Munich: Fink, pp. 153–66.

Grieser, T. 1999. 'Buchhandel und Verlag in der Inflation: Studien zu wirtschaftlichen Entwicklungstendenzen des deutschen Buchhandels in der Inflation nach dem Ersten Weltkrieg', *Archiv für Geschichte des Buchwesens* 51: 1–187.

Groebner, V. 2008. *Das Mittelalter hört nicht auf. Über historisches Erzählen*. Munich: Beck.

Grünewald, E. 1982. *Ernst Kantorowicz und Stefan George. Beiträge zur Biographie des Historikers bis zum Jahre 1938 und zu seinem Jugendwerk Kaiser Friedrich der Zweite.* Wiesbaden: Steiner.

Grütter, H.T. 1994. 'Warum fasziniert die Vergangenheit? Perspektiven einer neuen Geschichtskultur', in K. Füßmann and H.T. Grütter (eds), *Historische Faszination. Geschichtskultur heute.* Cologne: Böhlau, pp. 45–57.

Häberle, P. 1997. *Europäische Rechtskultur.* Frankfurt am Main: Suhrkamp.

Habermas, J. 1954. 'Die Dialektik der Rationalisierung. Vom Pauperismus in Produktion und Konsum', *Merkur* 8: 701–24.

Haffner, S. 1967. *Winston Churchill.* Reinbek: Rowohlt.

——— 1968. *Die verratene Revolution. Deutschland 1918/19.* Bern: Scherz.

——— 1978. *Anmerkungen zu Hitler.* Munich: Kindler.

——— 1979. *Preußen ohne Legende.* Hamburg: Gruner and Jahr.

——— 1982. *Zur Zeitgeschichte. 36 Essays.* Munich: Kindler.

——— 1987. *Von Bismarck zu Hitler.* Munich: Kindler.

——— 2000. *Geschichte eines Deutschen. Die Erinnerungen 1914–1933.* Stuttgart: Deutsche Verlagsanstalt.

Hagner, M. 2004. *Geniale Gehirne. Zur Geschichte der Elitegehirnforschung.* Göttingen: Wallstein.

Hakelberg, D. 2004. 'Adliges Herkommen und bürgerliche Nationalgeschichte. Hans von Aufseß und die Vorgeschichte des Germanischen Nationalmuseums in Nürnberg', in H. Beck (ed.) *Zur Geschichte der Gleichung 'germanisch-deutsch' – Sprache und Namen, Geschichte und Institutionen.* Berlin: de Gruyter, pp. 523–76.

Halbwachs, M. 1950. *La Mémoire collective.* Paris: Presses Universitaires de France.

——— 1985[1925]. *Das Gedächtnis und seine soziale Bedingung.* Frankfurt am Main: Suhrkamp.

Hall, S. (ed.) 1997. *Representation: Cultural Representations and Signifying Practices.* London: Sage.

Hamann, B. 1981. *Elisabeth. Kaiserin wider Willen.* Vienna: Amalthea.

——— 1996. *Elisabeth. Kaiserin wider Willen,* 15th edn. Vienna: Amalthea.

Hamann, B. (ed.) 1984. *Das poetische Tagebuch. Kaiserin Elisabeth.* Vienna: Österreichische Akademie der Wissenschaften.

Hamburger Instituts für Sozialforschung (ed.) 1996. *Vernichtungskrieg. Verbrechen der Wehrmacht 1941 bis 1944. Ausstellungskatalog.* Hamburg: Hamburger Edition.

——— (ed.) 1998a. *Besucher einer Ausstellung. Die Ausstellung 'Vernichtungskrieg. Verbrechen der Wehrmacht 1941 bis 1944' in Interview und Gespräch.* Hamburg: Hamburger Edition.

——— (ed.) 1998b. *Krieg ist ein Gesellschaftszustand. Reden zur Eröffnung der Ausstellung 'Vernichtungskrieg. Verbrechen der Wehrmacht 1941 bis 1944'.* Hamburg: Hamburger Edition.

————— (ed.) 1999. *Eine Ausstellung und ihre Folgen. Zur Rezeption der Ausstellung 'Vernichtungskrieg. Verbrechen der Wehrmacht 1941 bis 1944'.* Hamburg: Hamburger Edition.

————— (ed.) 2002. *Verbrechen der Wehrmacht. Dimensionen des Vernichtungskrieges 1941–1944. Ausstellungskatalog.* Hamburg: Hamburger Edition.

Hardtwig, W. 1979. 'Theorie oder Erzählung - eine falsche Alternative', in J. Kocka and T. Nipperdey (eds), *Theorie und Erzählung in der Geschichte.* Munich: Deutscher Taschenbuch-Verlag, pp. 290–99.

————— 1982. 'Die Verwissenschaftlichung der Historie und die Ästhetisierung der Darstellung', in R. Koselleck and H. Lutz (eds), *Formen der Geschichtsschreibung.* Munich: Deutscher Taschenbuch-Verlag, pp. 147–91.

————— 1990a. 'Erinnerung, Wissenschaft, Mythos. Nationale Geschichtsbilder und politische Symbole in der Reichsgründungsära und im Kaiserreich', in idem, *Geschichtskultur und Wissenschaft.* Munich: Deutscher Taschenbuch-Verlag, pp. 224–63.

————— 1990b. 'Geschichte als Wissenschaft oder Kunst', in idem, *Geschichtskultur und Wissenschaft.* Munich: Deutscher Taschenbuch-Verlag, pp. 92–102.

————— 1990c. 'Vorwort', in idem, *Geschichtskultur und Wissenschaft.* Munich: Deutscher Taschenbuch-Verlag, pp. 7–11.

————— 1990d. 'Von Preußens Aufgabe in Deutschland zur Deutschlands Aufgabe in der Welt. Liberalismus und borussianisches Geschichtsbild zwischen Revolution und Imperialismus', in idem, *Geschichtskultur und Wissenschaft.* Munich: Deutscher Taschenbuch-Verlag, pp. 103–60.

————— 1990e. 'Geschichtsstudium, Geschichtswissenschaft und Geschichtstheorie. Deutschland von der Aufklärung bis zur Gegenwart', in idem, *Geschichtskultur und Wissenschaft.* Munich: Deutscher Taschenbuch-Verlag, pp. 13–57.

————— 1990f. *Geschichtskultur und Wissenschaft.* Munich: Deutscher Taschenbuch-Verlag.

————— 1997. 'Jacob Burckhardt (1818–97)', in V. Reinhardt (ed.) *Hauptwerke der Geschichtsschreibung.* Stuttgart: Körner, pp. 74–78.

————— 1998. 'Die Verwissenschaftlichung der neueren Geschichtsschreibung', in H-J. Goertz (ed.) *Geschichte: Ein Grundkurs.* Reinbek: Rowohlt, pp. 245–69.

————— 2002a. 'Fiktive Zeitgeschichte? Literarische Erzählung, Geschichtswissenschaft und Erinnerungskultur in Deutschland', in K.H. Jarausch and M. Sabrow (eds), *Verletztes Gedächtnis. Erinnerungskultur und Zeitgeschichte im Konflikt.* Frankfurt am Main: Campus, pp. 99–123.

————— 2002b. 'Geschichtskultur', in S. Jordan (ed.) *Lexikon Geschichtswissenschaft. Hundert Grundbegriffe.* Stuttgart: Reclam, pp. 112–16.

————— 2005a. 'Kugler, Menzel und das Bild Friedrichs des Großen', in idem, *Hochkultur des bürgerlichen Zeitalters.* Göttingen: Vandenhoeck and Ruprecht, pp. 306–22.

———— 2005b. 'Der Literat als Chronist. Tagebücher aus dem Krieg 1939–1945', in idem (ed.) *Geschichte für Leser. Populäre Geschichtsschreibung in Deutschland im 20. Jahrhundert.* Stuttgart: Steiner, pp. 147–80.

———— 2005c. 'Die Krise des Geschichtsbewußtseins in Kaiserreich und Weimarer Republik und der Aufstieg des Nationalsozialismus', in idem, *Hochkultur des bürgerlichen Zeitalters.* Göttingen: Vandenhoeck and Ruprecht, pp. 77–102.

———— 2005d. 'Geschichte für Leser. Populäre Geschichtsschreibung in Deutschland im 20. Jahrhundert. Einleitung', in W. Hardtwig and E. Schütz (eds), *Geschichte für Leser. Populäre Geschichtsschreibung in Deutschland im 20. Jahrhundert.* Stuttgart: Steiner, pp. 11–32.

———— and A. Schug (eds). 2009. *History Sells. Angewandte Geschichte als Wissenschaft und Markt.* Stuttgart: Steiner.

Hartmann, C. 2004. 'Verbrecherischer Krieg – verbrecherische Wehrmacht? Überlegungen zur Struktur des deutschen Ostheeres 1941–1944', *Vierteljahrsheft für Zeitgeschichte* 52: 1–75.

Hartmann, C. and J. Hürter. 2005. *Verbrechen der Wehrmacht. Bilanz einer Debatte.* Munich: Beck.

Haslip, J. 1965. *The Lonely Empress.* Cleveland, OH: World Publisher.

Haupt, H.-G. and D. Langewiesche (eds). 2001. *Nation und Religion in der deutschen Geschichte.* Frankfurt am Main: Campus.

Heer, H. and V. Ullrich. 1985. *Geschichte entdecken. Erfahrungen und Projekte der neuen Geschichtsbewegung.* Reinbek: Rowohlt.

Heigl, R. 2000. *Wüstensöhne und Despoten. Das Bild des Vorderen Orients in deutschsprachigen Weltgeschichten des 19. Jahrhunderts.* Regensburg: Lehrstuhl für Neuere Deutsche Literaturwissenschaft der Universität Regensburg.

Heimann, T. 2000. 'Erinnerung als Wandlung. Kriegsbilder im frühen DDR-Film', in M. Sabrow (ed.) *Geschichte als Herrschaftsdiskurs. Der Umgang mit der Vergangenheit in der DDR.* Cologne: Böhlau, pp. 37–85.

Heimrod, U. (ed.) 1999. *Der Denkmalstreit – das Denkmal? Die Debatte um das Denkmal für die ermordeten Juden Europas. Eine Dokumentation.* Berlin: Philo Verlagsgesellschaft.

Heinßen, J. 2003. *Historismus und Kulturkritik. Studien zur deutschen Geschichtskultur im späten 19. Jahrhundert.* Göttingen: Vandenhoeck and Ruprecht.

Heit, A. 1994. 'Die ungestillte Sehnsucht. Versuch über ein Movens historischer Faszination in Umberto Ecos Roman *Der Name der Rose*', in K. Füßmann and H.T. Grütter (eds), *Historische Faszination. Geschichtskultur heute.* Cologne: Böhlau, pp. 113–28.

Helmolt, H.F. (ed.) 1899–1907. *Weltgeschichte*, 9 vols. Leipzig: Bibliographisches Institut.

Hentschel, A. and G. Grasshoff. 2005. *Albert Einstein. 'Jene glücklichen Berner Jahre'.* Bern: Stämpfli.

Herbert, U. 1996. *Best. Biographische Studien über Radikalismus, Weltanschauung und Vernunft 1903–1989*. Bonn: Dietz.

———— 1998. 'Vernichtungspolitik. Neue Antworten und Fragen zur Geschichte des "Holocaust"', in idem (ed.) *Nationalsozialistische Vernichtungspolitik 1939–1945. Neue Forschungen und Kontroversen*. Frankfurt am Main: Fischer, pp. 9–66.

Hermann, A. 1994. *Einstein. Der Weltweise und sein Jahrhundert. Eine Biographie*. Munich: Piper.

Hermann, M. 2005. 'Historische Quellen. Sachbericht und autobiographische Literatur. Berichte von Überlebenden der Konzentrationslager als populäre Geschichtsschreibung? (1946–1964)', in W. Hardtwig (ed.) *Geschichte für Leser. Populäre Geschichtsschreibung in Deutschland im 20. Jahrhundert*. Stuttgart: Steiner, pp. 123–46.

Herre, P. (ed.) 1910. *Quellenkunde zur Weltgeschichte. Ein Handbuch*. Leipzig: Dieterich.

Herrmann, E.M. 1963. *Zur Theorie und Praxis der Presse in der Sowjetischen Besatzungszone Deutschlands. Berichte und Dokumente*. Berlin: Colloquium.

Herrmann, U. 1991. 'Pädagogisches Denken und Anfänge der Reform-pädagogik', in C. Berg (ed.) *Handbuch der deutschen Bildungsgeschichte*, vol. 4. *1870–1918. Von der Reichsgründung bis zum Ende des Ersten Weltkrieges*. Munich: Beck, pp. 147–78.

Hertfelder, T. and G. Hübinger (eds). 2000. *Kritik und Mandat. Intellektuelle in der deutschen Politik*. Stuttgart: Deutsche Verlagsanstalt.

Herz, E. 1994. *Denk ich an Deutschland in der Nacht*. Warburg: Hermes.

Heuss, A. 1976. 'Über die Schwierigkeit, Weltgeschichte zu schreiben', *Saeculum* 27: 1–35.

Heuss, T. 1932. *Hitlers Weg. Eine historisch-politische Studie über den Nationalsozialismus*. Stuttgart: Union.

———— 1951. *Deutsche Gestalten*, 3rd edn. Tübingen: Wunderlich.

Heyden-Rynsch, V. v.d. (ed.) 1983. *Elisabeth von Österreich. Tagebuchblätter von Constantin Christomanos*. Munich: Matthes and Seitz.

Hicks, P. 2002. 'Catharine Macaulay's Civil War: Gender, History and Republicanism in Georgian Britain', *Journal of British Studies* 41: 170–98.

Highfield, R. and P. Carter. 1993. *The Private Lives of Albert Einstein*. London: Faber.

———— 1994. *Die geheimen Leben des Albert Einstein: Eine Biographie*, trans. A. Ehlers. Munich: Deutscher Taschenbuch-Verlag.

Hiller, H. 1966. *Zur Sozialgeschichte von Buch und Buchhandel*. Bonn: Bouvier.

Hobsbawm, E. and T. Ranger (eds). 1992. *The Invention of Tradition*. Cambridge: Cambridge University Press.

Hochbruck, W. 2006. *Geschichtstheater. Dramatische Präsentationen historischer Lebenswelten*. Remseck: Geschichtstheatergesellschaft.

Hockerts, G. 2002. 'Zugänge zur Zeitgeschichte. Primärerfahrung, Erinnerungskultur, Geschichtswissenschaft', in K.H. Jarausch and M.

Sabrow (eds), *Verletztes Gedächtnis. Erinnerungskultur und Zeitgeschichte im Konflikt*. Frankfurt am Main: Campus, pp. 39–74.

Hodenberg, C. von. 2006. *Konsens und Krise. Eine Geschichte der westdeutschen Medienöffentlichkeit 1944–1973*. Göttingen: Wallstein.

Hoffmann, B. and H. Dukas. 1972. *Albert Einstein: Creator and Rebel*. New York: Viking Press.

Hoffmann, D. 2006. *Einsteins Berlin. Auf den Spuren eines Genies*. Weinheim: Wiley-VCH.

Hofmann, F. and J. Schmitt. 1978[1903]. *Vollständiges Generalregister der Gartenlaube vom 1. bis 50. Jahrgang (1853–1902)*. Hildesheim: Gerstenberg.

Holz, H.H. 1993. 'Das Zeitalter der Weltgeschichte', in H.H. Holz and D. Losurdo (eds), *Weltgeschichte*. Bonn: Pahl-Rugenstein, pp. 13–38.

Holzweißig, G. 1996. 'Konrad Adenauer in den Medien der DDR. Kampagnen der SED-Agitationsbürokratie', in H.G. Hockerts (ed.) *Das Adenauer-Bild in der DDR*. Bonn: Bouvier, pp. 75–106.

———— 2002. *Die schärfste Waffe der Partei. Eine Mediengeschichte der DDR*. Cologne: Böhlau.

Horn, S. 2002. '"Jetzt aber zu einem Thema, das uns in dieser Woche alle beschäftigt". Die westdeutsche Fernsehberichterstattung über den Frankfurter Auschwitz-Prozeß (1963–1965) und den Düsseldorfer Majdanek-Prozeß (1975–1981) – ein Vergleich', *1999* 17: 13–43.

———— and M. Sauer (eds). 2009. *Geschichte und Öffentlichkeit. Orte – Medien – Institutionen*. Stuttgart: UTB.

Huber, T. 1834. *Geschichte des Cevennen-Kriegs. Ein Lesebuch für Ungelehrte. Nach Memoiren und geschichtlichen Nachrichten erzählt von der verstorbenen Therese Huber*. Stuttgart: Cotta.

Hübinger, G. 1988. 'Geschichte als leitende Orientierungswissenschaft im 19. Jahrhundert', *Berichte zur Wissenschaftsgeschichte* 11: 149–58.

———— 1994. 'Die europäischen Intellektuellen 1890–1930', *Neue Politische Literatur* 39: 34–54.

———— 1997. 'Heinrich von Treitschke (1834–96)', in V. Reinhardt (ed.) *Hauptwerke der Geschichtsschreibung*. Stuttgart: Körner, pp. 650–52.

Hübinger, G. (ed.) 1996. *Versammlungsort moderner Geister. Der Eugen Diederichs Verlag – Aufbruch ins Jahrhundert der Extreme*. Munich: Diederichs.

Hübinger, G. and W.J. Mommsen (eds). 1993. *Intellektuelle im Deutschen Kaiserreich*. Frankfurt am Main: Fischer.

Hughes-Warrington, M. 2005a. 'Readers, Responses and Popular Culture', in idem (ed.) *Palgrave Advances in World Histories*. Basingstoke: Palgrave Macmillan, pp. 215–37.

———— 2005b. 'World Histories', in idem (ed.) *Palgrave Advances in World Histories*. Basingstoke: Palgrave Macmillan, pp. 1–17.

Hume, D. 1754–62. *History of England: From the Invasion of Julius Caesar to the Revolution in 1688*, 6 vols. London: A. Millar.

Hunt, T. 2006. 'Reality, Identity, and Empathy: The Changing Face of Social History Television', *Journal of Social History* 39: 843–58.

Hüser, D. 2006. 'Staat – Zivilgesellschaft – Populärkultur. Zum Wandel des Gedenkens an den Algerienkrieg in Frankreich', in C. Kohser-Spohn and F. Renken (eds), *Trauma Algerienkrieg. Zur Geschichte und Aufarbeitung eines Konflikts*. Frankfurt am Main: Campus, pp. 95–111.

Iggers, G.G. 1968. *The German Conception of History: The National Tradition of Historical Thought from Herder to the Present*. Middletown, CT: Wesleyan University Press.

———— 1996. *Geschichtswissenschaft im 20. Jahrhundert*, 2nd edn. Göttingen: Vandenhoeck and Ruprecht.

———— 1997. *Deutsche Geschichtswissenschaft. Eine Kritik der traditionellen Geschichtsauffassung von Herder bis zur Gegenwart*. Vienna: Böhlau.

Illy, J. 2006. *Albert Meets America: How Journalists Treated Genius during Einstein's 1921 Travels*. Baltimore, MD: Johns Hopkins University Press.

Insdorf, A. 1989. *Indelible Shadows: Film and the Holocaust*. Cambridge: Cambridge University Press.

Jäger, M. 1994. *Kultur und Politik in der DDR 1945–1990*. Cologne: Verlag Wissenschaft und Politik.

Jäger, O. 1887–89. *Weltgeschichte in vier Bänden*, 1st edn. Bielefeld: Velhagen and Klasing.

———— 1890–94. *Weltgeschichte in vier Bänden*, 2nd edn. Bielefeld: Velhagen and Klasing.

Janosi, F.E. von. 1969. 'Grundeinstellungen der Moderne', in A. Randa (ed.) *Mensch und Weltgeschichte. Zur Geschichte der Universalgeschichtsschreibung*. Salzburg: Pustet, pp. 239–57.

Jarausch, K.H. 2002. 'Zeitgeschichte und Erinnerung. Deutungskonkurrenz oder Interdependenz?' in K.H. Jarausch and M. Sabrow (eds), *Verletztes Gedächtnis. Erinnerungskultur und Zeitgeschichte im Konflikt*. Frankfurt am Main: Campus, pp. 9–38.

Jarausch, K.H. and M. Sabrow (eds). 2002. *Verletztes Gedächtnis. Erinnerungs-kultur und Zeitgeschichte im Konflikt*. Frankfurt am Main: Campus.

Jenke, M. 1999. 'Hörfunk im Wettbewerb', in D. Schwarzkopf (ed.) *Rundfunkpolitik in Deutschland. Wettbewerb und Öffentlichkeit*. Munich: Deutscher Taschenbuch-Verlag, pp. 643–700.

Jens, I. (ed.) 1984. *Hans Scholl. Sophie Scholl. Briefe und Aufzeichnungen*. Frankfurt am Main: Fischer.

Joliot-Curie, I. 1955. 'Etude sur les Carnets de laboratoire de la découverte du polonium et du radium', in *M. Curie, Pierre Curie*, 2nd edn. Paris: Denoël, pp. 135–66.

Jonas, K.W. and H.R. Stunz. 2004. *Golo Mann. Leben und Werk 1929–2003. Bibliographie und Lebenschronik*. Wiesbaden: Harrassowitz.

Jo Nye, M. 2006. 'Scientific Biography: History of Science by Another Means?' *Isis* 97: 322–29.

Jordanova, L. 2000. *History in Practice*. London: Arnold.

Kaelble, H. 2004. 'Welche Chancen für eine Weltgeschichte?' *Zeithistorische Forschungen/Studies in Contemporary History*. Retrieved 3 January 2007 from: http://www.zeithistorische-forschungen.de/16126041-Kaelble-3-2004.

Kaes, A. 1987. *Deutschlandbilder. Die Wiederkehr der Geschichte als Film*. Munich: Text and Kritik.

Kagan, D. 1984. 'The Changing World of World Histories', *The New York Times*, 11 November. Retrieved 5 September 2006 from: http://query.nytimes.com/gst/fullpage.html?res=9C05E3DC1139F932A25752C1A962948260andsec=andpagewanted=print.

Kansteiner, W. 2003. 'Ein Völkermord ohne Täter? Die Darstellung der "Endlösung" in den Sendungen des Zweiten Deutschen Fernsehens', in M. Zuckermann (ed.) *Medien – Politik – Geschichte*. Göttingen: Wallstein, pp. 253–86.

———— 2006. *In Pursuit of German Memory: History, Television, and Politics after Auschwitz*. Athens: Ohio University Press.

Kassal-Mikula, R. 1987. '"Kaiserin-Elisabeth-Denkmäler" in Wien 1854–1914', in *Elisabeth von Österreich. Einsamkeit, Macht und Freiheit. 99. Sonderausstellung des Historischen Museums der Stadt Wien*, 2nd edn. Vienna: Eigenverlag der Museen der Stadt Wien, pp. 82–101.

Keefer, E. (ed.) 2006. *Lebendige Vergangenheit. Vom Archäologischen Experiment zur Zeitreise*. Stuttgart: Konrad Theiss.

Keilbach, J. 2002. 'Fernsehbilder der Geschichte. Anmerkungen zur Darstellung des Nationalsozialismus in den Geschichtsdokumentationen des ZDF', *1999* 17: 102–14.

———— 2008. *Geschichtsbilder und Zeitzeugen. Zur Darstellung des Nationalsozialismus im bundesdeutschen Fernsehen*. Münster: Lit.

Kelley, R. 1978. 'Public History: Its Origins, Nature, and Prospects', *Public Historian* 1: 16–28.

Kelly, A. 1981. *The Descent of Darwin: The Popularization of Darwinism in Germany 1860–1914*. Chapel Hill: University of North Carolina Press.

Kershaw, I. 1998–2000. *Hitler*, 2 vols. London: Deutsche Verlags-Anstalt.

———— 2000. *The Nazi Dictatorship: Problems and Perspectives of Interpretation*. London: Arnold.

Kiefer, M. 1993. *Auf der Suche nach nationaler Identität und Wegen zur deutschen Einheit. Die deutsche Frage in der überregionalen Tages- und Wochenpresse der Bundesrepublik 1949–1955*, 2nd edn. Frankfurt am Main: Lang.

Kielmannsegg, P. von. 2000. *Nach der Katastrophe. Eine Geschichte des geteilten Deutschland*. Berlin: Siedler.

Kirsch, J.-H. 2003. *Nationaler Mythos oder historische Trauer? Der Streit um ein zentrales 'Holocaust-Mahnmal' für die Berliner Republik*. Cologne: Böhlau.

Kirst, H.H. 1954a. *08/15 Die abenteuerliche Revolte des Gefr. Asch*. Munich: Kurt-Desch-Verlag.

——— 1954b. *08/15 Die seltsamen Kriegserlebnisse des Soldaten Asch.* Munich: Kurt-Desch-Verlag

——— 1955. *08/15 Der gefährliche Endsieg des Soldaten Asch.* Munich: Kurt-Desch-Verlag.

Kistner, T. and L. Schulze. 2001. *Die Spielmacher. Strippenzieher und Profiteure im deutschen Fußball.* Stuttgart: Deutsche Verlagsanstalt.

Kittsteiner, H.D. 1998. *Listen der Vernunft. Motive geschichtsphilosophischen Denkens.* Frankfurt: Fischer.

——— 2005. 'Oswald Spengler zwischen "Untergang des Abendlandes" und "Preußischem Sozialismus"', in W. Hardtwig (ed.) *Geschichte für Leser. Populäre Geschichtsschreibung in Deutschland im 20. Jahrhundert.* Stuttgart: Steiner, pp. 309–32.

Klingler, W. 1983. 'Nationalsozialistische Rundfunkpolitik 1942–1945. Organisation, Programm und Hörer', Ph.D. dissertation. Mannheim: University of Mannheim.

Klotz, J. 2001. 'Die Ausstellung "Vernichtungskrieg, Verbrechen der Wehrmacht 1941 bis 1944". Zwischen Geschichtswissenschaft und Geschichtspolitik', in D. Bald and J. Klotz (eds), *Mythos Wehrmacht. Nachkriegsdebatten und Traditionspflege.* Berlin: Aufbau, pp. 116–76.

Knilli, F. and S. Zielinksi (eds). 1983. *Betrifft 'Holocaust'. Zuschauer schreiben an den WDR.* Berlin: Spiess.

Knoch, H. 2005. 'Die lange Dauer der Propaganda. Populäre Kriegsdarstellung in der frühen Bundesrepublik', in W. Hardtwig (ed.) *Geschichte für Leser. Populäre Geschichtsschreibung in Deutschland im 20. Jahrhundert.* Stuttgart: Steiner, pp. 205–26.

Knopp, G. and S. Quandt (eds). 1988. *Geschichte im Fernsehen. Ein Handbuch.* Darmstadt: Wissenschaftliche Buchgesellschaft.

Knorr-Cetina, K. 1984. *Die Fabrikation von Erkenntnis. Zur Anthropologie der Naturwissenschaften.* Frankfurt am Main: Suhrkamp.

Koch, M. 2003. *Nationale Identität im Prozess nationalstaatlicher Orientierung, dargestellt am Beispiel Deutschlands durch die Analyse der Familienzeitschrift 'Die Gartenlaube' von 1853–1890.* Frankfurt: Lang.

Kocka, J. 1990. 'Wozu Geschichte (1975/1989)', in W. Hardtwig (ed.) *Über das Studium der Geschichte.* Munich: Deutscher Taschenbuch Verlag, pp. 427–43.

Kocka, J. and T. Nipperdey (eds). 1979. *Theorie und Erzählung in der Geschichte.* Munich: Deutscher Taschenbuch-Verlag.

Koebner, R. 1990 [1941–43]. 'Die Idee der Zeitwende', in idem, *Geschichte, Geschichtsbewußtsein und Zeitwende. Vorträge und Schriften aus dem Nachlaß.* Gerlingen: Bleicher, pp. 147–93.

Koepnick, L. 2002. 'Reframing the Past: Heritage Cinema and the Holocaust in the 1990s', *New German Critique* 87: 47–82.

Kohser-Spohn, C. and F. Renken (eds). 2006. *Trauma Algerienkrieg. Zur Geschichte und Aufarbeitung eines Konflikts.* Frankfurt am Main: Campus.

Korff, G. (ed.) 1990. *Das historische Museum. Labor, Schaubühne, Identitäts-fabrik.* Frankfurt am Main: Campus.

Kors, A.C. 1999. 'The Future of History in an Increasingly Unified World', in E. Fox-Genovese and E. Lasch-Quinn (eds), *Reconstructing History: The Emergence of a New Historical Society.* New York: Routledge, pp. 12–17.

Korte, B. and S. Paletschek (eds). 2008. *Der Erste Weltkrieg in der populären Erinnerungskultur.* Essen: Klartext.

———— (eds). 2009. *History goes Pop. Zur Repräsentation von Geschichte in populären Medien und Genres.* Bielefeld: Transcript.

Korte, H. 1999. 'Hollywoodästhetik und die deutsche Geschichte. Schindlers Liste (Spielberg 1993)', in idem (ed.) *Einführung in die systematische Filmanalyse.* Berlin: Erich Schmidt, pp. 157–94.

Koselleck, R. 1979. 'Historia Magistra Vitae. Über die Auflösung des Topos im Horizont neuzeitlich bewegter Geschichte', in idem, *Vergangene Zukunft. Zur Semantik geschichtlicher Zeiten.* Frankfurt am Main: Suhrkamp, pp. 38–66.

———— 1989. *Vergangene Zukunft. Zur Semantik geschichtlicher Zeiten.* Frankfurt am Main: Suhrkamp.

———— 1997. 'Vom Sinn und Unsinn der Geschichte', in K.E. Müller and J. Rüsen (eds), *Historische Sinnbildung. Problemstellungen, Zeitkonzepte, Wahr-nehmungshorizonte, Darstellungsstrategien.* Reinbek: Rowohlt, pp. 79–97.

———— 2003. 'Erfahrungswandel und Methodenwechsel. Eine historisch-anthropologische Skizze', in idem, *Zeitschichten. Studien zur Historik.* Frankfurt am Main: Suhrkamp, pp. 27–77.

Koselleck, R. and H. Lutz (eds). 1982. *Formen der Geschichtsschreibung.* Munich: Deutscher Taschenbuch-Verlag.

Kössler, T. 2005. 'Zwischen Milieu und Markt. Die populäre Geschichtsschreibung der sozialistischen Arbeiterbewegung 1890–1933', in W. Hardtwig (ed.) *Geschichte für Leser. Populäre Geschichtsschreibung in Deutschland im 20. Jahrhundert.* Stuttgart: Steiner, pp. 259–85.

Kraul, M. 1982. 'Gymnasium, Gesellschaft und Geschichtsunterricht im Vormärz', in K. Bergmann and G. Schneider (eds), *Gesellschaft, Staat, Geschichtsunterricht. Beiträge zu einer Geschichte der Geschichtsdidaktik und des Geschichtsunterrichts von 1500–1980.* Düsseldorf: Paedagogischer Verlag Schwann, pp. 44–103.

Kraus-Kautzky. P. 1987. 'Filme über Elisabeth von Österreich', in *Elisabeth von Österreich. Einsamkeit, Macht und Freiheit. 99. Sonderausstellung des Historischen Museums der Stadt Wien,* 2nd edn. Vienna: Eigenverlag der Museen der Stadt Wien, pp. 117–18.

Kretschmann, C. (ed.) 2003. *Wissenspopularisierung. Konzepte der Wissenverbreitung im Wandel.* Berlin: Akademieverlag.

Krockow, C. von. 1988. *Die Stunde der Frauen: Bericht aus Pommern 1944 bis 1947.* Stuttgart: Deutsche Verlagsanstalt.

———— 1991. *Fahrten durch die Mark Brandenburg.* Stuttgart: Deutsche Verlagsanstalt.

————— 2000. *Zu Gast in drei Welten. Erinnerungen*, 2nd edn. Stuttgart: Deutsche Verlagsanstalt.

Kuhlemann, F.M. 1991. 'Niedere Schulen', in C. Berg (ed.) *Handbuch der deutschen Bildungsgeschichte*, vol. 4. Munich: Beck, pp. 179–227.

Kumpfmüller, M. 1995. *Die Schlacht von Stalingrad. Metamorphosen eines deutschen Mythos*. Munich: Fink.

Kunz, G. 2000. *Verortete Geschichte. Regionales Geschichtsbewußtsein in den deutschen historischen Vereinen des 19. Jahrhunderts*. Göttingen: Vandenhoeck and Ruprecht.

Kunze, M. and S. Levay. 1993. *Elisabeth. Songbook*. Gründwald: Roswitha Kunze.

Kyhring, A. 1945. *Gutta på skauen*. Oslo: Gyldendal Norsk Forlag.

Laclau, E. and C. Mouffe. 2000. *Hegemonie und radikale Demokratie. Zur Dekonstruktion des Marxismus*. Vienna: Passagen.

Lagny, M. 1997. 'Kino für Historiker', *Österreichische Zeitschrift für Geschichtswissenschaft* 8: 457–83.

Lahme, T. and H.R. Stunz. 2005. 'Der Erfolg als Mißverständnis? Wie Golo Mann zum Bestsellerautor wurde', in W. Hardtwig (ed.) *Geschichte für Leser. Populäre Geschichtsschreibung in Deutschland im 20. Jahrhundert*. Stuttgart: Steiner, pp. 371–98.

Langewiesche, D. 2000. 'Föderativer Nationalismus als Erbe der deutschen Reichsnation. Über Föderalismus und Zentralismus in der deutschen Nationalgeschichte', in idem, *Nation, Nationalismus und Nationalstaat in Deutschland und Europa*. Munich: Beck, pp. 55–79.

————— 2003. 'Geschichtswissenschaft in der Postmoderne?' in idem, *Liberalismus und Sozialismus. Gesellschaftsbilder – Zukunftsvisionen – Bildungskonzeptionen*. Bonn: Dietz, pp. 8–38.

————— 2008a. *Zeitwende. Geschichtsdenken heute*. Göttingen: Vandenhoeck and Ruprecht.

————— 2008b. 'Über das Umschreiben der Geschichte. Zur Rolle der Sozialgeschichte', in idem, *Zeitwende. Geschichtsdenken heute*. Göttingen: Vandenhoeck and Ruprecht, pp. 56–68.

————— 2008c. 'Zeitwende – eine Grundfigur neuzeitlichen Geschichtsdenkens. Richard Koebner im Vergleich mit Francis Fukuyama und Eric Hobsbawm', in idem, *Zeitwende. Geschichtsdenken heute*. Göttingen: Vandenhoeck and Ruprecht, pp. 41–55.

————— 2008d. 'Die Geschichtsschreibung und ihr Publikum. Zum Verhältnis von Geschichtswissenschaft und Geschichtsmarkt', in idem, *Zeitwende. Geschichtsdenken heute*. Göttingen: Vandenhoeck and Ruprecht, pp. 85–100.

————— 2008e. 'Das Alte Reich nach seinem Ende. Die Reichsidee in der deutschen Politik des 19. und frühen 20. Jahrhunderts. Versuch einer nationalgeschichtlichen Neubewertung in welthistorischer Perspektive', in idem, *Reich, Nation, Förderation. Deutschland und Europa*. Munich: Beck, pp. 211–34.

Langewiesche, D. and G. Schmidt (eds). 2000. *Föderative Nation. Deutschlandkonzepte von der Reformation bis zum Ersten Weltkrieg*. Munich: Oldenbourg.

Larsen, S.U. (ed.) 1999. *I krigens kjølvann. Nye sider ved norsk krigshistorie og etterkrigstid*. Oslo: Universitetsforlaget.

Lasch-Quinn, E. 1999. 'Democracy in the Ivory Tower? Towards the Restoration of an Intellectual Community', in E. Fox-Genovese and E. Lasch-Quinn (eds), *Reconstructing History: The Emergence of a New Historical Society*. New York: Routledge, pp. 23–34.

Latour, B. and S. Woolgar. 1979. *Laboratory Life: The Social Construction of Scientific Facts*. London: Sage.

Lehmann, A. 1992. 'Erinnerungen an die Kriegsgefangenschaft', in W. Wette and G.R. Ueberschär (eds), *Stalingrad. Mythos und Wirklichkeit einer Schlacht*. Frankfurt am Main: Fischer, pp. 178–89.

Lehndorff, H.G. von. 1961. *Ostpreußisches Tagebuch: Aufzeichnungen eines Arztes aus den Jahren 1945–1947*. Munich: Biederstein.

Leggewie, C. and E. Meyer. 2005. 'Ein Ort, an den man gerne geht'. *Das Holocaust-Mahnmal und die deutsche Geschichtspolitik nach 1989*. Munich: Hanser.

Lemke, M. 2000. 'Nationalismus und Patriotismus in den frühen Jahren der DDR', *Aus Politik und Zeitgeschichte* 50: 11–19.

Lenger, F. 1992. 'Wissenschaftsgeschichte und die Geschichte der Gelehrten 1890–1933. Von der historischen Kulturwissenschaft zur Soziologie', *Internationales Archiv für Sozialgeschichte der deutschen Literatur* 17: 150–80.

Lenz, C. 2004. 'Erinnerungskultur und Geschichtspolitik – politische Autorisierung, Hegemoniebildung und Narrationen des Widerstandes in Norwegen', in C. Fröhlich and H.-A. Heinrich (eds), *Geschichtspolitik. Wer sind ihre Akteure, wer ihre Rezipienten?* Stuttgart: Franz Steiner, pp. 81–94.

——— 2007. 'Vom Widerstand zum Weltfrieden. Der Wandel nationaler und familiärer Konsenserzählungen über die Besatzungszeit in Norwegen', in H. Welzer (ed.) *Krieg der Erinnerung. Krieg der Erinnerungen. Holocaust, Kollaboration und Widerstand im europäischen Gedächtnis*. Frankfurt am Main: S. Fischer, pp. 41–75.

Leonhard, W. 1978. *Die Revolution entläßt ihre Kinder*, 16th edn. Frankfurt am Main: Ullstein.

Lepsius, R.M. 1993. 'Parteiensystem und Sozialstruktur', in idem, *Demokratie in Deutschland. Soziologisch-historische Konstellationsanalysen*. Göttingen: Vandenhoeck and Ruprecht, pp. 25–50.

Le Roy Ladurie, E. 1982. *Der Karneval in Romans*. Stuttgart: Klett-Cotta.

——— 1983. *Die Bauern des Languedoc*. Stuttgart: Klett-Cotta.

Lersch, E. and R. Viehoff. 2007. *Geschichte im Fernsehen. Eine Untersuchung zur Entwicklung des Genres und der Gattungsästhetik geschichtlicher Darstellungen im Fernsehen 1995 bis 2003*. Berlin: Vistas.

Leuschner, B. (ed.) 1999. *Der Briefwechsel zwischen Therese Huber (1764–1829) und Karoline von Woltmann (1782–1847). Ein Diskurs über Schreiben und Leben.* Marburg: Tectum.

Levin, I. 2007. *Flukten – Jødenes flukt til Sverige under annen verdenskrig.* Oslo: HL-Senteret.

Lewy, G. 2005a. *The Armenian Massacres in Ottoman Turkey: A Disputed Genocide.* Salt Lake City: University of Utah Press.

———— 2005b. 'Revisiting the Armenian Genocide', *Middle East Quarterly* 12: 3–12.

Lindner, T. 1901–16. *Weltgeschichte seit der Völkerwanderung*, 9 vols. Stuttgart: Cotta.

———— 1993. *Die Peripetie des Siebenjährigen Krieges. Der Herbstfeldzug 1760 in Sachsen und der Winterfeldzug 1760/61 in Hessen.* Berlin: Duncker and Humblot.

Loewy, H. 1995. 'Schindler. Held, Spieler oder Kapitalist?' *Historische Anthropologie* 2: 309–23.

———— 2002. 'Bei Vollmond, Holokaust. Genretheoretische Bemerkungen zu einer Dokumentation des ZDF', *1999* 17: 114–27.

Looser, D. 2000. *British Women Writers and the Writing of History, 1670–1820.* Baltimore, MD: Johns Hopkins University Press.

Lorenz, M. 2006. 'Wikipedia. Zum Verhältnis von Struktur und Wirkungsmacht eines heimlichen Leitmediums', *WerkstattGeschichte* 43: 84–95.

Lottes, G. 2005. 'Erinnerungskulturen zwischen Psychologie und Kulturwissenschaft', in G. Oesterle (ed.) *Erinnerung, Gedächtnis, Wissen. Studien zur kulturwissenschaftlichen Gedächtnisforschung.* Göttingen: Vandenhoeck and Ruprecht, pp. 163–84.

Lübbe, H. 2001. *'Ich entschuldige mich'. Das neue politische Bußritual.* Berlin: Siedler.

Maase, K. 1997. *Grenzenloses Vergnügen. Der Aufstieg der Massenkultur 1850–1970.* Frankfurt am Main: Fischer.

Macaulay, C. 1763–83. *The History of England from the Accession of James I to the Elevation of the House of Hanover*, 8 vols. London: J. Nourse.

Maier, F.G. 1973. 'Das Problem der Universalität', in G. Schulz (ed.) *Geschichte heute. Positionen, Tendenzen und Probleme.* Göttingen: Vandenhoeck and Ruprecht, pp. 84–108.

Malley, M. 1976. 'From Hyperphosphorescence to Nuclear Decay: A History of the Early Years of Radioactivity, 1896–1914', Ph.D. dissertation. Berkeley: University of California.

Mann, G. 1982. *Nachtphantasien. Erzählte Geschichte.* Frankfurt am Main: Fischer.

Mann, T. 1974. 'Über die Lehre Spenglers', in idem, *Gesammelte Werke*, vol. 10, 2nd edn. Frankfurt am Main: Fischer, pp. 172–81.

Manus, M. 1945. *Det vil helst gå godt.* Oslo: Steensballe.

Marßoleck, I. 2001. 'Radio in Deutschland. Zur Sozialgeschichte eines Mediums', *Geschichte und Gesellschaft* 27: 207–39.

Märthesheimer P. and I. Frenzel (eds). 1979. *Im Kreuzfeuer. Der Fernsehfilm 'Holocaust'. Eine Nation ist betroffen.* Frankfurt am Main: Fischer.

Marx, K. and F. Engels. 1959 [1848]. 'Manifest der kommunistischen Partei', in K. Marx and F. Engels, *Werke*, vol. 4. Berlin: Dietz, pp. 459–93.

Mayer, H.F. and G. Vogl. 1998. *Sisi-Kult und Kreisky-Mythos. Ein österreichisches Jahrhundert in Anekdoten.* Vienna: Kremayr and Scheriau.

McLuhan, M. and Q. Fiore. 1967. *The Medium is the Message: An Inventory of Effects.* New York: Bantam Books.

Megill, A. 1995. 'Grand Narrative and the Discipline of History', in F. Ankersmit and H. Kellner (eds), *A New Philosophy of History.* Chicago: University of Chicago Press, pp. 151–73, 263–71.

Meier, C. 1982. *Caesar.* Berlin: Severin and Siedler.

Melman, B. 1993. 'Gender, History and Memory: The Invention of Women's Pasts in the Nineteenth and Early Twentieth Centuries', *History and Memory* 5: 5–41.

Meyer, B. 2004. 'Geschichte im Film. Judenverfolgung, Mischehen und der Protest in der Rosenstraße 1943', *Zeitschrift für Geschichtswissenschaft* 52: 23–36.

Meyer, H. 1985. *Velhagen und Klasing. Einhundertfünfzig Jahre 1835–1985.* Berlin: Cornelsen-Velhagen and Klasing.

Michel, K. 2004. 'Wo ist Einsteins Denkorgan?' *Die Zeit,* 11 March, B37.

Michel, R. 2004. *Deutschland ist Weltmeister. Meine Erinnerungen an das Wunder von Bern.* Munich: Südwest-Verlag.

Middell, M. 1993. 'Universalgeschichte heute', in G. Diesener et al. (eds), *Karl Lamprecht weiterdenken. Universal- und Kulturgeschichte heute.* Leipzig: Leipziger Universitätsverlag, pp. 386–404.

———— 2005a. 'Universalgeschichte, Weltgeschichte, Globalgeschichte, Geschichte der Globalisierung – ein Streit um Worte?' in M. Grandner and D. Rothermund (eds), *Globalisierung und Globalgeschichte.* Vienna: Mandelbaum, pp. 60–82.

———— 2005b. *Weltgeschichtsschreibung im Zeitalter der Verfachlichung und Professionalisierung. Das Leipziger Institut für Kultur- und Universalgeschichte 1890–1990.* Leipzig: Akademische Verlagsanstalt.

———— 2005c. 'Kulturtransfer und Weltgeschichte. Eine Brücke zwischen Positionen um 1900 und Debatten am Ende des 20. Jahrhunderts', in H. Mitterbauer and K. Scherke (eds), *Ent-grenzte Räume. Kulturelle Transfers um 1900 und in der Gegenwart.* Vienna: Passagen, pp. 43–73.

Mittenzwei, W. 2001. *Die Intellektuellen: Literatur und Politik in Ostdeutschland von 1945 bis 2000.* Leipzig: Faber and Faber.

Moeller, R.G. (ed.) 1997. *West Germany under Construction: Politics, Society, and Culture in the Adenauer Era.* Ann Arbor: University of Michigan Press.

Mögenburg, H. 1993. *Kalter Krieg und Wirtschaftswunder. Die Fünfziger Jahre im geteilten Deutschland (1949–1961).* Frankfurt am Main: Diesterweg.

Mohr, R. 2000. 'Mirakel der Erinnerung', *Der Spiegel* 48: 306–8.

Mohr, R. et al. 2001. 'Macht damit was ihr wollt', *Der Spiegel* 34: 183–86.

Moltmann, G. 1975. 'Das Problem der Universalgeschichte', in E. Jäckel and E. Weymar (eds), *Die Funktion der Geschichte in unserer Zeit.* Stuttgart: Klett, pp. 135–49.

Moore, R.I. 1997. 'World History', in M. Bentley (ed.) *Companion to Historiography.* London: Routledge, pp. 941–59.

Mraz, G. and U. Fischer-Westhauser. 1998. *Elisabeth. Prinzessin in Bayern, Kaiserin von Österreich, Königin von Ungarn. Wunschbilder oder Die Kunst der Retouche.* Vienna: Brandstätter.

Muchembled, R. 1984. *Kultur des Volks – Kultur der Eliten. Die Geschichte einer erfolgreichen Verdrängung,* 2nd edn. Stuttgart: Klett-Cotta.

———— 1990. *Die Erfindung des modernen Menschen. Gefühlsdifferenzierung und kollektive Verhaltensweisen im Zeitalter des Absolutismus.* Reinbek: Rowohlt.

Muhlack, U. 1991. *Geschichtswissenschaft im Humanismus und in der Aufklärung. Die Vorgeschichte des Historismus.* Munich: Beck.

———— 1997. 'Leopold von Ranke (1795–1886)', in V. Reinhardt (ed.) *Hauptwerke der Geschichtsschreibung.* Stuttgart: Körner, pp. 503–7.

Müller. S.L. and A. Schwarz. 2008. 'A Ready-made Set of Ancestors: Re-enacting a Gendered Past', in A. Schwarz and S.L. Müller (eds), *Iterationen: Geschlecht im kulturellen Gedächtnis.* Göttingen: Wallstein, pp. 89–110.

Müller, W. 2005. 'Vom "papistischen Jubeljahr" zum historischen Jubiläum', in P. Münch (ed.) *Jubiläum, Jubiläum. Zur Geschichte öffentlicher und privater Erinnerung.* Essen: Klartext, pp. 29–44.

Münch, P. (ed.) 2005. *Jubiläum, Jubiläum: Zur Geschichte öffentlicher und privater Erinnerung.* Essen: Klartext.

Mütter, B. 1992. 'Grenzen der weltgeschichtlichen Perspektive in der deutschen Geschichtsschreibung vom Zeitalter der Aufklärung bis zur Epoche des Imperialismus. Das Beispiel Lateinamerika', in W. Fürnrohr (ed.) *Geschichtsbewußtsein und Universalgeschichte. Das Zeitalter der Entdeckungen und Eroberungen in Geschichtsschreibung, Unterricht und Öffentlichkeit.* Frankfurt am Main: Diesterweg, pp. 45–72.

Niethammer, L. 1999. 'Geschichte und Gedächtnis', in idem, *Deutschland danach. Postfaschistische Gesellschaft und nationales Gedächtnis.* Bonn: Dietz, pp. 536–607.

Nipperdey, T. 1968. 'Nationalidee und Nationaldenkmal in Deutschland im 19. Jahrhundert', *Historische Zeitschrift* 206: 529–85.

———— 1983. *Deutsche Geschichte 1800–1866. Bürgerwelt und starker Staat.* Munich: Beck.

Nissen, M. 2009. *Populäre Geschichtsschreibung. Historiker, Verleger und die deutsche Öffentlichkeit (1848–1900).* Cologne: Böhlau.

Noakes, J. 1996. 'Nationalsozialismus in der Provinz. Kleine und mittlere Städte im Dritten Reich 1933–1945', in H. Möller and A. Wirsching (eds), *Nationalsozialismus in der Region. Beiträge zur regionalen und lokalen*

Forschung und zum internationalen Vergleich. Munich: Oldenbourg, pp. 238–51.

Nora, P. 2002. 'Gedächtniskonjunktur', Transit: Europäische Revue 22. Retrieved 18 August 2008 from: http://www.iwm.at/index.php?option= com_contentandtask=viewandid=155andItemid=362.

Nora, P. (ed). 1984-1992. *Les lieux de mémoire.* Paris: Gallimard.

O'Dowd, M. and I. Porciani (eds). 2004. *Storia della Storiografia,* vol. 46: *History Women.* Mailand: Jaca Book.

Oels, D. 2005. 'Ceram – Keller – Pörtner. Die archäologischen Bestseller der fünfziger Jahre als historischer Projektionsraum', in W. Hardtwig (ed.) *Geschichte für Leser. Populäre Geschichtsschreibung in Deutschland im 20. Jahrhundert.* Stuttgart: Steiner, pp. 345–70.

Oexle, O.G. 1996. 'Das Mittelalter als Waffe. Ernst H. Kantorowicz. Kaiser Friedrich der Zweite in den politischen Kontroversen der Weimarer Republik', in idem, *Geschichtswissenschaft im Zeichen des Historismus.* Göttingen: Vandenhoeck and Ruprecht, pp. 163–215.

Olsen, K. 1999. 'Da freden brøt løs: norske myndigheters behandling av tyskerjenter', in: S.U. Larsen (ed.) *I krigens kjølvann. Nye sider ved norsk krigshistorie og etterkrigstid.* Oslo: Universitetsforlaget, pp. 275–95.

Ortega y Gasset, J. 1931. *The Revolt of the Masses.* London: Unwin Books.

Osterhammel, J. 1992. 'Nation und Zivilisation in der britischen Historiographie von Hume bis Macaulay', *Historische Zeitschrift* 254: 281–340.

——— 1994. 'Raumerfassung und Universalgeschichte im 20. Jahrhundert', in G. Hübinger and J. Osterhammel (eds), *Universalgeschichte und Nationalgeschichten. Ernst Schulin zum 65. Geburtstag.* Freiburg: Rombach, pp. 51–72.

Oswalt, V. and H.-J. Pandel (eds). 2009. *Geschichtskultur: Die Anwesenheit von Vergangenheit in der Gegenwart.* Schwalbach/Ts.: Wochenshau-Verlag.

Paletschek, S. 2002. 'Duplizität der Ereignisse. Die Gründung des Historischen Seminars 1875 an der Universität Tübingen und seine Entwicklung bis 1914', in W. Freitag (ed.) *Halle und die deutsche Geschichtswissenschaft um 1900.* Halle: Mitteldeutscher Verlag, pp. 37–64.

——— 2007. 'Historiographie und Geschlecht', in J.R. Regnath and M. Riepl-Schmidt (eds), *Eroberung der Geschichte. Frauen und Tradition.* Münster: Lit, pp. 105–42.

Pandel, H.J. 1997. 'Geschichtsunterricht in der Haupt- und Realschule', in K. Bergmann et al. (eds), *Handbuch der Geschichtsdidaktik.* Seelze-Velber: Kallmeyer, pp. 526–30.

Pater, M. 1998. 'Rundfunkangebote', in I. Marßoleck and A. von Saldern (eds), *Zuhören und Gehörtwerden,* vol. 1. *Radio im Nationalsozialismus. Zwischen Lenkung und Ablenkung.* Tübingen: Edition Diskord, pp. 129–241.

Paul, J. and H. Köhler. 2001. 'Anmerkungen zu Haffner. Haffners posthumer Bestseller "Geschichte eines Deutschen" ist nicht historisch authentisch', *Frankfurter Allgemeine Zeitung,* 16 August, B7–8.

Peter, J. 1995. *Der Historikerstreit und die Suche nach einer nationalen Identität der achtziger Jahre.* Frankfurt am Main: Peter Lang Verlag.

Petersen, T. 2005. *Flucht und Vertreibung aus Sicht der deutschen, polnischen und tschechischen Bevölkerung.* Bonn: Stiftung Haus der Geschichte der Bundesrepublik Deutschland.

Peukert, D.J. 1989. *Weimarer Republik. Krisenjahre der klassischen Moderne.* Frankfurt am Main: Suhrkamp.

Pflaum, R. 1989. *Grand Obsession: Madame Curie and Her World.* New York: Doubleday.

Pflugk-Harttung, J. von. (ed.) 1907–10. *Weltgeschichte. Die Entwicklung der Menschheit in Staat und Gesellschaft, in Kultur und Geistesleben,* 6 vols. Berlin: Ullstein.

Pigulla, A. 1996. *China in der deutschen Weltgeschichtsschreibung vom 18. bis zum 20. Jahrhundert.* Wiesbaden: Harrassowitz.

Pinthus, K. (ed.) 1920. *Menschheitsdämmerung. Symphonie jüngster Dichter.* Berlin: Rowohlt.

Piozzi, H. 1801. *Retrospection or A Review of the Most Striking and Important Events, Characters, Situations and Their Consequences, which the Last Eighteen Hundred Years have Presented to the View of Mankind,* 2 vols. London: Stockdale.

Pirker, E.U. et al. (eds). 2010. *Echte Geschichte. Authentizitätsfiktionen in populären Geschichtskulturen.* Bielefeld: Transcript.

Planert, U. 2007. *Der Mythos vom Befreiungskrieg. Frankreichs Kriege und der deutsche Süden. Alltag – Wahrnehmung – Deutung, 1792–1841.* Paderborn: Schöningh.

Plumb, J.H. 1969. *The Death of the Past.* London: Macmillan.

Plumpe, G. 1990. *Die I.G. Farbenindustrie AG. Wirtschaft, Technik und Politik 1904–1945.* Berlin: Duncker und Humblot.

Poblocki, K. 2002.'Becoming-state: The Bio-cultural Imperialism of Sid Meier's Civilization', *Focaal: A Journal of Anthropology* 39: 163–77.

Pocock, J. 1998. 'Catharine Macaulay, Patriot Historian', in H. Smith (ed.) *Women Writers and the Early Modern British Political Tradition.* Cambridge: Cambridge University Press, pp. 243–58.

Pohl, D. 1996. *Nationalsozialistische Judenverfolgung in Ostgallizien 1941–1944. Organisation und Durchführung eines staatlichen Massenverbrechens.* Munich: Oldenbourg.

Potthast, B. 2007. *Die Ganzheit der Geschichte. Historische Romane im 19. Jahrhundert.* Göttingen: Wallstein.

Pretzel, O. 2001. 'Diese Kritik will den Rufmord', *Die Zeit,* 28 August.

Puntscher Riekmann, S. (ed.) 2004. *The State of Europe: Transformations of Statehood from a European Perspective.* Frankfurt am Main: Campus.

Puschner, U. 2005. 'Völkische Geschichtsschreibung. Themen, Autoren und Wirkungen völkischer Geschichtsideologie', in W. Hardtwig (ed.) *Geschichte*

für Leser. Populäre Geschichtsschreibung in Deutschland im 20. Jahrhundert.
Stuttgart: Steiner, pp. 287–308.

Quinn, S. 1995. *Marie Curie: A Life.* New York: Simon and Schuster.

Ranke, L. von. 1937. *Englische Geschichte,* 4 vols. Meersburg: Hendel.

———— 1970[1854]. *Über die Epochen der neueren Geschichte.* Darmstadt:
Wissenschaftliche Buchgesellschaft.

———— 1975a[1831–32]. 'Idee der Universalhistorie', in idem, *Aus Werk und
Nachlass,* vol. 4: *Vorlesungseinleitungen.* Munich: Oldenbourg, pp. 72–83.

———— 1975b[1864]. 'Parlamentarische Geschichte von England in den beiden
letzten Jahrhunderten', in idem, *Aus Werk und Nachlass,* vol. 4: *Vorlesungseinleitungen.* Munich: Oldenbourg, pp. 362–75.

Raphael, L. 2003. *Geschichtswissenschaft im Zeitalter der Extreme. Theorien,
Methoden, Tendenzen von 1900 bis zur Gegenwart.* Munich: Beck.

Rauch, J. 1990. 'Die Mutter der Relativitätstheorie', *Emma* 10: 42–49.

Regnath, J.R. and M. Riepl-Schmidt (eds). 2007. *Eroberung der Geschichte.
Frauen und Tradition.* Münster: Lit.

Reichel, P. 1995. *Politik mit der Erinnerung. Gedächtnisorte im Streit um die
nationalsozialistische Vergangenheit.* Munich: Hanser.

———— 2001. *Vergangenheitsbewältigung in Deutschland. Die Auseinandersetzung
mit der NS-Diktatur von 1945 bis heute.* Munich: Beck.

Reich-Ranicki, M. 1999. *Mein Leben.* Stuttgart: Deutsche Verlagsanstalt.

Reid, R. 1974. *Marie Curie.* London: Collins.

Reill, P.H. 1975. *The German Enlightenment and the Rise of Historicism.*
Berkeley: University of California Press.

Reisinger, B. 1998. *Elisabeth. Kaiserin von Österreich. Ein Frauenleben.* Vienna:
Niederösterreichisches Pressehaus.

Reitemeier, F. 2001. *Deutsch-englische Literaturbeziehungen. Der historische
Roman Sir Walter Scotts und seine deutschen Vorläufer.* Paderborn: Schöningh.

Reitz, E. 1984. *Liebe zum Kino.* Cologne: Köln 78.

Renan, E. 1947[1882]. 'Qu'est-ce qu'une nation?' in H. Psichari (ed.) *Œuvres
Complètes d'Ernest Renan,* vol. 1. Paris: Lévy, pp. 887–906.

Renn, J. (ed.) 2005. *Albert Einstein: Chief Engineer of the Universe.* Weinheim:
Wiley-VCH.

Ribuffo, L.P. 1999. 'Confessions of an Accidental (or Perhaps Overdetermined)
Historian', in E. Fox-Genovese and E. Lasch-Quinn (eds), *Reconstructing
History: The Emergence of a New Historical Society.* New York: Routledge, pp.
143–63.

Ricœur, P. 1998. *Das Rätsel der Vergangenheit. Erinnern – Vergessen – Verzeihen.*
Göttingen: Wallstein.

Ritzmann, I. 2006. 'Ideengeschichtliche Aspekte des Hermannsdenkmals bei
Detmold', *Lippische Mitteilungen* 75: 193–229.

Rödder, A. 2004. *Wertewandel und Postmoderne. Gesellschaft und Kultur in der
Bundesrepublik Deutschland 1965–1990.* Stuttgart: Stiftung Bundespräsident
Theodor-Heuss-Haus.

Rodik, B. 2006. *Der gestohlene Geigenkasten. Ein Ratekrimi um Albert Einstein.* Loewe: Bindlach.

Rosenzweig, R. 2006. 'Can History be Open Source? Wikipedia and the Future of the Past', *Journal of American History* 96: 117–46.

Rosenzweig, R. and D. Thelen. 1998. *The Presence of the Past: Popular Uses of History in American Life.* New York: Columbia University Press.

Rossiter, M. 1993. 'The Matthew Matilda Effect in Science', *Social Studies of Science* 23: 325–41.

Rothermund, D. 2005. 'Globalgeschichte und Geschichte der Globalisierung', in M. Grandner and D. Rothermund (eds), *Globalisierung und Globalgeschichte.* Vienna: Mandelbaum, pp. 12–35.

Rothfels, H. 1953, 'Zeitgeschichte als Aufgabe'. *Vierteljahrshefte für Zeitgeschichte* 1: 1–8.

Rüsen, J. 1994a. 'Was ist Geschichtskultur? Überlegungen zu einer neuen Art, über Geschichte nachzudenken', in K. Füßmann and H.T. Grütter (eds), *Historische Faszination. Geschichtskultur heute.* Cologne: Böhlau, pp. 3–26.

——— 1994b. *Historische Orientierung. Über die Arbeit des Geschichtsbewußtseins, sich in der Zeit zurechtzufinden.* Cologne: Böhlau.

Rüsen, J. and F. Jäger. 1992. *Die Geschichte des Historismus. Eine Einführung.* Munich: Beck.

Rutschky. M. 2005. 'Monumentalfeuilleton: Egon Friedells Kulturkritik der Neuzeit', in W. Hardtwig (ed.) *Geschichte für Leser. Populäre Geschichtsschreibung in Deutschland im 20. Jahrhundert.* Stuttgart: Steiner, pp. 333–44.

Sabrow, M. 2000. 'Planprojekt Meistererzählung. Die Entstehungsgeschichte des "Lehrbuchs der deutschen Geschichte"', in M. Sabrow (ed.) *Geschichte als Herrschaftsdiskurs. Der Umgang mit der Vergangenheit in der DDR.* Cologne: Böhlau, pp. 227–314.

——— 2001. *Das Diktat des Konsenses. Geschichtswissenschaft in der DDR 1949–1969.* Munich: Oldenbourg.

Saldern, A. von. 1996. 'Überfremdungsängste. Gegen die Amerikanisierung der deutschen Kultur in den zwanziger Jahren', in A. Lüdtke and I. Marßoleck (eds), *Amerikanisierung. Traum und Alptraum im Deutschland des 20. Jahrhunderts.* Stuttgart: Steiner, pp. 213–45.

Salt, J. 2003. 'The Narrative Gap in Ottoman Armenian History', *Middle Eastern Studies* 39: 19–36.

Samuel, R. 1994. *Theatres of Memory,* vol.1: *Past and Present in Contemporary Culture.* London: Verso.

Sandkühler, T. 1996. *'Endlösung' in Galizien. Der Judenmord in Ostpolen und die Rettungsinitiativen von Berthold Beitz 1941–1944.* Bonn: Dietz.

Sarkowski, H. 1976. *Das Bibliographische Institut. Verlagsgeschichte und Bibliographie 1826–1976.* Mannheim: Bibliographisches Institut.

Schäfer, D. 1907. *Weltgeschichte der Neuzeit,* 2 vols. Berlin: Mittler and Sohn.

Schaller, D.J. 2004. '"La question arménienne n'existe plus". Der Völkermord an den Armeniern während des Ersten Weltkriegs und seine Darstellung in der Historiographie', in I. Wojak (ed.) *Völkermord und Kriegsverbrechen in der ersten Hälfte des 20. Jahrhunderts.* Frankfurt am Main: Campus, pp. 99–128.

Scharpf, F.W. 1999. *Regieren in Europa. Effektiv und demokratisch?* Frankfurt am Main: Campus.

Schatzker, C. 1988. 'Die Rezeption der "Schoa" durch das israelische Bildungs-wesen und die israelische Gesellschaft', in W. Scheffler and W. Bergmann (eds), *Lerntag über den Holocaust als Thema im Geschichtsunterricht und in der politischen Bildung.* Berlin: Universitäts-Bibliothek der Technischen-Universität Berlin, pp. 77–85.

Scheffler, W. 1979. 'Anmerkungen zum Fernsehfilm Holocaust und zu Fragen zeithistorischer Forschung', *Geschichte und Gesellschaft* 5: 570–79.

Schenda, R. 1988. *Volk ohne Buch: Studien zur Sozialgeschichte der populären Lesestoffe 1770–1910,* 3rd edn. Frankfurt am Main: Klostermann.

Schildt, A. 1995. *Moderne Zeiten. Freizeit, Massenmedien und 'Zeitgeist' in der Bundesrepublik der 50er Jahre.* Hamburg: Christians.

———— 1999. *Zwischen Abendland und Amerika. Studien zur westdeutschen Ideenlandschaft der 50er Jahre.* Munich: Oldenbourg.

Schivelbusch, W. 1977. *Geschichte der Eisenbahnreise. Zur Industrialisierung von Raum und Zeit im 19. Jahrhundert.* Munich: Hanser.

Schlak, S. 2001. 'Geschichtsschreibung im George-Kreis', Ph.D. dissertation. Berlin: Humboldt University.

Schlögel, K. 1988. *Jenseits des Großen Oktober. Das Laboratorium der Moderne, Petersburg 1909–1921.* Berlin: Siedler.

———— 2001. *Promenade in Jalta und andere Städtebilder.* Munich: Hanser.

———— 2003. *Im Raume lesen wir die Zeit. Über Zivilisationsgeschichte und Geopolitik.* Munich: Hanser.

Schlosser, C.F. 1815–41. *Weltgeschichte in zusammenhängender Erzählung,* 4 vols. Frankfurt: Varrentrapp.

———— 1823. *Geschichte des 18. Jahrhunderts in gedrängter Uebersicht. Mit steter Beziehung auf die völlige Veränderung der Denk- und Regierungsweise am Ende derselben,* 2 vols. Heidelberg: Mohr.

———— 1843–57. *Weltgeschichte für das deutsche Volk,* 20 vols. Frankfurt: Varrentrapp.

———— 1892–93. *Fr. Chr. Schlossers Weltgeschichte für das deutsche Volk, von neuem durchgesehen und ergänzt von Oskar Jäger und Franz Wolff,* 19 vols, 23rd edn. Berlin: Seehagen.

Schmid, H. 2001. *Erinnern an den 'Tag der Schuld'. Das Novemberpogrom von 1938 in der deutschen Geschichtspolitik.* Hamburg: Ergebnisse.

Schmitt, C. 1950. *Ex Captivitate Salus. Erfahrungen der Zeit 1945/47.* Cologne: Greven.

Schneider, G. 1997. 'Geschichtsunterricht als Institution', in K. Bergmann et al. (eds), *Handbuch der Geschichtsdidaktik.* Seelze-Velber: Kallmeyer, pp. 495–509.

Schneider, M. 1995. '*Volkspädagogik' von rechts. Ernst Nolte, die Bemühungen um die 'Historisierung' des Nationalsozialismus und die 'selbstbewußte Nation'*. Bonn: Friedrich-Ebert-Stiftung.

Schönemann, B. 2002. 'Geschichtskultur als Forschungskonzept der Geschichtsdidaktik', *Zeitschrift für Geschichtsdidaktik* 1: 78–86.

Schopenhauer, J. 1810. *Carl Ludwig Fernows Leben*. Tübingen: Cotta.

Schröder, I. and S. Höhler. 2005. 'Welt-Räume: Annäherungen an eine Geschichte der Globalität im 20. Jahrhundert', in I. Schröder and S. Höhler (eds), *Welt-Räume. Geschichte, Geographie und Globalisierung seit 1900*. Frankfurt am Main: Campus, pp. 9–47.

Schulin, E. 1974. 'Einleitung', in idem (ed.) *Universalgeschichte*. Cologne: Kiepenheuer and Witsch, pp. 11–65.

———— 1998. 'Neue Diskussionen über Historismus', *Storia della Storiografia* 33: 109–17.

Schulte-Althoff, F.-J. 1971. *Studien zur politischen Wissenschaftsgeschichte der deutschen Geographie im Zeitalter des Imperialismus*. Paderborn: Schöningh.

Schultz, H.-D. 2005. 'Europa: (k)ein Kontinent? Das Europa deutscher Geographen', in I. Schröder and S. Höhler (eds), *Welt-Räume. Geschichte, Geographie und Globalisierung seit 1900*. Frankfurt am Main: Campus, pp. 204–31.

Schulz, G.-M. 2002. 'Docu-Dramas – oder. Die Sehnsucht nach der Authentizität. Rückblicke auf Holocaust von Marvin Chomsky und Schindlers Liste von Steven Spielberg', in W. Wende (ed.) *Geschichte im Film. Mediale Inszenierungen des Holocaust und kulturelles Gedächtnis*. Stuttgart: Metzler, pp. 159–80.

Schulze, H. 1996. *Kleine deutsche Geschichte*. Munich: Beck.

Schütz, E. 2005. 'Von Lageropfern und Helden der Flucht. Kriegs-gefangenschaft Deutscher – Popularisierungsmuster in der Bundesrepublik', in W. Hardtwig (ed.) *Geschichte für Leser. Populäre Geschichtsschreibung in Deutschland im 20. Jahrhundert*. Stuttgart: Steiner, pp. 181–204.

Schwab, U. (ed.) 2007. *Fiktionale Geschichtssendungen im DDR-Fernsehen. Einblicke in ein Forschungsgebiet*. Leipzig: Leipziger Universitätsverlag.

Schwab-Felisch, H. 1977. 'Bücher bei Ullstein', in W.J. Freyburg and H. Wallenberg (eds), *Hundert Jahre Ullstein 1877–1977*. Frankfurt am Main: Ullstein, pp. 179–216.

Schwarz, A. 1999. *Der Schlüssel zur modernen Welt. Wissenschaftspopularisierung in Großbritannien und Deutschland im Übergang zur Moderne (ca. 1870–1940)*. Stuttgart: Steiner.

Schweer, J. 1994. '*Der Sieg von Bern'. V. Fußball-Weltmeisterschaft 1954*. Kassel: Agon.

Schwentker, W. 2005. 'Globalisierung und Geschichtswissenschaft. Themen, Methoden und Kritik der Globalgeschichte', in M. Grandner and D. Rothermund (eds), *Globalisierung und Globalgeschichte*. Vienna: Mandelbaum, pp. 36–59.

Shapin, S. 1990. 'Science and the Public', in R. Olby (ed.) *Companion to the History of Modern Science*. London: Routledge, pp. 990–1007.

Shinn, T. and R. Whitley (eds). 1985. *Expository Science: Forms and Functions of Popularisation*. Dordrecht: Reidel.

Shortland, M. and R. Yeo (eds). 1996. *Telling Lives: Essays on Scientific Biography*. Cambridge: Cambridge University Press.

Siemann, W. 1998. 'Die Revolution von 1848/49 zwischen Erinnerung, Mythos und Wissenschaft: 1848–1998', *Geschichte in Wissenschaft und Unterricht* 49: 272–81.

Simon, C. 1996. *Historiographie. Eine Einführung*. Stuttgart-Hohenheim: Ulmer.

Sinclair, A. 2000. *Elisabeth, Kaiserin von Österreich*. Munich: Econ.

Smith, B. 1995. 'Gender and the Practices of Scientific History: The Seminar and Archival Research in the Nineteenth Century', *American Historical Review* 100: 1150–76.

———— 1998. *The Gender of History: Men, Women, and Historical Praxis*. Cambridge, MA: Harvard University Press.

Sobel, D. 1995. *Longitude: The True Story of a Lone Genius Who Solved the Greatest Scientific Problem of His Time*. New York: Walker.

Söderqvist, T. (ed.) 2007. *The History and Poetics of Scientific Biography*. Ashgate: Aldershot.

Sønsteby, G. 1960. *Rapport fra 'Nr. 24'*. Oslo: Mortensen.

Soukup, U. 2001. *Ich bin nun mal Deutscher. Sebastian Haffner: Eine Biographie*. Berlin: Aufbau.

Speer, A. 1969. *Erinnerungen*. Berlin: Propyläen.

Speitkamp, W. 1996. *Die Verwaltung der Geschichte. Denkmalpflege und Staat in Deutschland 1871–1933*. Göttingen: Vandenhoeck and Ruprecht.

Spier, F. 1998. *Big History. Was Geschichte im Innersten zusammenhält*. Darmstadt: Wissenschaftliche Buchgesellschaft.

Stein, P. 1984. 'Vormärz', in W. Beutin (ed.) *Deutsche Literaturgeschichte von den Anfängen bis zur Gegenwart*, 2nd edn. Stuttgart: Metzler, pp. 204–50.

Steinbach, P. and J. Tuchel (eds). 1994. *Widerstand gegen den National-sozialismus*. Bonn: Bundeszentrale für Politische Bildung.

Steinle, M. 2008. 'Der Erste Weltkrieg als großes Fresko auf dem kleinen Bildschirm. "1914–1918" im deutschen und französischen Fernsehen', in B. Korte and S. Paletschek (eds), *Der Erste Weltkrieg in der populären Erinnerungskultur*. Essen: Klartext, pp. 183–200.

Sternberger, D. 1954. 'Unter uns Weltmeistern gesagt … Untersuchung einiger Reaktionen auf den Berner Fußballsieg', *Die Gegenwart* 212: 461–64.

Stiftung Haus der Geschichte der Bundesrepublik Deutschland (ed.) 2005. *Flucht, Vertreibung, Integration*. Bielefeld: Kerber.

Stöve, E. 1982. 'Zeitliche Differenzierung und Geschichtsbewußtsein in der neuzeitlichen Historiographie', in E. Rudolph and E. Stöve (eds), *Geschichtsbewußtsein und Rationalität. Zum Problem der Geschichtlichkeit in der Theoriebildung*. Stuttgart: Klett-Cotta, pp. 11–50.

Stråth, B. (ed.) 2000. *Myth and Memory in the Construction of Community: Historical Patterns in Europe and Beyond.* Brussels: Lang.

Strathern, P. 1999. *Curie and die Radioaktivität,* trans. X. Osthelder. Frankfurt am Main: Fischer.

Stuchtey, B. and E. Fuchs. 2003. 'Problems of Writing World History: Western and Non-Western Experiences, 1800–2000', in idem (eds), *Writing World History 1800–2000.* Oxford: Oxford Univsity Press, pp. 1–44.

Sundhaussen, H. 2003. 'Die "Genozidnation". Serbische Kriegs- und Nachkriegsbilder', in N. Buschmann and D. Langewiesche (eds), *Der Krieg in den Gründungsmythen europäischer Nationen und der USA.* Frankfurt am Main: Campus, pp. 351–71.

Süssmann, J. 2000. *Geschichtsschreibung oder Roman. Zur Konstitutionslogik von Geschichtserzählungen zwischen Schiller und Ranke (1780–1824).* Stuttgart: Steiner.

Sveri, E. 1998. *Vindu til fortiden.* Oslo: Kvinners Frivillige Beredskap.

——— 2002. *Kvinner i norsk motstandsbevegelse 1940–45.* Oslo: Norges Hjemmefrontmuseum.

Szöllösi-Janze, M. 2004. 'Wissensgesellschaft in Deutschland: Überlegungen zur Neubestimmung der deutschen Zeitgeschichte über Verwissenschaftlichungsprozesse', *Geschichte und Gesellschaft* 30: 277–313.

Tacke, C. 1995. *Denkmal im sozialen Raum. Nationale Symbole in Deutschland und Frankreich im 19. Jahrhundert.* Göttingen: Vandenhoeck and Ruprecht.

Tempelhof, G.F. von. 1783–1801. *Geschichte des siebenjährigen Krieges in Deutschland zwischen dem Könige von Preußen und der Kaiserin Königin mit ihren Alliierten als eine Fortsetzung der Geschichte des General Lloyd,* 6 vols. Berlin: Unger.

Treskow, R.v. 1990. *Erlauchter Vertheidiger der Menschenrechte! Die Korrespondenz Karl von Rottecks,* vol. 1. *Einführung und Interpretation.* Freiburg: Ploetz.

Tschudi, C. 1901. *Elisabeth, Kaiserin von Österreich und Königin von Ungarn.* Leipzig: Reclam.

Tyrell, I. 2005. *Historians in Public: The Practice of American History, 1890–1970.* Chicago: University of Chicago Press.

Ulf, C. (ed.) 2003. *Der neue Streit um Troia. Eine Bilanz.* Munich: Beck.

Ullmann, H.-P. 1995. *Das Deutsche Kaiserreich 1871–1918.* Frankfurt am Main: Suhrkamp.

Ullrich, S. 2001. 'Im Dienste der Republik von Weimar: Emil Ludwig als Historiker und Publizist', *Zeitschrift für Geschichtswissenschaft* 49: 119–40.

——— 2005. '"Der Fesselndste unter den Biographen ist heute nicht der Historiker". Emil Ludwig und seine historischen Biographien', in W. Hardtwig (ed.) *Geschichte für Leser. Populäre Geschichtsschreibung in Deutschland im 20. Jahrhundert.* Stuttgart: Steiner, pp. 35–56.

Ullrich, V. 1999a. *Die nervöse Großmacht. Aufstieg und Untergang des deutschen Kaiserreichs 1871–1918,* 2nd edn. Frankfurt am Main: Fischer.

——— 1999b. 'Der helle Klang', *Die Zeit,* 7 January, p. 7.

Unterreiner, K. 2001. *Sisi. Mythos und Wahrheit.* Vienna: Brandstätter.

Uriccio, W. 2005. 'Simulation, History, and Computer Games', in J. Raessens and J. Goldstein (eds), *Handbook of Computer Game Studies.* Cambridge, MA: MIT Press, pp. 327–34.

Vallentin, A. 1955. *Das Drama Albert Einsteins. Eine Biographie.* Stuttgart: Günther.

Vierhaus, R. 1977. 'Einrichtungen wissenschaftlicher und populärer Geschichtsforschung im 19. Jahrhundert', in B. Deneke and R. Kahsnitz (eds), *Das kunst- und kulturgeschichtliche Museum im 19. Jahrhundert.* Munich: Prestel, pp. 109–17.

Vogel, J. 1992. *Elisabeth von Österreich. Momente aus dem Leben einer Kunstfigur.* Vienna: Brandstätter; 2nd edn. Frankfurt am Main: Neue Kritik.

Völkel, M. 2006. *Geschichtsschreibung. Eine Einführung in globaler Perspektive.* Cologne: Böhlau.

Voll, B. 1998. *Das Sisi-Syndrom. Wenn die Seele die Balance verliert – Wie Sie Ihr inneres Gleichgewicht wieder finden.* Munich: Droemer Knaur.

Wagner, H.-U. 1997. *'Der gute Wille, etwas Neues zu schaffen'. Das Hörspielprogramm in Deutschland von 1945 bis 1949.* Potsdam: Verlag für Berlin-Brandenburg.

Wahl, R. 2003. *Verfassungsstaat, Europäisierung, Internationalisierung.* Frankfurt am Main: Suhrkamp.

Wallenrodt, J.I.E. von. 1797. *Das Leben der Frau von Wallenrodt in Briefen an einen Freund. Ein Beitrag in Seelenkunde und Weltkenntniß,* 2 vols. Leipzig: Stiller.

Weber, G. 2006. 'Neue Kämpfe um Troia. Genese, Entwicklung und Hintergründe einer Kontroverse', *Klio* 88: 7–33.

Weber, R. 2000. 'Einleitung', in J. Schopenhauer, *Im Wechsel der Zeiten, im Gedränge der Welt. Jugenderinnerungen, Tagebücher, Briefe.* Düsseldorf: Artemis and Winkler, pp. 5–23.

Weber, W.E.J. 2001. 'Universalgeschichte', in M. Maurer (ed.) *Aufriß der Historischen Wissenschaften,* vol. 2: *Räume.* Stuttgart: Reclam, pp. 15–98.

Webson, D.P. 1998. *Sisi lebt!* Munich: Droemer Knaur.

Weckel, U. 1998. *Zwischen Häuslichkeit und Öffentlichkeit. Die ersten deutschen Frauenzeitschriften im späten 18. Jahrhundert und ihr Publikum.* Tübingen: Niemeyer.

Wegmann, W. 1980. 'Der westdeutsche Kriegsfilm der fünfziger Jahre', Ph.D. dissertation. Cologne: University of Colgne.

Weichlein, S. 2005. '"Meine Peitsche ist die Feder". Populäre katholische Geschichtsschreibung im 19. und 20. Jahrhundert', in W. Hardtwig (ed.) *Geschichte für Leser. Populäre Geschichtsschreibung in Deutschland im 20. Jahrhundert.* Stuttgart: Steiner, pp. 227–58.

Weidauer, A. 1996. *Berliner Panoramen der Kaiserzeit.* Berlin: Mann.

Weiss, C. (ed.) 1995. *'Der gute Deutsche'. Dokumente zur Diskussion um Steven Spielbergs 'Schindlers Liste' in Deutschland.* St. Ingbert: Röhrig.

Welzer, H. 2002. *Das kommunikative Gedächtnis. Eine Theorie der Erinnerung.* Munich: Beck.

Welzer, H. (ed.) 2001. *Das soziale Gedächtnis. Geschichte, Erinnerung, Tradierung.* Hamburg: Hamburger Edition.

Welzer, H. et al. 2002. *'Opa war kein Nazi': Nationalsozialismus und Holocaust im Familiengedächtnis.* Frankfurt am Main: Fischer.

Wende, W. 2002. 'Die Geschichte hinter der Geschichte – Aimée und Jaguar von Erica Fischer (1994) und Max Färberböck (1998)', in idem (ed.) *Geschichte im Film. Mediale Inszenierungen des Holocaust und kulturelles Gedächtnis.* Stuttgart: Metzler, pp. 252–89.

Wildt, M. 1995. 'Das Erfundene und das Reale. Historiographische Anmerkungen zu einem Spielfilm', *Historische Anthropologie* 2: 324–34.

———— 2002. *Generation des Unbedingten. Das Führungskorps des Reichssicherheitshauptamtes.* Hamburg: Hamburger Edition.

Willms, J. 1988. *Paris: Hauptstadt Europas 1789–1914.* Munich: Beck.

Winkler, H.A. 1993. 'Nationalismus, Nationalstaat und nationale Frage in Deutschland seit 1945', in H.A. Winkler and H. Kaelble (eds), *Nationalismus – Nationalitäten – Supranationalität.* Stuttgart: Klett-Cotta, pp. 12–33.

———— 2000. *Der lange Weg nach Westen,* 2 vols. Munich: Beck.

Wirtz, R. 2008. 'Alles authentisch: so war's. Geschichte im Fernsehen oder TV-History', in T. Fischer and R. Wirtz (eds), *Alles authentisch? Popularisierung der Geschichte im Fernsehen.* Konstanz: UVK, pp. 9–32.

Wiseman, S. 2001. 'Catharine Macaulay: History and Republicanism', in E. Eger et al. (eds), *Women, Writing and the Public Sphere, 1700–1830.* Cambridge: Cambridge University Press, pp. 181–99.

Wittmann, R. 1991. *Geschichte des deutschen Buchhandels. Ein Überblick.* Munich: Beck.

Wolfgram, M.A. 2002. 'West German and Unified German Cinema's Difficult Encounter with the Holocaust', *Film and History* 32: 24–37.

Wolfrum, E. 1999. *Geschichtspolitik in der Bundesrepublik Deutschland. Der Weg zur bundesrepublikanischen Erinnerung 1948–1990.* Darmstadt: Wissenschaftliche Buchgesellschaft.

———— 2001. *Geschichte als Waffe. Vom Kaiserreich bis zur Wiedervereinigung.* Göttingen: Vandenhoeck and Ruprecht.

Zamseil, F. 2007. *Zwischen Nation und Region. Die Zeitschrift 'Gartenlaube' in der 2. Hälfte des 19. Jahrhunderts.* Hamburg: Diplomica.

Zimmerman, A. 2004. 'Ethnologie im Kaiserreich. Natur, Kultur und "Rasse" in Deutschland und seinen Kolonien', in S. Conrad and J. Osterhammel (eds), *Das Kaiserreich transnational. Deutschland in der Welt 1871–1914.* Göttingen: Vandenhoek and Ruprecht, pp. 191–212.

Zweig, S. 2000. *Joseph Fouché. Bildnis eines politischen Menschen,* 43rd edn. Frankfurt am Main: Fischer.

Notes on Contributors

Hartmut Bergenthum is Curator of the Special Collections for Africa South of the Sahara and Oceania at the University Library, Frankfurt am Main. He previously worked as a research assistant in the Collaborative Research Centre on Memory Cultures at Giessen University, and has published on the historiography of Germany and Kenya. His publications include *Weltgeschichten im Zeitalter der Weltpolitik* (2004) and *Geschichtswissenschaft in Kenia in der zweiten Hälfte des 20. Jahrhunderts* (2004).

Frank Bösch is Professor of History and Journalism in the Department of History at the University of Giessen; in 2005 he was a fellow at the German Historical Institute London. His fields of research include the history of media and communications, and the cultural and political history of Britain and Germany in the nineteenth and twentieth centuries. His publications include *Öffentliche Geheimnisse. Skandale, Politik und Medien in Deutschland und Großbritannien, 1880–1914* (2009) and he has co-edited the volume *Public History. Öffentliche Darstellungen des Nationalsozialismus jenseits der Geschichts-wissenschaft* (2009).

Franz-Josef Brüggemeier is Professor of Economic, Social and Environmental History at the University of Freiburg. He has published widely on the social and environmental history of Germany from the eighteenth to the twentieth century and on the history of German football. His recent publications include *Zurück auf dem Platz. Deutschland und die Fußball-Weltmeisterschaft 1954* (2004) and *Geschichte Grossbritanniens in 20. Jahrhundert* (2010). In addition to writing books he has also organized several major historical exhibitions.

Beate Ceranski is Lecturer in the Department of the History of Science and Technology at the University of Stuttgart. Her research interests include the history of physics, the genesis of scientific disciplines, and the history of gender in science and technology. Her publications include *Und sie fürchtet sich vor* *niemandem. Die Physikerin Laura Bassi (1711–1778)* (1996) and she is currently completing a forthcoming book on the history of radioactivity research.

Christoph Classen is a research fellow at the Center for Research on Contemporary History at Potsdam. His main areas of research are the history of media, the legacy of Naziism in both parts of Germany, and the impact of modern mass media on political cultures and their transnational and nationalizing effects. His recent publications include 'Two Types of Propaganda? Thoughts on the Significance of Mass-Media Communications in the Third Reich and the GDR', *Totalitarian Movements and Political Religions* 8 (2007) and he has co-edited with Wulf Kanshire the issue 'Historical Representation and Historical Truth', *History and Theory* 47 (2009).

Angelika Epple is Professor of Modern History at the University of Bielefeld. She has published on the history of historiography, historical theory, gender history, and the cultural and economic history of globalization. Her publications include *Empfindsame Geschichtsschreibung: Eine Geschlechtergeschichte der Historiographie zwischen Aufklärung und Historismus* (2003), *Der Unternehmen Stollwerck. Eine Mikrogeschichte der Globalisierung* (2010) and two co-edited volumes, *Globale Waren* (2007) and *Gendering Historiography: Beyond National Canons* (2009).

Wolfgang Hardtwig is Emeritus Professor of Modern History at Humboldt University, Berlin. In 1993/4 he was a fellow at the Institute for Advanced Studies, Princeton, and a fellow at the Historisches Kolleg in Munich in 2000/1. His research interests range from the cultural and social history of Germany between the sixteenth and twentieth centuries to the history of historiography and the theory of history. His publications include *Hochkultur des bürgerlichen Zeitalters* (2005), *Politische Kulturgeschichte der Zwischenkriegszeit 1918–1939* (2005), and two co-edited collections, *Geschichte für Leser. Populäre Geschichtsschreibung in Deutschland im 20. Jahrhundert* (2005) and *Keiner kommt davon. Zeitgeschichte in der Literatur nach 1945* (2008).

Dieter Langewiesche is Emeritus Professor of History at the University of Tübingen and was Pro-rector of the newly created University of Erfurt in the 1990s. His research interests broadly include nineteenth and twentieth century political and social history. Among his works are *Liberalism in Germany* (2000), *Nation, Nationalismus, Nationalstaat in Deutschland und Europa* (2000), *Europa zwischen Restauration und Revolution 1815–1849* (5th edn 2007), *Reich, Nation, Föderation. Deutschland und Europa* (2008) and *Zeitwende. Geschichtsdenken heute* (2008).

Claudia Lenz is research coordinator at the European Wergeland Centre on Education for Intercultural Understanding, Human Rights and Democratic

Citizenship in Oslo and a research consultant on the project Futures and Pasts in Transition: Family Conversations on Occupational and Personal Ambitions and Perspectives in Luxembourg (University of Luxemburg). Her primary area of research covers historical consciousness, memory politics and historical culture relating to the Second World War and Holocaust in Scandinavia. Her recent publications are the co-authored paper 'De-coding the Gendered Order of Memory in the German TV series *Hitlers Frauen*', in *German Politics and Society* 4 (2008) and 'A Kind of Fraternization That Was Totally Unacceptable: The Drawing of Boundaries Within the National Identity and the Regulation of Female Sexuality', in *NachRichten* 18 (2008).

Sylvia Paletschek is Professor of Modern History at the University of Freiburg, and in 2006/7 she was Visiting Fellow at St Antony's College, Oxford. Her research interests include gender and women's history, the history of universities, memory culture and the history of historiography. Her publications include *Die permanente Erfindung einer Tradition. Die Universität Tübingen im Kaiserreich und in der Weimarer Republik* (2001) and she has co-edited a number of volumes: *Women's Emancipation Movements in the Nineteenth Century: A European Perspective* (2004), *The Gender of Memory: Cultures of Remembrance in Nineteenth- and Twentieth-Century Europe* (2008) and *History Goes Pop. Geschichte in populären Medien und Genres* (2009).

Sylvia Schraut is Professor of Modern History in the Department of History, University of Bundeswehr München. Her fields of research include social history, the history of nobility, and gender and women's history. Her publications include *Sozialer Wandel im Industrialisierungsprozess, Esslingen 1800–1870* (1989), *Flüchtlingsaufnahme in Württemberg-Baden 1945–1949. Amerikanische Besatzungsziele und demokratischer Wiederaufbau im Konflikt* (1995), *Das Haus Schönborn. Eine Familienbiographie. Katholischer Reichsadel 1640–1840* (2005) and the co-edited volume *The Gender of Memory: Cultures of Remembrance in Nineteenth- and Twentieth-Century Europe* (2008).

Index

CPSIA information can be obtained at www.ICGtesting.com
Printed in the USA
LVOW050800280212

270753LV00007B/32/P